THE PALESTINIAN PROBLEM

edited by ANDREW C. KIMMENS

THE REFERENCE SHELF

Volume 61 Number 1

THE H. W. WILSON COMPANY

New York   1989

THE REFERENCE SHELF

The books in this series contain reprints of articles, excerpts from books, and addresses on current issues and social trends in the United States and other countries. There are six separately bound numbers in each volume, all of which are generally published in the same calendar year. One number is a collection of recent speeches; each of the others is devoted to a single subject and gives background information and discussion from various points of view, concluding with a bibliography of books and pamphlets, and selected abstracts of periodical articles. Books in the series may be purchased individually or on subscription.

Library of Congress Cataloging in Publication Data

Main entry under title:

The Palestinian problem.

(The Reference shelf ; v. 61, no. 1)
Bibliography: p.
1. Jewish-Arab relations—1917-   . I. Kimmens,
Andrew C.   II. Series.
DS119.7.P28833 1989   956.085'4   88-33947
ISBN 0-8242-0780-7

Printed in the United States of America

CONTENTS

IV. No Way Out? The Palestinian Intifada
   and the Triumph of the Israeli Right

PREFACE

Nothing is immutable or absolute in relations between peoples, and reconciliation after long antagonism is always possible. Yet hardly anyone alive today can remember a time when there were not very bad feelings between Jews and Palestinian Arabs over the land they both claim as their own. A tremendous leap of imagination is required now, after decades of bloodshed and bitter invective, to realize that a change for the better could ever occur.

The unsettled Palestinian problem has doomed every move toward regional peace the world has recently seen. The apparent breakthrough offered by Anwar Sadat's historic visit to Jerusalem and the resulting 1979 treaty between Israel and Egypt led to no real peace because the Palestinians' cause was unresolved. Shimon Peres's and Hosni Mubarak's proclamation at the end of their 1986 summit meeting in Alexandria that 1987 would be the year for a comprehensive negotiated Middle East peace came to nothing because they failed to acknowledge the centrality of the Palestinian issue. It does no good to cast doubts on the intentions of such would-be peacemakers, but it has become abundantly clear to all sane observers that only a dramatic change in attitudes on the part of Israelis, Palestinians, and Arabs can hope to bridge the widening chasm at present dividing them. If Israel is to feel secure, to live at peace with its Arab neighbors, the national aspirations of the Palestinian people must be satisfied.

Every conflict has its history, and this book attempts to outline the one which has as its basis the Palestinians' burning sense of having been wronged—by their former Jewish neighbors, by their friends among the neighboring Arab countries, by the superpowers, by the United Nations. Internationally assisted Jewish immigration into Palestine, which began around the turn of the century, helped fan nascent flames of disaffection. British support for the political aims of Zionism and the failure of internationally agreed-upon plans for partition between the communities led to mortal fear among the Palestinians that their rights were being flouted in full view of the world. The imposition by force of the state of Israel led to a large-scale exodus of Palestinians from their homeland, which turned into a rout during and after the 1948 Arab-Israeli war. Forty years of life in the appalling squalor of refugee camps have produced only extreme bitterness and a desire for revenge among the displaced, along with, among the Israelis, a querulous sense of being unable to put right a terrible wrong.

It is one of the bitterest ironies of twentieth-century history that the birth of the state of the Jews, given such a large impetus by the consciousness of the horror of the Jewish Holocaust of only a few years before, should have entailed the victimization of yet another people, whose only "fault," once again, was to have lived at the wrong time and in the wrong place. Now, after decades of murder and revenge on both sides, and the studious ignoring by the Israelis of their former neighbors' national rights, mere mutual recognition and coexistence will surely not be enough. Forbearance and magnanimity will be required on the part of Israel, now grown into the world's fourth-greatest military power, a wholehearted willingness, officially and privately, to forget the past and to welcome and support the national aspirations of a people who are far weaker in military might and international financial support, but who yet have feelings and rights remarkably similar to those of the Israelis themselves. Israel must only connect. As the late Simha Flapan wrote (see pp. 200ff.), "Diaspora Jewry and friends of Israel abroad must realize that present Israeli policy is doomed to reproduce over and over again the cycle of violence that shocks our sensibilities every time we read or hear of [it], whether the hand that perpetrates it detonates a bomb or fires a pistol. The collective revenge of an army for the murder of one of its citizens is no more righteous or admirable than the individual revenge of a desperate youth for the murder of one of his people. It is only propaganda and distorted vision that labels one 'terrorism' and the other 'national defense.'"

ANDREW C. KIMMENS

February 1989

I. THE ORIGINS OF THE CONFLICT: THE BALFOUR DECLARATION AND THE BRITISH MANDATE

EDITOR'S INTRODUCTION

The conflict between Jews and Arabs over the land called Israel by the former and Palestine by the latter is as old as the twentieth century, but not much older. Though it is often imagined to be, it is certainly not one of those ethno-religious disputes—the world contains a great many of them—which began centuries ago and whose original causes have been long forgotten. The few thousand Jews who participated in the first wave of settlement in Palestine, which dates from about 1878 (the founding of the first Jewish town, Petah Tikvah), aroused little resentment among the indigenous Arabs, who in any case had lived harmoniously side by side in the Holy Land with Jewish neighbors for centuries.

The rapid rise of Zionism as a political force, beginning in the mid-1890s with Theodor Herzl's influential pamphlet *The Jewish State* (1896) and his convening of the First Zionist Congress in Basel, Switzerland (1897), led to gradually exacerbated tensions in the region. The Zionists' primary goal was the creation in Palestine of a "home" for the Jewish people, and to this end land began to be purchased from Arab owners at an ever-accelerating rate. During World War I Zionist leaders were able to secure from the British war cabinet an expression of sympathy for Zionist aspirations (the Balfour Declaration of 1917), which greatly increased Arab fears of Jewish domination.

Relations became truly strained just after the war, when a desultory and inefficient Ottoman rule over Palestine yielded to a much more active and intrusive British presence. The British mandate, which began in 1922, embodied a provision for the implementation of the Balfour Declaration, further facilitating Jewish immigration into Palestine.

This section examines the history of the mandatory period and the ways in which Jewish-Arab tensions were allowed and even encouraged to increase and fester. The first article, by the

French orientalist Maxime Rodinson from his important book *Israel and the Arabs,* sets the stage by examining the rival nationalisms—Arab and Jewish—which came into seemingly inevitable conflict. The second article, by the American historian D. Edward Knox, is an examination of the geopolitical background to the Balfour Declaration and its immediate aftermath. The third article, by Simha Flapan, an Israeli who spent his entire adult life working for Israeli-Palestinian reconciliation, is a terse summation of the findings of his first, highly significant book. He holds that the beliefs formed by Zionist leaders during the mandatory period—in particular, the refusal to recognize the Palestinians' national aspirations—continued into the post-mandatory period and formed important parts of the domestic policies of the Israeli state. The fourth article comprises excerpts from Chaim Weizmann's summation before the Palestine Royal Commission in 1936 of the dire situation of world Jewry and of the absolute necessity for increased Jewish migration to Palestine. In the fifth article Moshe Aumann asserts in the mid-1980s that there has never been a Palestinian people per se, and that most of the growth of the non-Jewish people of Palestine has occurred only during the twentieth century, as a direct result of economic opportunities created by Jewish immigration to the area.

JEWISH NATIONALISM AND ARAB NATIONALISM[1]

Once again the course of human history, events in a tiny Middle Eastern province (in area about the size of Wales or of three French *départements*) have shaken the world and unleashed fierce passions from San Francisco to Karachi. The province is that little patch of Palestinian soil, barren and inhospitable, in which only the imaginations of half-starved nomads could see "a land flowing with milk and honey." But it is from here that a sizeable proportion of mankind have chosen to derive their God, their ideas, and everything that governs their life, customs, loves and hates.

[1]By Maxime Rodinson, emeritus professor of old Ethiopic and Old South Arabian in the École Pratique des Hautes Études at the Sorbonne and lecturer in Middle Eastern Anthropology. From *Israel and the Arabs,* by Maxime Rodinson. Copyright © 1968 by Michael Perl. Reprinted by permission of Pantheon Books, a division of Random House, Inc.

A new epoch in the history of this land opened less than a century ago. This new phase, strange as it seems, was heralded by events and situations which arose in territories far removed from that land in distance, customs, social structure and ideas. Just as at the time of the Crusades almost a thousand years ago, Palestine's tribulations stemmed from the fact that far away men and women longed for her, and were ready to die for her, like lovers pining for an absent mistress.

In the eleventh century, Palestine's lovers were Western Christians moved by the memory of their God and the danger threatening his tomb. In the nineteenth century, they were Eastern European Jews. For almost two thousand years, Jews all over the world had dreamt of their old homeland as the land in which God would reign in their midst, a dream-world where the wolf would lie down with the lamb and a little child would lead them. But then God discreetly disappeared from the vision, and a very terrestrial kingdom emerged instead. Far from any Messianic prophecy, it was hoped that this would be an "ordinary" kingdom where the rulers and the ruled, the rich and the poor, wise men and fools would live side by side, just as anywhere else. There would even be, like everywhere else, murderers, thieves and prostitutes—from which no anti-Jewish inference should be drawn.

The Jews, once inhabitants of Palestine, had emigrated and scattered over almost the whole of the earth's surface—like their Syrian neighbours and many other peoples. The independence of their national home, again like many others, was destroyed by the Romans. But the cult of their national god Yahweh had certain characteristics which rendered it peculiarly attractive to many people. Their prophets had proclaimed that he was not only their God but the God of all peoples, although he had conferred a special privilege on the people of Israel, as they called themselves. One of their heresies, Christianity, had conquered the Roman world and spread beyond it. Many Jews were converted to pagan cults, then to Christianity, and later still, in the East, to Islam, a new religion born in the heart of the Arabian peninsula, which also drew its authority from their God, their laws and their prophets.

But as predicted by its prophets, a "remnant" of the Jewish people was left, scattered over a multitude of different communities, remaining faithful to the old law, to the old scriptures, to ancient, complicated, archaic and cumbersome rituals. These, Jews in the true sense of the word, practising a minority religion, had been tolerated by the Christian states, but came to be viewed with increasing mistrust and hostility. Their failure to recognize the divine nature of one of themselves, Jesus of Nazareth, appeared more and more scandalous. After centuries of more or less grudging tolerance came the era of violent persecutions, of torture and the stake. Again, many became Christians. But as before, a "remnant" was left, and multiplied in Eastern Europe where the Jews were at first welcomed. In the territory of Islam they were, like their Christian rivals, tolerated and "protected," at the price of certain special taxes and discriminatory measures, and at the price also, from time to time and under special circumstances, of outbreaks of intolerance on the part of the Muslim mob—the "poor white" reaction of those who cling to the last vestige of their superiority, their membership of the dominant community.

Within this network of self-contained minority communities, interpolated like cysts in states professing a rival ideology, the hope of salvation survived. This salvation was to be prepared by God on behalf of his chosen people, whom in his mysterious but infinite love he had allowed to suffer, no doubt so that the happiness they were to inherit should be all the more splendid. The old homeland, Palestine, the land of Israel as they called it, together with its centre the Holy City of Jerusalem, were still worshipped as the place appointed for the final victory, the kingdom of peace and plenty at the end of time. The Jews visited it whenever possible; they hoped to die there; they had themselves buried there. But the task of preparing their return to the promised land was left to God.

After the fall of the Jewish State of Palestine and the last struggles for Jewish independence from the Romans in the years 70 and 135, up to the fateful day of 1948, only two Jewish states were ever formed. The first appeared in the Yemen in the course of the fifth century, and took the form of a core of original Jews ruled by natives of southern Arabia converted to Judaism. The other was likewise and empire of the converted: the Khazars, a people of Turco-Mongoloid stock dwelling on the lower Volga. It lasted from about the eighth to the tenth century. For nineteen centuries these were the only instances when Judaism was anything other than a group of minority communities, and became itself a state religion.

The new spirit running through Western Europe in the eighteenth century was to change all this. Terrestrial communities were no longer built up around a god, but only within the framework of a state. The world of religious communities began to disappear, to be replaced by the world of nations. And for many men and women, God himself gradually receded from the earthly scene, to the point of disappearing altogether. The French Revolution drew the logical conclusions from these new conditions and new ideas. It proclaimed aloud and carried through to the end the abolition of every act of discrimination—a change already accepted by the enlightened despot Joseph II and by the young American Republic. Faith in a system of dogmas, the practice of certain rites, adherence to one or other religious community were no longer relevant critieria by which citizens of the same nation could be isolated from one another. Jews became Frenchmen like any other. They worshipped their own God after their own fashion, within the framework, if they so desired, of their own religious association, just as did the Catholics.

The logic of the French solution conformed so well with the social and ideological conditions of the time that Western Europe and America gradually came to accept it. The consequences for the Jewish situation were enormous. In this new world, religious communities no longer formed nations or quasi-nations to which the individual was bound, whether by choice or by force, but had become hardly more than free associations much like political parties or chess clubs. In this situation, a Jew who lost faith in the religion of his ancestors was no longer obliged either to be converted to another religion or somehow to sidestep the innumerable practical and moral problems with which he was faced as the subject of a community whose creed he did not accept. He became a Frenchman, an Englishman or a Belgian, of Jewish origin, and even this fact would probably fade from men's memories. No one could hold him to account for his religious opinions. No bond tied him to Judaism. And in conformity with the general tendencies at work in European society, such cases occurred with increasing frequency.

Of course not all Jews went as far as this. But cultural assimilation, which had always existed, became much greater. The notion of a "Jewish people" had now become outdated. It had some justification when Jewish communities were universally regarded as foreign bodies encapsulated in the different nations, or as minority groups with no right of participation in the government of their states, when a multiple network of common interests united them wherever they might happen to be. Under the new order, all were full citizens of the various states; some of them happened to practise a certain religion, while others were descendants of practitioners of that religion. Even if their common religion created a bond between the Jews of different countries, the example of the Catholics and others showed that this common membership was easily reconciled with total commitment to each separate fatherland, a commitment which extended as far as mutual bloodletting without a trace of remorse or bad conscience.

Thus assimilation triumphed, to a greater or lesser degree. This is not to say that it was accepted and recognized by all non-Jews. For too long the Jews had been denounced as God's murderers and the servants of Satan. The Catholic Church and reactionary elements in every Christian confession smelt the hand of the Jew in every enterprise which undermined, to a degree increasingly dangerous to them, their ideological monopoly and the many advantages they drew from it. It is a commonplace of conservative ideological conventions to refuse to recognize that a progressive movement which attacks acquired privilege is the normal reaction of those classes in society who are discriminated against and oppressed. To denounce the motives of such a movement as a dark conspiracy of the forces of evil is much more convenient for the conscience of the privileged and much better propaganda material to direct at the ignorant masses. And who better to represent these forces than the Jews, to whom liberalization opened the doors of Christian society?

Moreover, it was true that the Jews detached themselves more easily than others from traditions in flagrant discord with the spirit of modern civilization; they were anxious to escape from the stigma of their underprivileged minority position to become a part of a larger society, and found themselves still the object of ancestral enmities. Hence in proportion their numbers they always provided a very large contingent of liberals, reformers, even revolutionaries.

From time to time—and this is especially evident in the history of British Jewry—almost total assimilation would be freshly imperilled by the arrival of immigrants from parts of the world where the old order still persisted. These immigrants came from communities closed in upon themselves, cysts in the body politic of states in whose life they played no part, and hence having developed, in differing degrees, their own peculiar cultural characteristics. This was true of the Russia of the Tsars and of the whole of Eastern Europe, where the Jews (who had mostly come from the western parts of Germany in the Middle Ages) even spoke their own special language, Yiddish, a Germanic dialect with its own literature, existing in the midst of Slav populations. And then the Jews from Eastern Europe would appear in the West, repopulate the deserted synagogues, and once again build up their own community life until they, in their turn, were assimilated.

In 1879 a fateful event took place. Bismarck, personally devoid of any prejudice against the Jews, found it expedient for his internal policy to launch a campaign of "anti-Semitism," to use the term which had recently become popular in Germany, where certain writers of small influence had been developing this theme as a stick with which to beat liberalism. The weapon proved effective, and it was taken up to meet similar political circumstances in Austria, France and Russia in the years which followed. As James Parkes very rightly says,

Political antisemitism had extremely little to do with the Jews as such. . . . The enemy was "liberalism," "industrialism," "secularism" —anything the reactionaries disliked; and they found by experience that there was no better way of persuading their electors to dislike these things also than to label them "Jewish." (*An Enemy of the People: Anti-Semitism*, Penguin Books, Harmondsworth, 1945, pp. 10–11)

Extremely violent verbally, political anti-Semitism provoked relatively little physical violence in Western Europe until the victory of Nazism. But in Russia, where Jewish communities of the medieval type still survived in large numbers, the reactionary Tsar Alexander III decided to avenge the death of his father on the Jews (Alexander II was killed by revolutionaries in 1881). The Tsarist administration likewise deliberately developed anti-Semitism as a political weapon against liberal ideas, and used it with great success among the more backward classes of the population, who were unleashed on the defenceless Jewish communities. The Russian pogroms filled the civilized world with horror.

The Jews reacted in various ways. Many of them gritted their teeth and waited for the storm to pass, remembering that similar persecutions had in the past struck at the French Protestants and the English Catholics. Some emphasized their assimilation, changed their name, and broadcast their attachment to the religion and cultural values of their adoptive homeland, in an effort to obliterate their origins. Others fought with intensified fury, side by side with liberals or revolutionaries of Christian origin, for a society from which anti-Semitism would be extirpated root and branch. In Eastern Europe, where the Jews still formed almost a nation of their own with its own Yiddish language and culture, a local cultural nationalism grew up, broadly socialist in spirit. This was the ideology of the Bund, the Jewish Socialist Party of the Russian Empire, founded in 1898.

Another reaction was openly nationalistic in spirit: this was political Zionism, created by a thoroughly assimilated Jew, the Viennese journalist Theodor Herzl. Appalled by the demonstrations of the French mob against Dreyfus, Herzl feverishly wrote his *A Jewish State* in 1896. In it, he showed himself converted to nationalism and in agreement with the anti-Semites on the diagnosis that the European Jews were an alien element, unassimilated for the most part, and in the long run unassimilable. They constituted a people, a nation. The remedy to the situation lay in departure, in the possession of a homeland, such as other nations had. Somewhere a Jewish State, purely Jewish, autonomous and independent, had to be created. But where? A number of possible solutions were canvassed, including the Argentine. But the clear preference was for the ancient homeland, Palestine, abandoned by most Jews for almost two millennia. The messianic fervour of religious Jews, the emotions aroused by Biblical texts, and traditions which retained their power even over Jews who had ceased to identify with Judaism, all contributed to an effective mobilization of Jewish opinion towards this end.

Palestine was at that time an Arab province of the Ottoman Empire. This did not appear a great obstacle. Around 1900 colonization projects did not have the unfavourable aura that surrounds them today. More or less backward populations were being introduced to progress and civilization, even at the cost of being displaced or somewhat subordinated. It is hardly surprising, therefore, that this project, originating in Europe, showed little concern for the fate of the inhabitants of the onetime promised land. Likewise, as was normal in the atmosphere of the times, the only strategy considered was a pact with some power or group of powers in exchange for favours which the would-be settlers might be in a position to bestow. The terms 'colonization' and 'colony' were used quite without inhibitions by the pioneers of political Zionism. Herzl wrote of Palestine: "We should there form a portion of the rampart of Europe against Asia, an outpost of civilization as opposed to barbarism." (*A Jewish State*, London, 1896, p. 29)

Small Jewish colonies did exist within Palestine. Jews of many different origins had come to settle in the Holy Land, side by side with an already motley population. In 1880 they numbered some 24,000 of a total of perhaps 500,000 inhabitants. After the new wave of anti-Semitism had begun in Russia in 1881, great numbers of Russian Jews fled to Westen Europe or the United States, but some directed their steps towards Palestine. A movement had sprung up among the Russian Jews advocating the establishment of Jewish agricultural settlements in Palestine or Syria. Agricultural labour was supposed to regenerate the Jewish people, degraded or at least denatured by centuries in the ghetto. A variety of Tolstoyan socialism became manifest in the movement of the "Lovers of Zion." It was possible that a true Jewish socialist society might grow up in Palestine. But the Jewish settlements in Palestine were not numerous, and before the advent of Herzl the prospect of a Jewish State was ignored or considered to be extremely far off. Then came Herzl, and the first Congress of the Zionist Movement held in Basle in 1897 marked a new departure.

Throughout all this, the actual inhabitants of Palestine were ignored by practically everybody. The philosophy prevailing in the European world at the time was without any doubt responsible for this. Every territory situated outside that world was considered empty—not of inhabitants of course, but constituting a kind of cultural vaccuum, and therefore suitable for colonization. And in fact the European nations were able to impose their will in most parts of the world without too much difficulty.

It was unfortunate for the form of Jewish nationalism represented by Zionism that just at the moment when it decided to direct its efforts towards achieving a Jewish State in Palestine, the natives of that country began to be affected by a similar ideological movement, namely Arab nationalism.

The Arabs were an ancient people from the Near East, whose language, like that of the ancient Hebrews, was a branch of the family known as "Semitic." Ancient Hebrew mythology recognized them as close relatives of the Hebrews, together with all the other neighbouring peoples, and it is certainly true that the same ethnic or racial characteristics appeared, perhaps in slightly varying degrees, in all these peoples of the ancient Middle East. Of course this by no means prevented bitter rivalries, sometimes going as far as outright hostility. The Arabs, inhabitants of the Arabian peninsula, began at a very early date to make frequent incursions into neighbouring territories. At the beginning of the seventh century they were politically and ideologically united by their prophet Muhammad (or Mahomet), who preached a new religion, Islam, which drew heavily for its inspiration on Judaism and Christianity. The Arabs subsequently conquered an enormous area of the earth's surface, extending from India and the fringes of China to Spain and Southern France. They did not force their religion on the conquered Jews and Christians, since they granted that these religions were in possession of a certain element of the truth. Religious minorities were "protected," though obliged to pay special taxes. However, the political and social conditions of the state ruled by the Muslim Arabs (soon to become fragmented) gradually induced the majority of its subjects to embrace the Islamic faith. Some of these subjects, between Mesopotamia and Morocco, were gradually "Arabized" and became indistinguishable from their Arab conquerors.

Arab domination was brief among those peoples—principally the Persians and the Turks—who, although they had become Muslims, had not been Arabized. Native Persian and Turkish dynasties very soon came to power and before long dominated the Arabs and their Arabized subjects. National feeling certainly existed at that time, in that part of the world as elsewhere, but had not as yet acquired an ideology. To be ruled by sovereigns of foreign origin was a perfectly normal phenomenon, in many cases accepted for thousands of years. Co-religionism between rulers and ruled (except for some minority groups) seemed a far more important characteristic.

From the fourteenth century a Muslim state, that of the Ottoman Turks, began to show its strength in Anatolia. By the sixteenth and seventeenth centuries it had subjugated most of the territories with Arab populations, in particular Egypt, Palestine and Syria, which had for two or three centuries been under the suzerainty of the Mamelukes, rulers who were themselves of Turkish origin. The Ottoman Empire was an immense structure, governed from Istanbul (previously Constantinople). The Sultan who resided there ruled over a tremendously varied population, extending from Belgrade and Bucharest to Algeria and the Yemen. His power was, of course, sanctified by Islam. The minority religions, Christianity and Judaism in particular, were allowed considerable autonomy; but the governors of the various provinces of the Empire made their authority felt by all their subjects through their highly arbitrary rule, and above all by extracting the maximum tribute in taxes, dues and rents.

Towards the end of the eighteenth century the preponderance of Europe began to make itself felt. The economic, technological and military superiority of this part of the world, which had for some time been foreshadowed by increasingly spectacular scientific advances, became more and more overwhelming. European merchants who had long had a foothold in the Muslim countries enjoyed an increasingly privileged position. European ambassadors who had earlier had little status were now admitted to the Sultan's counsels and even began to dictate policy. They were frequently aided and abetted by the local Christian community, their common ideology providing a means of mutual understanding, and also by the local Jews, many of whom came from Europe, and who in any case maintained close relations with their European co-religionists. The Ottomans, who as recently as 1683 had stood before the gates of Vienna, now retreated through the Balkans before the Christian powers. The Balkan subject peoples revolted one by one, with European encouragement, eroding the frontiers of the Empire. The French took Algiers in 1830, the British Aden in 1839, thus beginning the movement of direct colonization. After a pause during which the European powers consolidated their indirect but terribly effective hold over the whole of the Ottoman Empire, Anglo-French colonial expansion moved inexorably forwards: Tunisia in 1881, Egypt in 1882, the Sudan in 1899, Libya and Morocco in 1912. At the same time, the cultural influence of Europe grew everywhere stronger. Its values, its forms of organizational, even its fashions had increasing impact, penetrating first the rich and cultured elite, then gradually the poverty-stricken masses. Europe brought domination and humiliation; but at the same time she introduced a new style of political and cultural life. She showed that a political structure was possible in which the state's subjects could also have their say in its government, and that a culture was conceivable in which the masses could be educated to a degree enabling them in principle to understand and participate in decisions taken at the topmost level. Moreover it was these organizational forms which appeared to express European superiority, enabling an advance along the path of infinite progress towards greater liberty and greater welfare. Slowly new aspirations, new loyalties, new ideas began to appear and to spread.

This new mentality, the new horizons which Europe had revealed, only served to make European domination, whether direct or indirect, even harder to bear. The most universal sentiment was an immense humiliation, shared by an entire people, from sultan to the humblest peasant. Moreover those who were most determined to learn European ways and share the secret of her power usually did so as a first step on the road towards an implacable revenge.

The Muslim rulers, who had to make decisions from one day to the next, reacted as best they could, according to the pressures acting on them and their different temperaments. Some clung to the old forms and structures on which their power was based, and resisted all change except under duress. Others attempted to introduce reforms, in a more or less consistent manner. In a society in which the old order of things largely persisted, under the watchful eye of the European powers who made sure that such reforms would in no way threaten their dominant position, these measures usually came to nought, or resulted in deadlock or crisis.

The future was being forged elsewhere. Intellectuals of a new type were gradually beginning to appear, who although educated in the traditional disciplines of the old culture were sensitive to the new situation, open to new ideas, and convinced of the need to lead their peoples out of the dark tunnel of backwardness and humiliation. Their level of culture was uneven and frequently superficial, they varied greatly in intellectual power and moral standards; it would be easy to highlight the unscrupulousness of some of them, the deficiencies of others, the defects of all. Nevertheless, it was their function as intellectuals to create dynamic and appealing ideologies; and they fulfilled this function. This was not done as an abstract exercise but with direct reference to the objective situation as they saw it. Their ideas, inasmuch as they reflected the situation accurately and held out some hope of a solution to universal problems, evoked an increasingly powerful response.

The men who won influence over increasingly wide sections of society and ultimately left their mark upon history were the prophets of immediate or eventual liberation. They expected a more or less Utopian breakthrough towards a new set of values: the suppression of privilege; liberty; welfare; in short, happiness. Naturally enough, this liberating upsurge was at first conceived within the old framework of society. The existing frameworks were the Muslim relgous community, the *umma*; and the political structures—the Ottoman Empire, Iran and the state of Egypt. The first great mobilizer of opinion was Jemal ad-din al-Afghani (1839–1897). He belonged to the select line of great nineteenth-century nationalist and liberal revolutionaries. Like them, he was a conspirator, and a secularist freemason. By plots, expedients and lies, he dedicated his life to the cause which he hoped to lead to victory. Actually a Persian Shiite, he posed as an Afghan Sunnite in order to gain greater influence over the orthodox Mohammedan world (hence his pseudonymous surname, al-Afghani, the Afghan). At some time in his career he had decided that religion was still a powerful force and not to be despised. He hoped, indeed, to exploit it in arousing the masses to revolt against reactionary despotism, allied in his view with foreign domination. He thus assumed the character of a Muslim Holy Man, not without revealing quite different features to his European friends. He attempted to play off one European power against others, frequently changing his tactics and running the risk of being himself more exploited than able to exploit these powers. But he sowed ideas; simple and sometimes wrong but always dynamic ideas. They were to fall on fertile ground.

He won many disciples, in Iran, in the Ottoman Empire and throughout the Muslim world. Their attitudes towards Islam, towards the modernization of their society and social progress, and towards the use of violence differed considerably. But they were united by one fundamental aspiration, the most common characteristic of that mass of society which they represented: the recapture of national independence from the European colonial powers.

This central theme was argued on different grounds and with different emphasis by the various ideologies. But it was always present. And around these ideologies there grew up very gradually small and at first insignificant groups of men dedicated to putting the programme of liberation into effect.

Who was to be liberated? The Muslim community, the Ottoman Empire, the Egyptian nation, the Arab people? It mattered little at first, since the enemy was in every case the same—the European imperialist powers, and especially the most dynamic of them at that time and the most actively interested in the area, Great Britain.

Nevertheless, European nationalist ideas infected all the political ideologues of the Muslim world; and they based themselves on a European model—the nation-state built up around a people defined by a common language. This alien model, which ultimately captured the imagination first of the elite and then of the masses, must have struck a chord in pre-national fellings of identification—inhibited no doubt by community of religion, but nonetheless always present in more or less repressed form.

The Turks were the first to be affected by this type of nationalism. The "Ottomanists" had originally wanted merely to create an Ottoman nation of the modern, liberal type in an atmosphere of romanticism. But because most of the members of this group were Turks, it was soon guided by feelings of specifically Turkish national pride. This found expression in increased interest in Turkish national origins, and a love for historic monuments to the ancient grandeur of the Turks. The Young Turk movement overthrew the despot Abdul Hamid in 1908, and replaced him by a regime which appealed to all the different national elements in the Ottoman Empire, but increasingly tended to maintain and reinforce the supremacy of the Turks in that Empire. This was bound to provoke a reaction among the other nationalities and favour the crystallization of Arab and other nationalist ideologies.

The broad outlines of such an ideology had already been drawn. Not surprisingly, a considerable number of the new ideologues were Christian Arabs from the Lebanon, who were not bound by any ties of religion to the Turks. After 1908, resistance to Turkish supremacy reinforced the movement in this direction. The minimum demand was for the decentralization of the Ottoman Empire; the maximum was Arab independence. But support for these demands was still hesitant. Most Arabs had not forgotten that "the principal contradiction" (as Mao Tse-Tung was to say half a century later) was the struggle against European imperialism, even if some did not hesitate to court the aid of, say, France against Great Britain. Moreover the Muslim Arabs shrank from conducting a ruthless struggle against the Turks.

In Palestine, which had an Arab majority, the situation was complicated by the gradual growth of the Jewish settlements. These had now generally accepted Herzl's doctrine of political Zionism. Herzl (who died in 1904) had attempted to win the support of various European powers and of the Sultan Abdul Hamid for the establishment of his Jewish State in Palestine. At first this was to take the relatively innocuous form of an autonomous territory under Ottoman suzerainty, on the pattern of the Lebanon. This scheme was unsuccessful. Herzl's successors then put off the achievement of the final objective for a more auspicious time, but never lost sight of it. Meanwhile they continued to found Jewish settlements in Palestine to help reinforce their claims. By 1914 the Jews comprised 85,000 out of a total population of 739,000.

The Palestinian Arabs, in direct contact with the Jewish settlers, had realized the danger of having grafted on to them a foreign community isolated from the life of the local inhabitants. It did not require great perspicacity to understand the aspirations of this alien community to form a new national entity, and hence to subjugate or displace the native peoples. They had protested vigorously in the Ottoman Parliament. However, the virile nationalism of the Young Turks made any early cession of territory seem extremely unlikely. Jewish immigration was restricted by the Ottoman state, although bureaucratic corruption made the restrictions easy to circumvent. Some Arab nationalist leaders, especially non-Palestinians, contemplated an alliance with the Zionist movement against Turkish supremacy. Contributions from the Diaspora put considerable funds at the disposal of the Jews, who were far more advanced both technologically and economically, and were culturally on a level with Europe. They would therefore have been a formidable ally to the young Arab movement, which was poor and inexperienced, with a thoroughly underdeveloped social basis, to express it in fashionable terminology. And some negotiations towards an Arab-Zionist alliance did in fact take place.

But on 2 November 1914, the Ottoman Empire under the rule of the Young Turks entered the world war on the side of Germany and Austria Hungary against Great Britain, France and Russia. A new era had opened.

GREAT BRITAIN AND PALESTINE IN THE WAR, 1914-1917[2]

British policy in regard to Palestine in the war years preceding 1917 was never formulated with any precision, despite an agreement with the French in 1916 to internationalize the administration of Palestine and despite exchanges of letters with the Arabs in 1915 and 1916 over the future of Arab territory. Many individuals, offices, and departments had concrete ideas and plans for Palestine's future, but the final working out of these ideas and plans, it was generally recognized, had to be left until the larger questions arising from the war were settled. At no time was it possible to say the British policy was monolithic in its approach to Palestine. Mark Sykes, the member of Lloyd George's "garden suburb" who was responsible for the Middle East from 1916 until his death in 1919, counted at one time eighteen authorities both in London and abroad who had to be consulted before a move involving the Middle East could be made. The Sharif Husayn, a British ally whose role in the fighting against the Ottoman Empire was a subject of controversy within the British government, noted once that he saw not one government, but five.

This uncertainty, vagueness, and lack of coordination was not, of course, unlimited. By 1917, as a result of the wartime need to deal with Russian, French and Arab claims for territory in the Middle East, the British had been forced into a delineation of interests that was a good deal firmer than they really wanted. For over a century, British policy toward the Eastern Question had been governed by the overriding need to guard the approaches to India by keeping the Asian portion of the Ottoman Empire intact and keeping Arabia, Persia, and Afghanistan together as a geographical bloc which Britain had no desire to occupy but which she was determined would not be occupied by any rival. When the Ottoman Empire drifted into hostilities against the Entente powers in late October 1914, the British had to reappraise traditional policy. Their reaction in terms of tactics was immediate, but it took much longer for a new strategic policy to emerge.

[2]By the historian D. Edward Knox, from his book *The Making of a New Eastern Question: British Palestine Policy and the Origins of Israel, 1917-1925*, pp. 9-21. Copyright © 1981 The Catholic University of America Press. Reprinted by permission.

Two days before Britain declared war on Turkey on 3 November 1914, she recognized Kuwait's independence from the Ottoman Empire. On 5 November she formally annexed Cyprus and on 18 December established a protectorate over Egypt. Militarily, Britain reacted even more swiftly. She reinforced Egypt, bombarded the Dardanelles forts, and landed in southern Mesopotamia an expeditionary force that had been standing by in the Persian Gulf.

Despite this evident departure from a "policy of conservation," due to the fundamental change in the British-Ottoman relationship, British policy continued to be guided by the principle of denying territory to all powers capable of threatening communication with India. True, modifications were necessary. In view of the great danger of war in the West, Ottoman hostility, and British sensitivity to the Russian alliance, Constantinople, no longer vital to British interests since about 1890, was considered expendable, if the Russians desired it. On the other hand, Egypt, which had acquired the Ottoman capital's former importance in British eyes, was significantly not annexed into the empire, though that had been the first impulse of the Foreign Office, but merely included under Britain's protection. In other particulars also, the British maintained traditional lines of policy. Because of a division of opinion between the Indian government on the one hand and Lord Kitchener and the Arabists of Cairo and Khartoum on the other, even Mesopotamia remained an undecided question so far as eventual territorial acquisition went. Palestine was wanted, not for itself, but for security of the head of the Persian Gulf and to deny France proximity to Egypt and a border with Arabia. Since the Entente powers were not prepared at any time during the war to permit one power to gain exclusive control of Palestine, except for a British base in Haifa, they were all reconciled to internationalizing its administration, in effect leaving it a buffer zone. In fact the most concrete conclusion to come from war committee meetings in March 1915 was that the government's territorial desiderata should be to preserve a Muslim political entity and to maintain the security of the Arabian holy places.

In reluctant pursuit of its policy of security for its own interests in the southern portion of the Ottoman Empire, the British government prior to 1917 entered into two major understandings with its French and Arab allies. The first, the Husayn-

McMahon correspondence, arose from a British desire to exploit Arab dissatisfaction with Turkish rule. The second, the Sykes-Picot Agreement of May 1916, resulted from an intense French diplomatic campaign to arrive at an early defintion of war aims.

In February and April 1914, Abdullah, the second son of Sharif Husayn of Mecca, had approached Lord Kitchener, British agent and consul general in Cairo, and Ronald Storrs, his oriental secretary, about a modest supply of arms for the sharif to use for defense against the Turks. He had, of course, been politely refused, but the visit was momentous nevertheless. In September, Storrs, after seeking and obtaining the approval of Captain Gilbert F. Clayton, then Sudan agent and director of intelligence of the Egyptian army, reminded Kitchener in a private letter of the encounter with Abdullah. Kitchener, now secretary of state for war in London, had long cherished the idea of an Arab kingdom under British auspices, and he fell in with the suggestion by issuing an immediate order for Storrs to send a "secret and carefully chosen messenger" to Abdullah to sound out the attitude of the Arabs toward an alliance with Great Britain should the sultan be forced into war.

Subsequent negotiations were protracted, formal views being exchanged over an eight-month period (14 July 1915 to 10 March 1916). In his initial letter, Sharif Husayn spelled out the Arab position to Sir Henry McMahon, the first British high commissioner for Egypt. The letter, based on the so-called Damascus Protocol drawn up by Arab nationalist groups in Syria, required that England "acknowledge the independence of the Arab countries" within certain specified boundaries, as a reward for an Arab revolt in the interests of the Entente. Months later, on 24 October 1915, after the Foreign Office had begged him at the urgent request of Sir Ian Hamilton at Gallipoli to take immediate steps to split the Arabs from the Turks for military reasons, McMahon replied to Husayn.

Aware of simultaneous negotiations with the French and of the need for caution, he adopted a policy of deliberate vagueness. He wrote Husayn that, subject to three reservations, "Great Britain is prepared to recognize and support the independence of the Arabs in all the regions within the limits demanded by the Sharif of Mecca. Among these controversial reservations were two that affected the later treatment of Palestine. The first excluded the "portions of Syria lying to the west of the districts of Damascus,

Homs, Hama and Aleppo" on the grounds that they were not purely Arab, and the second excluded those regions where Britain's freedom to act alone was limited by the "interests of her ally, France."

There is a large literature on the question of whether or not Palestine was included in McMahon's limitation of Arab independence. McMahon and Clayton always maintained in later years that the sharif understood and initially accepted that Palestine's future had not yet been determined. Unfortunately, these official explanations came long enough after the event to cast considerable doubt on their complete veracity, and the controversy has continued to grow. Currently the weight of evidence clearly supports the British contention that Palestine was not promised to the Arabs in 1915. First, in March 1916, Foreign Secretary Sir Edward Grey proposed to the French and Russian governments that the Allies offer the Jews "an arrangement in regard to Palestine completely satisfactory to Jewish aspirations," a firm indication, even though the proposal came to nothing, that the secretary considered Palestine excluded from McMahon's promise. Second, the De Bunsen Committee (named after its chairman, Sir Maurice de Bunsen), appointed in April 1915 to study British war aims in the Middle East, recommended in June that Palestine should be the subject of "special negotiations, in which both belligerents and neutrals are alike interested." Thus the committee fully recognized that Britain was not free to act on Palestine without consulting French and Russian interests, and in the circumstances, a promise of Palestine to the Arabs would not have been contemplated. Third, Lord Kitchener, a staunch supporter of the idea of an Arab caliphate under Husayn and with British backing, failed to point out to the British government that the Sykes-Picot Agreement of May 1916 might contradict the pledges given Husayn. The least this indicates is that British promises regarding the Middle East were considered to be of secondary importance, tentative or speculative, and open to redefinition. Fourth, and most conclusive, in April 1918, almost two years after the beginning of the Arab uprising, events in Europe caused the British to withdraw elements from east of the Jordan in order to send reinforcements to the western front. Clayton, at the time Allenby's chief political officer, wrote Mark Sykes that he expected no difficulty with Faysal, out on the right wing of the British army, regarding the pullback of troops. He pointed out that the Arab leader had "always been apprehensive of our operating east of the Jordan in case it should lead to permanent occupation." Clayton continued significantly:

He will, therefore, regard our withdrawal as a loyal consequence of the policy which we have always laid down in our dealings with him, e.g. that we regard the country east of the Jordan as his sphere so far as he is able to make good in it.

The implication of a delineation of territories is clear. The area east of the Jordan was to be open to Faysal's influence, while cis-Jordan would remain uncommitted to the Arabs and at the disposal of Britain and her allies. This unsolicited statement, a rare instance of direct contemporary evidence on this controversial problem, came from the pen of a man who was "in daily touch with Sir Henry McMahon throughout the negotiations with King Hussein, and made the preliminary drafts of all the letters." It offers strong support for the claim Clayton made in 1923, at Sir Herbert Samuel's request, that McMahon never intended that "Palestine should be included in the general pledge given the Sherif" and that the Arab leaders understood this fact.

No matter which way the evidence points, however, and there is more evidence of an inferential nature that could be added, Palestine was not specifically mentioned in their correspondence by either Husayn or McMahon. But even if the Sharifians clearly understood the reservations concerning Palestine, and even if the subsequent British arguments were legally sound, it remains to be demonstrated that the people of Palestine were encouraged to draw any other inference than that they were to be included in an independent Arabia. Even such an authority on the East as Lord Curzon, who was not in the government at the time of the pledges, labored under a misapprehension as he attempted to articulate British policy in 1918. At that time he declared without contradiction in the presence of several other foreign policy experts at a meeting of the Eastern Committee that

If we deal with our commitments, there is first the general pledge to Hussein in October 1915, under which Palestine was included in the areas as to which Great Britain pledged itself that they should be Arab and independent in the future.

The statement was inaccurate, but even so, to British politicians it obviously presented no significant deterrent to strengthening British interests in Palestine. The argument regarding 1915 is a very subtle one, and the ambiguity of Britain's attitude toward

Palestine did not decrease as the war progressed. In fact, the situation became much more difficult when, at the end of the war, Britain appeared to have the power to dispose of Palestine as it wished, in which case, the Arab argument is, Palestine should have reverted to the area of Arab independence. However, as will be seen, Britain was able to gain its way over Palestine only by using Zionism as a lever to force the French to give up their claims to the Holy Land. The Anglo-French Entente could stand—barely—the strain of fulfilling Zionism, whereas satisfying Arab aspirations might not have reconciled the French to the loss of their traditional goal. . . .

By late 1916 Britain had secured its basic interests in Palestine: it had acquired a base and denied administrative and political control to any other single power. Events, however, were moving swiftly. During the revolutionary year of 1917, Britain's inital attempts to solve the Eastern Question were quickly rendered meaningless and even dangerously out of date, and the Palestine question reached a new and more central position British thinking.

The motivating force behind the dynamic changes in British policy in 1967 was supplied by Britain's new prime minister, David Lloyd George. Within a few days of his taking power in December 1916, preparations were begun for stepping up military activity in the Middle East and obtaining the support of Jewish world opinion for an Allied victory. Agitation for the British government to adopt a Zionist policy had begun early in the war when Herbert Samuel, then president of the Local Government Board, suggested to the foreign secretary that "the opportunity might arise" in the course of a war with the Ottoman Empire "for the fulfillment of the ancient aspiration of the Jewish people and the restoration in Palestine of a Jewish State." Sire Edward Grey confessed his sympathy with the idea and said that he would do what he could if an opportunity arose. Lloyd George was also approached on the subject by Samuel, who reported that he "was very keen to see a Jewish state established there." Little came officially of these early expressions of interest largely because of Prime Minister H. H. Asquith's lack of sympathy with Zionist ideals. However, a number of influential men in government service had become converted to Zionism by 1917. Of particular importance were the outstanding and forceful personalities of Lord Robert Cecil, General Smuts, and Lord Milner. Also of importance were several men—Philip Kerr, L. S. Amery, William Orms-by-Gore, and the famous Mark Sykes—who were to be included in Lloyd George's "garden suburb," where they were well placed to reintroduce the discussion of Zionist objectives in the Cabinet whenever more pressing business crowded it out. . . .

Lloyd George, already a most persistent "easterner," now bent on acquiring a British Palestine and on using an assumed Jewish international power, pressed for an active military program in the East to break the wartime stalemate. Although impressed by the prime minister's desire for a winter offensive, General Sir Archibald Murray, commander-in-chief of the Egyptian Expeditionary Force (EEF), timidly postponed an attack on Gaza, the gateway to Palestine, until 26 March 1917. Though the assault was a disastrous failure, the War Cabinet gained the impression that success was around the corner. On 2 April the Cabinet approved a resolute forward policy in Palestine designed to sweep the Turks out of southern Palestine and take Jerusalem. On 3 April, as he was about to leave for Egypt to become the head of the political mission attached to Murray's force, Mark Sykes received his instructions from Lloyd George and Lord Curzon, then lord president of the council. They stressed "the importance of not prejudicing the Zionist movement and the possibility of its development under British auspices." Sykes was specifically enjoined by the prime minister from entering into any political pledges to the Arabs, "and particularly none in regard to Palestine." Any problems they expected would come from the French, not the Arabs, who "probably realized that there was no prospect of their being allowed any control over Palestine." With Arabs out of the running in Palestine, military possession by a British army could be decisive so far as the French were concerned, and if that were not sufficient, perhaps the addition of a moral factor—Jewish opinion throughout the world—would impress the French.

Despite Murray's second failure at Gaza late in April, the War Cabinet, on 23 April, decided to adhere to an offensive policy in Palestine. The Russian revolution in March and the evaporation of the Russian army, the failure of the Nivelle offensive in France, and the fear of a renewed Turkish drive on Baghdad combined to provide cogent military reasons for an increased effort on the Palestine front. The British still had a strong army on the front, and it was felt that an impressive victory in Palestine and the conquest of Jerusalem would give a badly needed lift to the morale of the British public. The spring of 1917 was thus the turning point for the Zionists. The impending British invasion of Palestine combined with the decline of power in Russia opened the way to sharpened diplomatic conflict between Britain and France over the domination of Palestine. In appreciation of this fact, the British began moving from a position of tolerant interest in Zionism to one approaching commitment.

British policy then seemed to lose its cohesion and consistency so far as Palestine was concerned. In April 1917, the Treaty of Saint-Jean de Maurienne was being concluded by Great Britain, France, and Italy; its provisions called for an international administration for Palestine, in confirmation of the 1916 agreement. At the same time the uncertainties over Russia in 1917 led to an official review of the 1916 agreement. On 12 April a Committee on Territorial Terms of Peace was set up under the chairmanship of Lord Curzon. The committee concluded on 28 April that the agreement had to be modified so that Palestine and Mesopotamia would be placed in the definite and exclusive control of Great Britain. So the mercurial British prime minister had indeed broken the logjam in the East, but he had also created conflicting lines of policy.

The 1916 agreement continued to hold official sway while attempts to subvert it came from all sides. In July, Commander D. G. Hogarth, director of Cairo's Arab Bureau under Clayton, wrote to London urging its revision in favor of strengthening Britain's position in Palestine and Arabia. One month later, on 14 August, Sykes, now wholly caught up by his Zionist zeal, proposed to scrap the whole agreement and "get Great Britain appointed trustee of the powers for the administration of Palestine." The Anglo-French Entente was still the cornerstone of his scheme, but it was to be cemented to an alliance of Jews, Arabs, and Armenians. The French, alerted by Sykes on 6 April 1917 to British ambitions for a protectorate in Palestine, were of the opinion that London considered the 1916 agreement dead. The agreement, however, clung tenaciously to life until the armistice with Turkey and even afterward.

The road to the Balfour Declaration had been cleared with surprising speed in the spring of 1917. The Sykes-Picot Agreement and the promises to the Arabs were of small importance in view of a fast-changing international picture and the new administration in London. On 25 April 1917, Lord Robert Cecil told Weizmann that if the Zionists were to ask for a British Palestine, it would strengthen Britain's hand in future negotiations. On 18 July the Zionists submitted to the government the invited draft declaration of British sympathy for Zionist aspirations. After much official discussion, at times very heated, the British government gave the Zionists their promise in the form of a letter from Foreign Secretary Balfour to Lord Rothschild. The statement authorized by the Cabinet amounted to only one sentence:

His Majesty's Government view with favour the establishment in Palestine of a national home for the Jewish people, and will use their best endeavours to facilitate the achievement of this object, it being clearly understood that nothing shall be done which may prejudice the civil and religious rights of existing non-Jewish communities in Palestine, or the rights and political status enjoyed by Jews in any other country.

Ambiguously and vaguely, the Cabinet looked forward to the eventual emergence of a Jewish "home," whatever that might mean, but definitely did not promise to take on the responsibility for bringing it about. On 31 October 1917, the day the declaration was approved, Balfour addressed himself in the Cabinet to the problem of the unfamiliar term *national home*. He said he understood it to mean

some form of British, American, or other protectorate, under which full facilities would be given to the Jews to work out their own salvation and to build up, by means of education, agriculture, and industry, a real centre of national culture and focus of national life. It did not necessarily involve the early establishment of an independent Jewish state, which was a matter for gradual development in accordance with the ordinary laws of political evolution.

Personally, Balfour hoped the Jews would establish a state, as he confided to Colonel Richard Meinerzhagen in February 1918, adding, "It is up to them now; we have given them their great opportunity." On the other hand, Balfour was not ready to predict where this opportunity would lead. According to Sir Maurice Hankey, Balfour thought the Jewish national home "might turn out to be anything from a religious and cultural centre, a kind of Jewish Vatican, to a Jewish State; time alone would show. . . .

In late October, Allenby began his Palestine campaign. He took Beersheba on 31 October, captured Gaza, and then rolled up the coastal plain. On 11 December 1917, he entered liberated Jerusalem. The time of groping for solution from afar was at an end; it was now necessary to grapple with real military, political, and human problems at first hand. The flexibility the British had managed to retain since 1914 was about to meet the harsh realities of occupation needs. . . .

IN PLACE OF A SUMMARY[3]

The Mandatory period was characterised by three main features of Zionist policy towards the Arabs. First, the Arab national movement as a whole was viewed *de haut en bas*. There was a dramatic under-estimation of the potential of the Arab world for modernisation, based on its enormous natural resources, and its capacity to mobilise social, intellectual and political ability to exploit them.

The importance of the Middle East, politically, economically and strategically, has increased many times over since 1917 or 1948. The dependence of the Western economies and military operations upon oil is far greater than it was. The weight of the bloc of the 17 Arab states in world councils has no comparison with their position during the Mandatory period.

No Zionist leader foresaw these developments. The Zionist movement believed that the qualitative superiority of the Jewish people, with their highly-educated scientific-technical cadres, would compensate for the superiority in numbers of the Arabs. While originally this had an economic context, during the Mandatory period it developed into a concept of military superiority, which, confirmed by the 1948 war, seemed to place Israel on par with all the Arab states combined. It was only in the wake of the war of October 1973 that a new and more realistic appraisal of the Jewish-Arab relationship began to emerge. It is only beginning because those who determine Israel's policy today are still committed to the old concept of maximising Israel's military potential based on its scientific-technical advantages over the Arabs

[3]By Simha Flapan (1911–1987), national secretary (1954–1981) of Israel's Mapam Party and director of its Arab affairs department, founder-editor of the monthly *New Outlook,* and founder-director of the Jewish-Arab Institute and the Israeli Peace Research Institute. From *Zionism and the Palestinians*, Croom Helm, 1979, pp. 353–354. Copyright © 1979 Simha Flapan. Reprinted with permission from Harper & Row Publishers, Inc.

disregarding the truth that while battles are won by military technology, wars, today, are determined by the economic potential of the combatants. The futility of this strategy today is expressed by Israel's desire for the ultimate weapon—the nuclear bomb—whose introduction into the Middle East can lead only to the mutual destruction of both sides.

The corollary of the military strategy towards the Arabs has been the search for a Great Power ally, the second tenet of Zionist strategy which was initiated in the Mandatory period. Until 1948, the Zionist movement staked its future on British support and strove to integrate itself into the strategic needs of the British Empire. Today it is seeking a similar alliance with the United States, without regard to the fact that the international scene has changed considerably, and the Great Powers can no longer exert untrammelled influence throughout the world. It also ignores the same disparity that existed with respect to Great Britain, that the strategic interests of the Great Power and the Zionist movement may not correspond. Today America is in a process of reappraising its strategic position in the Middle East. Just as with Great Britain, it must assess its interests in the Arab world, and the possible role of the Arab factor in an international confrontation, without regard to Israel's dependence on American support.

The third tenet of Zionist policy, inherited from the Mandatory period, was the non-recognition of the national aspirations of the Palestinians. This was a consistent feature of Zionist strategy, initiated by Weizmann and carried out by Ben-Gurion and his followers (Golda Meir, etc.). This policy has been followed despite the abundant proof of the tenacity with which the Palestinians have clung to their national identity in the most adverse circumstances of dispersion. The Palestinian question was seen as the major stumbling block by even the most farseeing and intellectual Zionist leaders (Ruppin, Arlozoroff), who were led to pessimism and despair of any solution.

From these strategic tenets certain erroneous policies were derived: (1) a policy of economic segregation of the two national economies; (2) the illusion that the Palestinian problem would disappear through a transfer of population to neighbouring Arab countries; and (3) a belief in the Hashemite connection—that the pro-Western regime of Jordan would solve the Palestinian problem.

All of these policies were realised by the state of Israel. The war of 1948 led to the flight of most of the Palestinians, and Jordan took over the West Bank. Yet, rather than resolving the conflict, these developments intensified it. Today the Palestinian people, though without a state, an army, or an economy, are the most important factor among the powerful Arab states, for one reason—because they alone hold the key to real peace in the Middle East. The Palestinians are a more decisive factor today than they were in 1948, and without a settlement with them on the basis of mutual recognition it will be difficult if not impossible to achieve a comprehensive and durable peace-settlement in the Middle East.

THE JEWISH CASE, PUT BEFORE THE PALESTINE ROYAL COMMISSION[4]

. . . I should like to put briefly before you the Jewish problem as it presents itself to us to-day. It is a two-fold problem; but its nature can perhaps be expressed in one word: it is the problem of the homelessness of a people. Speaking of homelessness, I should like at once to state that individual Jews, and individual groups of Jews, may have homes and sometimes very comfortable homes. Indeed, if one thinks of the small communities in the west of Europe beginning with England and continuing further down to the South—France, Switzerland, Italy (In December 1936 Italy had not yet imitated Germany's policy of "aryanisation."), Belgium, and Holland—these Jewish communities are, as compared to the Jews in Central, Eastern and South-Eastern Europe, in a fairly comfortable position. Then again, the position of the great Jewish community further west in America is, economically, and to a certain extent politically and morally such that Jews there are

[4]By Chaim Weizmann (1874–1952), president of the Zionist Organization and of the Jewish Agency for Palestine, later first president (1949–1952) of Israel. The Palestine Royal Commission was appointed by the British government in August 1936 under the chairmanship of Earl Peel; Dr. Weizmann presented the Jewish case on November 25, 1936. Reprinted in Barnet Litvinoff, ed., *Israel: A Chronology and Fact Book, 2500 B.C.–1972*, Oceana Publications, Inc., 1974, pp. 59–83. Copyright© 1974 Oceana Publications, Inc. Reprinted by permission.

free to work and labour without let or hindrance. But if one draws a line and takes the Rhine as the geographical boundary, almost everything to the east of the Rhine is to-day in a position, politically and economically, which may be described—and I am not given, I think, to exaggeration—as something that is neither life nor death; and one may add that if Europe to-day were in the same state as it was in 1914 before the War, with the highways and byways of Europe and the world in general open, then we should have witnessed an emigration of Jews that would probably have dwarfed the pre-war emigration—and the pre-war emigration was not by any means small. I think that in the year 1914 alone there emigrated out of Russia, which then included Poland as well, something in the neighbourhood of 120,000 Jews.

They went in the majority of cases to America, where they could readily be absorbed in a highly developed industrial country. The emigrant found his livelihood almost immediately on arrival. This, as Your Lordship and the members of the Commission are well aware, cannot happen to-day. The world is closed; and we have recently heard it said in authoritative quarters in Geneva, in Poland, and in England, that there are a million Jews too many in Poland. This is not the place to enter into a discussion as to why exactly a million *Jews*? They are citizens of Poland; their fate and their destinies have been bound up with the fate and destinies of Poland for well-nigh a thousand years. They passed through all the vicissitudes of the Polish nation. They desire to make their contribution, good, bad or indifferent—like everybody else—to Polish development. Why should they be singled out as being a million too many? No doubt these elementary facts as to the state of the world to-day are known in Poland just as they are known to every intelligent newspaper reader here. What does it mean? Where can they go? Is there any place in the world which can rapidly absorb a million people, whoever they may be, Jews or non-Jews? . . .

I do not want to press the point any further. I shall not waste the time of the Commission by describing in any way what is happening in Germany. It is too well known to need elaboration. This accounts for the position of something like 3,600,000 Jews. Poland has slightly over three millions; Germany had in 1932 or 1933 something like 600,000, but that number has since diminished. If one goes further afield, and takes the Jewries of Roumania, Latvia, Austria, one sees practically the same picture, and it is no exaggeration on my part to say that today almost six million Jews—I am not speaking of the Jews in Persia and Morocco and such places, who are very inarticulate, and of whom one hears very little—there are in this part of the world six million people pent up in places where they are not wanted, and for whom the world is divided into places where they cannot live, and places into which they may not enter.

I shall say a word here about Russia. In Russia there are about three million Jews. We have very little contact with them. Russia is a closed country at present. The situation has, I think, materially improved because many who could not be integrated into the present structure of Russia are in process of disappearing. They all seem to have gone or to be about to go. The old Jewish communities of Russia with their tradition—it was a venerable tradition, a tradition of culture and learning, a religious tradition—are destroyed. The younger generation are spread and scattered among the 170,000,000 Russians, and are gradually being integrated into the new social structure which has been created or is about to be created. But in the sense in which we understand Judaism, it is disappearing in Russia.

. . . But leaving the conditions in Russia aside, I think the brief description I have given of the position of the Jews in the rest of the world, with the exception of the western communities, is substantially correct, and if I may say so with respect, errs on the side of understatement.

Now we think this is not merely a problem which concerns the Jewish community. It is in our view a world problem of considerable importance. Naturally it is one which affects primarily the Jewish community, and secondarily the state of affairs in that particular part of the world, a part of the world which since the War has moved towards new forms of political and social life, and which is not yet very strong or very mature either politically or economically. These six million people to whom I have referred are condemned to live from hand to mouth, they do not know today what is going to happen to-morrow. I am not speaking now of organised anti-Semitism; even assuming the host-nations were quite friendly, there would still be purely objective reasons in those parts of the world, which would tend to grind down the Jewish community and make it into the flotsam and jetsam of the world—grind it into economic dust, so to speak. . . .

. . . In all countries we try to do our best, but somehow in many countries we are not entirely accepted as an integral part of the communities to which we belong. This feeling is one of the causes which have prompted Jews throughout the ages, and particularly in the last hundred years, to try to make a contribution towards the solution of the problem and to normalise—to some extent to normalise—the position of the Jews in the world. We are sufficiently strong, My Lord, to have preserved our identity, but an identity which is *sui generis* and not like the identity of other nations. When one speaks of the English or the French or the German nation, one refers to a definite State, a definite organization, a language, a literature, a history, a common destiny; but it is clear that when one speaks of the Jewish people, one speaks of a people which is a minority everywhere, a majority nowhere, which is to some extent indentified with the races among which it lives, but still not quite identical. It is, if I may say so, a disembodied ghost of a race, without a body, and it therefore inspires suspicion, and suspicion breeds hatred. There should be one place in the world, in God's wide world, where we could live and express ourselves in accordance with our character, and make our contribution towards the civilized world, in our own way and through our own channels. Perhaps if we had, we would be better understood in ourselves, and our relation to other races and nations would become more normal. We would not have to be always on the defensive or, on the contrary, become too aggressive, as always happens with a minority forced to be constantly on the defensive. . . .

What has produced this particular mentality of the Jews which makes me describe the Jewish race as a sort of disembodied ghost—an entity and yet not an entity in accordance with the usual standards which are applied to define an entity? I believe the main cause which has produced the particular state of Jewry in the world is its attachment to Palestine. We are a stiff-necked people and a people of long memory. We never forget. Whether it is our misfortune or whether it is our good fortune, we have never forgotten Palestine, and this steadfastness, which has preserved the Jew throughout the ages and throughout a career that is almost one long chain of inhuman suffering, is primarily due to some physiological or psychological attachment to Palestine. We have never forgotten it nor given it up. We have survived our Babylonian and Roman conquerors. The Jews put up a fairly severe fight and the Roman Empire, which digested half of the civilized world, did not digest small Judea. And whenever they once got a chance, the slightest chance, there the Jews returned, there they created their literature, their villages, towns, and communities. And, if the Commission would take the trouble to study the post-Roman period of the Jews and the life of the Jews in Palestine, they would find that during the nineteen centuries which have passed since the destruction of Palestine as a Jewish political entity, there was not a single century in which the Jews did not attempt to come back.

It is, I believe, a fallacy to regard those 1,900 years as, so to say, a desert of time; they were not. When the material props of the Jewish commonwealth were destroyed, the Jews carried Palestine in their hearts and in their heads wherever they went. That idea continued to express itself in their ritual and in their prayers. In the East End of London the Jew still prays for dew in the summer and for rain in the winter, and his seasons and festivals are all Palestinian seasons and Palestinian festivals. When Rome destroyed their country, the intellectual leader of the Jewish community came to the Roman commander and said, "You have destroyed all our material possessions; give us, I pray, some refuge for our houses of learning." A refuge was found; the place still exists, it was then a big place, and is now a tiny railway station by the name of Yebna, in Hebrew "Yavneh." There were schools there, and there the Jews continued their intellectual output, so that those schools became, so to speak, the spiritual homes, not only of Palestinian Jewry, but of Jewry at large, which was gradually filtering out of Palestine and dispersing all over the world. They replaced the material Palestine, the political Palestine, by a moral Palestine which was indestructible, which remained indestructible; and this yearning found its expression in a mass of literature, sacred and non-sacred, secular and religious. . . .

Before I close, I should like to mention two or three things which preceded the Balfour Declaration. When we first started our work in 1897, at the first Zionist Congress, and Dr. Herzl, who was then the leader of the Movement, tried to negotiate with the Sultan for our return to Palestine, the Sultan, in the usual Turkish way, never said "Yes" and never said "No," and things were uncertain. But the Jewish position grew worse from day to day and finally, in 1903, there was a massacre in Kishinev which started a wave of pogroms that swept over the whole of Russia. The position of the Jews became desperate.

The hope of ever obtaining anything definite from the Turkish Government dwindled, and the leader of the Zionist Movement, who always hoped that some day England might help us with the Return, met Joseph Chamberlain. Joseph Chamberlain had then just returned from a tour to Africa, and he made an offer of a country which then was called Uganda (and is now part of Kenya) to the Jews. And so we found ourselves—a Movement far from any practical realisation of its aspirations—treated very seriously by the mightiest government in the world who made us a generous offer, an offer of a territory almost as big as the mandated territory of Palestine. I think the territory which was then discussed was something like 8,000 square miles, a plateau in Uganda—I have have never been there, but as far as I know, good land. We had the rope round our necks; and yet, when this offer was brought to the Zionist Congress, a great discussion ensued and finally the offer was accepted in this form: that a Commission should be sent to the country in question to see what it was. But that was carried by a small majority; the minority, a very important minority, consisted primarily of Jews from Eastern Europe (I myself was amongst them), and they refused the offer for one reason only: "It is not Palestine, and it never will be Palestine." I remember we proposed that our leader should write a letter to the British Government and say something like this to the British Government: "We are extremely grateful for your generous offer, but we cannot accept it, just as we could not agree to cease to be Jews. Some day it may be given to you to make us another offer." We said, "We have waited two thousand years, and we shall wait a few more years; and in the fullness of time God will keep His promise to His people." Our Leader died, and the offer was refused. Twelve or thirteen years later, Mr. Balfour, who was Prime Minister in the Cabinet which had made the Uganda offer, gave us the Balfour Declaration. . . .

. . . Of course, we have always borne in mind, and our teachers and mentors at that time, British statesmen, repeatedly told us: "There is a second half to the Balfour Declaration. That second part provides that nothing should be done which might injure the interests of the non-Jewish communities in Palestine." Well, I must leave it to the Commission to test this and to ascertain whether, throughout the work of these last sixteen years, we have done anything which has in any way injured the position of the non-Jewish population. I go further than that. The Balfour

Declaration says that the civil and religious rights of the non-Jewish communities should not be interfered with. I would humbly ask the Commission to give the broadest possible interpretation to that, not merely a narrow interpretation of civil and religious rights; put it as broadly as the Commission may wish, and test it, and I think I can say before the Commission, before God, and before the world, that in intention, consciously, nothing has been done to injure their position. . . .

THE PALESTINIANS: WHENCE AND WHEN DID THEY COME?[5]

The people of Palestine has lost not only political control over its country but physical occupation of its country as well.

FAYEZ A. SAYEGH,
"Zionist Colonization in Palestine,"
Research Center,
Palestine Liberation Organization, Beirut,
page v

. . . land acquired by Jews became extra-territorialized. It ceased to be land from which the Arabs could ever hope to gain any advantage.

SAMI HADAWI,
Palestine in Focus,
Palestine Research Center, Beirut,
1968, page 20

Sayegh and Hadawi have served, for decades, as two of the most active and prolific spokesmen in presenting the Palestinian-Arab cause. In numerous books and pamphlets and lectures throughout the world, they and their colleagues have reiterated the theme of the "physical expulsion of the Arabs from Palestine" until this claim became a central axiom of Arab propaganda against Israel. How much truth is in this allegation?

Unbiased examination of the period in question will demonstrate that it was as a result of Jewish settlement and development in Palestine that the Arab sector expanded and flourished as nev-

[5]By Moshe Aumann, Zionist publicist, from David Niv, ed., *Know the Facts: A Historical Guide to the Arab-Israeli Conflict*, pp. 159–166. Copyright© 1985 the Department of Education and Culture, World Zionist Organization. Reprinted by permission.

er before, and precisely in those areas, both urban and rural, of
dense Jewish settlement. Examination of sources will show that
even before the beginning of Zionist settlement in the 1880s,
when the predominant demographic trend was large-scale emigration from the land rather than immigration toward it—even
then, the influx of both Arab and non-Arab elements, for various
reasons, was prevalent. For example, many of the Egyptians who
invaded Palestine in 1831 with Mohammed Ali's conquering
army remained in the country even after the Turkish reconquest
in 1840. Several thousand Egyptians who were brought in along
with the conquerors to settle vacant areas of the land joined the
considerable number of deserters who had previously fled Egypt
in order to escape compulsory army service. "In 1831," wrote the
French scholar Mohammed Sabry, "over six thousand fellahin
crossed the Egyptian border and Abdallah [governor of Acre], in
his great generosity, refused to return them" (*L'Empire Egyptien
sous Mohammed Ali et la question d'Orient*). After the conquest as
well, Mohammed Ali continued to bring settlers from Egypt to
Palestine. some of them settled in the Hula Valley, among them
Bedouin from the tribes of Ghawarna and Arb-el-Zweid. The al-
Hanadi tribe settled in the Jordan Valley. The Hadera region was
settled by the Arb Damaira tribe, and Wadi Hawarat (Emek-
Hefer) by the Arb Ofi tribe. Most of the city of Jaffa, according
to an 1878 British Palestine Exploration Society map of the area,
was made up of Egyptian neighborhoods. The Egyptians estab-
lished eight villages on the coastal plain, not far from the spot
where Tel Aviv was to be established fifty years later (see the entry on "Palestine" in the 1911 edition of the "Encyclopedia
Britannica"). Notable in the Tel Aviv area were the villages of
Feja, Jeljilya, Sumail, Sheikh-Mounis, Salame, and Umlabis (later
Petah-Tikvah). Egyptians also inhabited the villages of Zarnuga,
Kubeibeh, and Qatra (later Gedera) in the south. The historian
DeHaas reports that "Ibrahim Pasha, who left Palestine in 1941,
had left behind him permanent Egyptian colonies at Beisan, Nablus, Irbid, Acre, and Jaffa, where some five hundred Egyptian soldiers' families established a new quarter" (*History of Palestine*, p.
419). That is, at least two thousand Egyptian immigrants settled
in one place alone (Jaffa) in the nineteenth century, and with the
passage of time their children and grandchildren were assimilated into that demographic conglomeration today known as "the
Palestinians." In 1844 the American expedition under William
Francis Lynch found some eight thousand Turks in Jaffa among

a population of thirteen thousand. Lynch also found that the Moslem population of Safed was largely descended from Algerian tribes that had fought against the French and fled to Damascus and from there to Safed, and from Kurds who had settled in the city during an earlier period (*Narrative of the US Expedition to the River Jordan and the Dead Sea*). The Algerians (popularly termed "Mograbim") established four villages in the Lower Galilee (Kafar Sabat, Ma'ader, Ulam, and Sha'ara), and in the Upper Galilee the villages of Dalton, Alma, and Dishon. In 1878 Circassian refugees from the Caucasus who had fled the Russian Christian rule arrived in Palestine. Some settled in eastern Transjordan and some in the western part, where they established the villages of Kafar Kama, Sarona, and Reihaniya. During the period of Turkish rule, Moslems from Bosnia also found refuge in Palestine and settled near Caesarea.

Lloyd George (in *The Truth about the Peace Treaties*, Vol. II, p. 1127) quotes a statement by Lord Milner to the effect that "colonies of Turkomans, Circassians, Kurds, and other savage races have been planted about to hold the country in subjection." The English historian James Parkes, in his book *Whose Land?*, enumerates over twenty villages in the Galilee alone whose inhabitants came from distant lands during the last hundred years. He describes the phenomenon in these terms: "Israelite, Syrian, Greek, Arab, Latin, Egyptian, and Balkan peoples have all contributed to the present population . . . In some cases, villages are populated wholly by settlers from other portions of the Turkish Empire within the nineteenth century. There are villages of Bosnians, Druzes, Circassians, and Egyptians." The Encyclopedia Britannica (Eleventh edition, 1911) also speaks of the mosaic of peoples and tribes that comprised the Land of Israel of that day, before they came to be called "Palestinians": Turks, Jews, "very large contingents from the Mediterranean countries, especially Armenia, Greece, and Italy," Persians, Afghans, Motawila, Kurds, Germans, Bosnians, Circassians, Sudanese, Algerians, and Samaritans.

Arab immigrants, mostly from Egypt, settled next to the Jewish colonies in the South which were established in the early 1880s—Rishon leZion, Nes-Ziona, Rehovot, Ekron and Gedera—and found employment there in the citurs groves and vineyards. The Belgian company which laid the Jaffa-Jerusalem railway (opened in 1892) brought in hundreds of Egyptian laborers. After the British conquest many Syrian and Lebanese were employed in such projects as the laying of the Haifa-Kuneitra railway (which also employed thousands of Egyptians), building army camps, paving roads, and building the Haifa port. Many of these imported laborers did not return to their countries of origin when the work was finished, but remained in the country.

In 1947, Yale University published a comprehensive study of the political, economic, and social situation in Palestine between the two world wars (Esco Foundation for Palestine, Inc., *Palestine: A Study of Jewish, Arab, and British Policies*). The study (Vol I, pp. 229–230) quotes the German jurist Ernst Frankenstein who wrote:

The present-day inhabitants of Palestine are not in the main the descendents of the ancient inhabitants of the land, nor are they predominantly the descendents of the Arab conquerors of Palestine [in the seventh century] . . . Authorities agree that the peasantry of Palestine who might be regarded as being most directly descended from the ancient inhabitants had, by the nineteenth century, greatly dwindled in numbers.

And the writer of the study continues:

Of the Arabs living in Palestine at the beginning of the first World War, no small proportion had immigrated from neighboring countries since 1882. His (Frankenstein's) calculations led him to believe that only some 228,000 descendants of the 1882 Moslem settled population were living in Palestine at the outbreak of World War II. He thus comes the conclusion: "In other words, 75 per cent of the Arab population of Palestine are either immigrants themselves or descendants of persons who immigrated into Palestine during the last hundred years, for the most part after 1882.

Frankenstein's assertion was corroborated by the 1937 Palestine Royal Commission ("the Peel Commission") which reported that after centuries during which the ill-fated land lost its inhabitants, there came a turning-point and after World War I the number of Arab immigrants to the land exceeded the number of emigrants from it (Palestine Royal Commission Report, p. 279). In a special section, the Commission report notes that to the official listing must be added a considerable number of illegal immigrants who came largely from Hedjaz and eastern Transjordan. The report emphasizes that "under the Immigration Ordinance persons habitually resident in Trans-Jordan may, unless the High Commisssioner otherwise directs, enter Palestine direct from Trans-Jordan although they are not in possession of passports or other similar documents" (par. 40). The Yale study also mentions this phenomenon in relation to both Jews and Arabs (p. 319). The nature of the situation makes it difficult to arrive at precise and authorized figures on Arab immigration to Palestine between the two world wars. Estimates range from 60,000 to 200,000. There is general agreement, however, on one point: The chief reason for the reversal of Arab population movement was the Jewish settlement and development of the land, which altered its aspect and created sources of livelihood previously non-existent. James Parkes elaborates this point his book *A History of Palestine from 135 A.D. to Modern Times* (p. 320): "The Arab population continued to grow at a phenomenal rate, there a was substantial illegal immigration of Arabs especially from the Hauran, and Arab prosperity increased through the increased activity of the Jewish community and the many new openings for employment which it offered." . . .

It is of course difficult, in the absence of hard statistical evidence from that period, to pinpoint 1882 as the precise year in which the Arab demographic movement toward Palestine began. Nor is it likely that the positive effects of Zionist settlement were felt in any considerable degree in Palestine before the turn of the century. Two facts, however, emerge clearly from this analysis: (1) Some time after 1882, the then predominant trend of emigration from the Land was reversed, as Jews as well as Arabs immigrated there. (2) The constant influx into the land of non-Palestinian elements, both Arab and non-Arab, even before 1882 and certainly after that year, changed entirely the picture of an ancient Arab-Palestinian people that had resided for centuries on its soil until evicted, as it were, by the Jewish pioneers. As noted, the Arab population of the land reached its peak in the period between the two world wars, and demographic statistics prove that this population grew, between 1922 and 1929 alone, by more than 75% (excluding Bedouins). Such growth cannot be the result of natural increase alone.

II. THE FAILURE OF PARTITION:
THE ESTABLISHMENT OF THE STATE OF ISRAEL
AND THE PALESTINIAN DIASPORA

EDITOR'S INTRODUCTION

Partition—dividing the land under contention between Arabs and Jews—came to be British policy under the mandate: it was recommended by the Palestine Royal Commission in 1937 and confirmed and implemented as United Nations policy a decade later. Partition was bitterly opposed by all segments of Palestinian Arab opinion, which saw it as a Zionist-inspired, Western-approved means of taking from them their industry, their best agricultural land, and indeed their very patrimony. For the Zionists, however, it represented a triumph: for the first time, Jewish settlers could claim a numerical majority within their own borders, which were realized by means of a covenant internationally agreed upon.

It was not, however, a convenant which kept the peace between the two sides. As communal strife worsened during 1947, more and more of the better-off Palestinians fled their homes in the Jewish zone to settle—temporarily, they thought—in Cairo, Beirut, or Amman. For the Arab poor, the *fellaheen* in the villages, the luxury of such resettlement was impossible. They watched with growing fear as their land became the focus of attacks by the highly organized Zionist military forces. Palestinian military resistance proved ineffectual, certainly no match for their opponents' zeal and tactical efficiency.

The proclamation of the state of Israel in the spring of 1948 was a fateful occasion. The Jewish people had at last a national entity to which they could all repair; for many this marked the end of the Jewish diaspora which had begun nineteen centuries before. For the Palestinians the occasion was no less epochal: during the ensuing war, which Israel won handily, hundreds of Arab villages were cleared of their impoverished inhabitants, who were forced to flee to hastily constructed refugee camps outside the borders of the new state. The misery and degradation suffered by the Palestinian Arabs in their diaspora did not diminish as the decades passed: their losses fueled among them all a bitter intransigence against the Israeli usurpers and a determination to win back by any means possible what had been taken from them.

In the first article of this section Walid Khalidi, a Palestinian political scientist, chronicles the events leading up to the Palestinians' flight from the new state of Israel; this description is taken from his exceptionally well-presented collection of photographs showing the variety of Palestinian Arab life before 1948. The second article, by Fawaz Turki, is a Palestinian's account of what it feels like to be forcibly deprived of one's homeland, to be, in his words, "stateless for nearly all of my twenty-nine years," and to have grown to manhood in a refugee camp. Turki's book is among the most passionate of many which have appeared since the late 1940s describing the plight of the exiled Palestinians. The third article, by the Israeli historian Benny Morris, is a detailed reconstruction, using much evidence newly released from Israeli archives, of the dense, complex history surrounding the beginning of the Palestinian diaspora in 1947-1948. In the fourth article Hal Draper, an American Socialist writer and publisher, using exclusively quotations from pro-Zionist sources, attempts to prove the brutality of the Israelis in taking over the property of their erstwhile Palestinian neighbors. Draper's article was originally published in mid-1956, only a few months before the Suez invasion; it is especially notable for its command of documentary sources from the 1948-1952 period. Much of its central part considers the notorious massacre of the Arab villagers of Deir Yassin, one of the bloodiest episodes in the entire history of the Israeli-Palestinian conflict. Yitshaq Ben-Ami, one of the leading members of the Irgun Zvai Leumi, the Jewish underground organization which carried out the attack, offers in the fifth article an explanation of the Irgun's actions. His account is notable for its expression of the anger and resentment still felt after fully two generations by the members of the Jewish underground—from which arose Menahem Begin, Yitzhak Shamir, and other leaders of the Likud bloc—for the quasi-official Jewish defense force, the Haganah, which itself gave rise to David Ben-Gurion, Yitzhak Rabin, Shimon Peres, and other leaders of the Israeli Labor alignment.

CIVIL WAR AND THE DESTRUCTION
OF THE PALESTINIAN COMMUNITY,
NOVEMBER 1947–MAY 1948[1]

The Palestine problem was now rapidly approaching its catastrophic climax. On 29 November 1947 the United Nations General Assembly passed a resolution recommending the partition of Palestine into a Jewish state, a Palestinian state, and a special international regime (*corpus separatum*) for Jerusalem and its environs; an economic union would be set up between the Jewish and Palestinian states. The Palestinians and other Arabs were as stunned as the Zionists and their sympathizers were jubilant. The very reactions of each side belied the claim that partition was a compromise solution.

Palestinian Opposition to Partition

The member states that championed and endorsed partition did so in the full knowledge of bitter Palestinian and Arab opposition to it. The Palestinians had lost some four thousand lives fighting partition from 1937 to 1939. Since its creation the Arab League had been warning against partition. The UN partition plan was based on the Zionist plan that President Truman had endorsed as early as August 1946. From the Palestinian perspective, partition was Zionist in provenance and conception, and tailored to meet Zionist needs and demands. That the UN resolution won 33 votes to 13, with abstentions and one delegation absent, was largely due to the enormous pressure brought to bear by the United States (including the personal intervention of President Truman) on member states to vote for it. To be sure, the Soviet Union voted for partition also, but only in order to end British rule in Palestine. Significantly, no African or Asian state voted in favor except Liberia and the Philippines. India, Pakistan, Turkey, and Afghanistan all voted against, while China abstained. Many Latin American countries (including Mexico) abstained.

[1]By Walid Khalidi, historian and political scientist, from his annotated photographic collection *Before Their Diaspora: A Photographic History of the Palestinians, 1876–1948*, pp. 305–313. Copyright© 1984 by the Institute for Palestine Studies. Reprinted with permission.

Even the Canadian representative was heard to say that his country supported partition "with a heavy heart and many misgivings." The United Kingdom coyly abstained.

Partition was seen by the Palestinians as imposing unilateral and intolerable sacrifices on themselves. The reasons for their opposition were the same as in 1937, except that the UN partition plan gave the proposed Jewish state 50 percent more territory than the 1937 plan had. The area of the Jewish state according to the UN plan would actually be larger than that of the proposed Palestinian state (5,500 square miles as compared with 4,500 square miles) at a time when the Jews constituted no more than 35 percent of the population and owned less than 7 percent of the land. Within the proposed Jewish state, Jewish landownership did not in fact exceed 600 square miles out of the total area of 5,500 square miles. Nearly all the citrus land (equally divided in ownership between Jews and Palestinians), 80 percent of the cereal land (entirely Palestinian-owned), and 40 percent of Palestinian industry would fall within the borders of the proposed Jewish state. Jaffa, the Palestinian state's major port on the Mediterranean, would be altogether cut off from its hinterland, and Gaza would lose its traditional links with the wheatlands of the Negev. Hundreds of villages would be separated from communal fields and pastures. The Palestinian state would lose direct access both to the Red Sea and to Syria. The economic union between the two states, on which partition had been postulated, was known beforehand to be impracticable. The patchwork of subunits into which partition would divide the country bore little relationship to the human and social realities on the ground.

The Palestinians failed to see why they should be made to pay for the Holocaust (the ultimate crime against humanity, committed in Europe by Europeans), and recalled that Zionism was born in the 1880s, long before the advent of the Third Reich. They failed to see why it was *not* fair for the Jews to be a minority in a unitary Palestinian state, while it *was* fair for almost half of the Palestinian population—the indigenous majority on its own ancestral soil—to be converted overnight into a minority under alien rule in the envisaged Jewish state according to partition.

The injustice of the UN partition resolution was further exposed in Palestinian and Arab eyes by the General Assembly's rejection of relevant draft resolutions proposed by the Arab delegates before the vote on partition. The Arab delegates pleaded that the International Court of Justice be consulted on whether the General Assembly was "competent to enforce or recommend the enforcement" of partition against the wishes of the majority of a country's population. The draft resolution to that effect was defeated in the Ad Hoc Committee by a 21 to 20 vote. Another draft resolution, proposing that all UN member states participate in alleviating the plight of Jewish refugees in Europe "in proportion to their area, economic resources . . . and other relevant factors," was not carried in a 16 to 16 vote (with 25 abstentions). In the circumstances the Palestinians and other Arabs felt that they were not bound by the partition resolution, which in any case was a nonmandatory recommendation by the General Assembly.

Zionist Preparations for War

As early as May 1942 the Zionist leadership had begun preparations to convert the whole of Palestine into a Jewish state, a polity embodied in the Biltmore Program. The Zionists were all the more capable of implementing a plan envisaging a Jewish state in part (albeit the greater part) of Palestine, i.e., partition. They had paid careful attention to the balance of power between themselves and the Palestinians. They had evolved strategies to offset and diminish the Palestinian quantitative advantage, and had foreseen a sequence of stages leading to the desired revolution in the local status quo. The classic exposition of these policies was made in 1932 by Chaim Arlosoroff, director of the Political Department in the Jewish Agency Executive. The European background of the Zionist immigrants and the Zionist leadership's ability to tap the professional, diplomatic, and financial resources of the Jewish communities in the industrialized Western countries stood the Zionist venture in good stead. By 1944 the government statistician in the Palestine administration could say: "The Jewish economy of Palestine is . . . radically different from the Arab economy and is in fact not very dissimilar from that of the United Kingdom.

Military organization was a high Zionist priority. The main armed force was the Haganah (Defense) under the command of the Jewish Agency. The Haganah had evolved in the early days of the Mandate as an offshoot of the pre-Mandatory Hashomer (Watchman), itself descended from the secret societies of Czarist

Russia. In 1947 the Haganah had had a continuous existence of at least thirty years. Although officially it was a secret, illegal paramilitary organization, the British not only tolerated the Haganah but assisted it both directly and indirectly. The 14,000-man Jewish Settlement Police for example, a force trained and supported by the British, became virtually the training cadre for Haganah reservists. By 1946 the Haganah had grown into a relatively formidable force; the Anglo-American committee reported Haganah strength to be about 62,000. In spite of repeated acts of Zionist terrorism (including Haganah attacks) against British security forces, Britain left the Haganah unscathed. So self-confident was the Haganah command that, in a memorandum submitted to the Anglo-American Committee on 25 March 1946 in Jerusalem, it said:

As far as the strength of the Arabs in Palestine is concerned, we are in possession of well-founded information. There is no doubt that the Jewish force is superior in organization, training, planning and equipment, and that we ourselves will be able to handle any attack or rebellion from the Arab side without calling for any assistance from the British or Americans. If you accept the Zionist solution [partition and a Jewish state in the greater part of Palestine] but are unable or unwilling to enforce it, please do not interfere, and we ourselves will secure its implementation.

The Zionist leadership began detailed military planning as early as 1945 in anticipation of the coming showdown. In a statement to his biographer, David Ben-Gurion confirmed that "the major preparations to convert Haganah into an army were begun three years before the birth of the state." On a special visit to the United States in 1945, Ben-Gurion (then chairman of the Jewish Agency Executive), called together nineteen leading American Jewish figures and persuaded them to contribute to the wholesale purchase of military industrial machinery being sold as scrap at the end of the war. The machinery was smuggled into Palestine under the Mandate and became the nucleus of a heavy Jewish military industry.

In May 1946 the Haganah developed a strategy embodied in the so-called May 1946 plan, in which the central concept was that of "counteraction." Such action was to be of two kinds: "warning" action generally confined to the area of the enemy's own operation, and "punitive" action unrestricted in its geographical scope. Because of inherent "difficulties," counteraction would not always be aimed at the specific Palestinian perpetrators of a previous action. Therefore, the human targets to be sought should be Palestinian political and military leaders, those who financed them, and those who incited them ("e.g., journalists") in addition to those who had carried out actual operations. The objective should be to "inflict physical harm," take the individuals in question "hostage," or "liquidate them." The material targets should be "clubs, cafés, and other meeting places, communication centers, flour mills, water plants and other vital economic installations." Villages, urban residential quarters, and farms used for planning operations or as bases for attack and withdrawal should be surrounded and occupied. "Everything possible in them should be burned and the houses of those who had incited or participated in operations should be blown up."

Soon after the UN partition decision, work began on a new plan, Plan Dalet (D). The objective of Plan Dalet was to take over and control the area of the proposed Jewish state. "It was obvious," in the words of Haganah historians, "that no Jewish colony outside the Jewish state—according to the UN partition resolution—would be abandoned or vacated and that the Haganah would do everything to organize their resistance." Within the Jewish state proper, Palestinian villages that resisted "should be destroyed . . . and their inhabitants expelled beyond the borders of the Jewish state." A similar strategy would be applied to the towns. "Palestinian residents of urban quarters which dominate access to or egress from the towns should be expelled beyond the borders of the Jewish state in the event of their resistance." Outside the Jewish state, towns such as Qalqilyah and Tulkarm should be occupied; Acre, Nazareth, Lydda, Ramleh, Bethlehem, Beit Jala, and Hebron should all be put under siege. "The inhabitants of Jaffa should be imprisoned within their municipal boundaries and not dare to leave them." All the villages between Tel Aviv and Jerusalem should be occupied. All the Palestinian quarters of West and East Jerusalem, as well as all the environs of the city, should be conquered.

Palestinian and Arab Countermeasures

On their side, the Palestinians had to start from scratch in reorganizing themselves. The 1946 report of the Anglo-American Committee, which estimated Zionist military strength to be ca. 62,000, made no mention of Palestinian military forces. The Palestinians looked to the Arab League to counterbalance Zionist military preponderance. But the League suffered from the constraints and divisiveness already noted. Its first tentative move to meet Palestinian defense needs was made in September 1947 when it formed the Technical Military Committee, headed by an Iraqi former chief of staff, General Ismail Safwat, to report on Palestinian defense requirements. Safwat's first report, submitted on October 8, was somber and realistic. He accurately assessed Zionist strength and asserted that the Palestinians possessed nothing remotely comparable to the Zionist forces "in manpower, organization, armament or ammunition." Urging the Arab states to "mobilize their utmost strength" promptly and form a general command, he warned that the Palestinians were in dire straits. The only Arab League reaction to Safwat's urgings was the allocation on October 15 of one million pounds sterling to the Technical Committee. On November 27, just before the UN partition vote, Safwat again warned: "It is well nigh impossible to overcome the Zionist forces with irregulars. . . . the Arab countries cannot afford a long war . . . ." He pleaded with the Arab countries to "ensure superiority in numbers and matériel and act with maximal speed."

The Arab League was loath to confront Britain, which had emphasized that it would remain solely responsible for the administration of Palestine until the end of the Mandate on 15 May 1948. At the same time a certain wishful thinking prevailed in many Arab capitals (a lingering residue of trust in Western liberalism) that somehow the justice of the Palestinian cause would be recognized and the Western powers would not allow the worst to befall the Palestinians. But with the rapidly deteriorating security situation in Palestine, the Arab countries could no longer postpone action, particularly after the UN partition resolution.

In December 1947 the Arab league decided to supply the Technical Military Committee with ten thousand rifles and to put at its disposal a force of three thousand irregulars. The latter were to form a volunteer Arab Liberation Army (ALA) composed of members from various Arab countries, among them five hundred from Palestine. After training in Damascus, ALA contingents would be sent to the threatened Palestinian areas. The formation of the ALA was the Arab League's compromise measure between exclusive reliance on diplomacy and Western good intentions on the one hand, and the serious action urged by Safwat on the other.

Since the UN partition vote in November, fighting had been escalating dramatically in Palestine. By January 1948 the Irgun and the Stern Gang had introduced the use of car bombs (originally directed against the British), and by March 1948 Palestinian irregulars were paying their opponents back in kind. Haganah attacks on villages and residential quarters were answered by Palestinian attacks on Zionist colonies, and vice versa. By 10 January 1948 the number of killed and wounded on both sides stood at 1,974.

Although militarily inferior, the Palestinians resisted firmly. This was partly a measure of their desperation and partly an effect of the infiltration from Syria of small ALA contingents during the period from January to March, which bolstered Palestinian strength and raised morale. But the real reason for the Palestinians' ability to hold their ground was that the military operations of the Haganah were still being conducted within the framework of the May 1946 Plan, i.e., the Zionist leadership had not begun to implement Plan Dalet. The Zionists were inhibited from doing so primarily because Plan Dalet required a high degree of Haganah mobilization, and the greater its mobilization the greater the chances of a confrontation with Britain, which claimed to be the de jure authority throughout the country until May 15.

Meanwhile, the appearance of a military stalemate in Palestine, the rising casualties on both sides, and the increasing involvement of ALA units in the fighting were having a considerable political impact in Washington and at the United Nations. A trend away from partition began to crystallize in March in the form of a call by the Truman administration for the General Assembly to reconsider the partition plan and to recommend the installation of a trusteeship regime instead. The American proposal created great alarm among the Zionists, who bitterly denounced it. Their alarm was all the greater because their line of communication with President Truman, their paramount champion, had broken down.

Truman Intervenes

For several months Truman had refused to meet with any American Zionist leader as a result of the intense pressure exerted on him by American Zionists since the partition resolution.

How intense this pressure must have been to so alienate Truman is perhaps indicated by the fact that 1948 was a presidential election year. On March 8 Truman declared his own candidacy in the presidential elections. On March 18 he finally agreed to meet the veteran British Zionist leader Chaim Weizmann. Weizmann had been sent to the United States by the Zionist leadership in Palestine for precisely this kind of contact, at the highest level of government.

The meeting between Truman and Weizmann took place secretly at the White House. Although Truman had approved his State Department's recommendation of trusteeship, he may not have fully grasped its implications. The Zionists were at a crossroads. There were only two months to go until the end of the Mandate. If the trusteeship proposal (which the Arab League accepted) received the full backing of the American president, this could mean the indefinite postponement of the establishment of the Jewish state. Moreover, Plan Dalet had been completed and was awaiting implementation. British evacuation was progressing steadily, as was Zionist military mobilization. The end of the Mandate on May 15 would leave a juridical vacuum, which the Arab countries could use to their advantage. The Jewish state had to be made an accomplished fact before then. But without the implementation of Plan Dalet, the Jewish state could not be established. What the Zionist leaders needed to know at first hand was the American president's own attitude toward the establishment of a Jewish state in these circumstances.

President Truman did not disappoint Weizmann. As he informs us in his memoirs: "When he [Weizmann] left my office I felt that he had reached a full understanding of my policy and that I knew what he wanted." And as Abba Eban confirms: "The President gave his visitor a specific commitment. He would work for the establishment and recognition of a Jewish state of which the Negev would be a part." There can be little doubt that Weizmann promptly sent the news to Tel Aviv and that the Zionist leadership there had little difficulty in understanding its significance.

On March 19, the day after the Truman-Weizmann meeting, the United States chief delegate to the United Nations Security Council, Warren Austin, unaware of this meeting and its outcome, proposed that action be suspended on the partition plan and the General Assembly convene to discuss the trusteeship solution. The Arab countries, equally unaware of the Truman-Weizmann meeting, welcomed with relief the American trusteeship proposal, and the Arabic press celebrated the occasion. But Safwat, chairman of the Military Committee, in command of the Arab Liberation Army, had no such illusions. With his eyes on the ground in Palestine, he warned on March 23: "The operational initiative in most of Palestine is in Zionist hands. . . . Our relatively stronger garrisons in Jaffa, Jerusalem, and Haifa are strictly on the defensive . . . ."

Plan Dalet

Plan Dalet went into effect during the first week of April. Its many subsidiary operations continued to unfold with devastating cumulative impact during the remaining six weeks of the Mandate. Some of these operations dovetailed with one another in a single region. Others took place concurrently in different parts of the country. Psychological offensives designed to induce civilians to flee were orchestrated with the military operations; the former involved broadcasting by radio or loudspeakers (carried in vehicles) and spreading rumors by word of mouth or leaflets.

Six major operations were launched in April. Two of them, Operations Nachshon (April 5–15) and Harel (April 15–20), were designed to occupy and destroy the Palestinian villages along the whole length of the Jaffa-Jerusalem road, thus splitting in two the central mass (according to the UN partition plan) of the Palestinian state. Palestinian villagers and irregulars fought desperately along the entire highway. A dramatic battle developed for the hilltop village of Castel, some five miles west of Jerusalem. The Palestinians fought under their charismatic commander Abd al-Qadir al-Husseini, and the village changed hands several times. Abd al-Qadir was killed on April 9 as he led a successful counter-attack. While the Castel battle was in progress, Irgun and Stern Gang units perpetrated the massacre of 245 civilian inhabitants of the village of Deir Yassin, about three miles from Castel. The Deir Yassin massacre was one of the more gruesome instances of "competition" between the Labour-dominated Haganah (in charge of Plan Dalet) and the right-wing Revisionist Irgun. Meanwhile, the ALA field commander, Fawzi al-Qawukji, opened a diversionary attack against the colony of Mishmar Haemek, southeast of Haifa; the attack was repulsed. Arab public opinion reacted with horror and alarm to these events.

On April 10 the Palestine Committee, a high-level political coordinating body set up by the Arab League, met to consider the three disasters that had just occurred: the death of Abd al-Qadir and the subsequent fall of Castel, the massacre at Deir Yassin, and Qawukji's defeat at Mishmar Haemek. For the first time, the assembled leaders gave serious consideration to the need for intervention by their regular army units in the wake of the failure of the Palestinian and ALA irregulars. But many more disasters were to follow before the Arab leaders would take their courage in their hands.

On April 18, in spite of their insistence on being the de jure authority in the country until the end of the Mandate, the British suddenly announced their withdrawal from Tiberias. This retreat paved the way for the conquest of Tiberias on the same day by the Haganah, and Tiberias became the first town to fall under Haganah control. Thousands of refugees streamed in panic into exile in Transjordan and Syria, creating a wave of shock and anger throughout the Arab world. Then on April 21 the British announced their withdrawal from Haifa; the Haganah promptly launched Operation Misparayim for the conquest of that city, which fell on April 22–23. Haifa was the first of the three major Palestinian cities (the other two being Jaffa and Jerusalem) to be conquered by the Haganah. Many more thousands of panic-stricken refugees fled either by sea to Lebanon and Egypt or overland across the Lebanese border.

During the last week of April, three other major operations were launched within the framework of Plan Dalet in different parts of the country: (1) Operation Chametz (April 25) to isolate and conquer Jaffa and the surrounding villages; (2) Operation Jevussi (April 26) to conquer the Palestinian residential quarters in West and East Jerusalem outside the Old City, as well as the villages in the northern and eastern suburbs; and (3) Operation Yiftach (April 28) to conquer the whole of eastern Galilee.

The Irgun anticipated Operation Chametz by launching its own offensive against Jaffa. By the end of April, the combined Haganah-Irgun offensives had completely encircled Jaffa, forcing most of the remaining civilians to flee by sea to Gaza or Egypt; many drowned in the process. A desperate attempt at resistance by a Palestinian ALA unit that penetrated into Jaffa was unsuccessful.

Operation Jevussi achieved its objectives within the city limits of West and East Jerusalem. The Palestinian residential quarters of Katamon, Talbiyya, the German Colony, the Greek Colony, Upper Bak'a, and Lower Bak'a, all in West Jerusalem, were conquered. Their inhabitants were driven into exile in Ramallah and Bethlehem, or across the Transjordanian border. The British, as the de jure authority, continued to hold certain enclaves in Jerusalem and to fly the Union Jack over the official residence of the high commissioner on the hill just south of the city, historically and appositely known as the Hill of Evil Counsel. Operation Jevussi was unsuccessful in the suburban villages to the north (Nabi Samu'il) and east (Tur), where Palestinian and ALA irregulars put up a stout resistance.

Operation Yiftach opened its first phase with the conquest of villages in the neighborhood of the Galilean town of Safed.

The pattern of attack in all three operations was the same: intensive, indiscriminate bombardment with mortars, of which the Haganah had an abundant supply, followed by coordinated attacks using infantry and armored cars. Great reliance was placed on simultaneous psychological warfare. The Palestinian collapse resulted from bad leadership, totally inadequate civil defense arrangements, and military disparity in planning, numbers, and firepower. By the end of April the Palestinian community was badly mangled. Tens of thousands of refugees were on the trek overland, with thousands more in transit at sea. The Arab governments could no longer ignore the pressure of public opinion on them to send their regular armies to help the Palestinians.

On April 30 Arab League leaders held a meeting in Amman, to which they summoned the chiefs of staff of their armies for counsel regarding the turn of events in Palestine. This was the very first such meeting of the Arab military heads. Accurately assessing Zionist strength, they estimated that the minimum force required to overcome the Haganah would be six divisions and six air squadrons. The political leaders, however, were unable or unwilling to bring themselves to believe this appraisal. Evidently, they still preferred to hope for a last-minute intervention by the Western powers, and to think that a mere show of force by their regular armies would bring it about. Therefore, they regarded the assessment of their military experts as exaggerated and unwarranted. They still could not countemplate intervention by the Arab armies before the formal end of the Mandate on May 15.

And when the time for intervention came, a force less than half the minimum considered necessary by the military heads was all that was sent.

Meanwhile, the Haganah command pressed on with the business of Plan Dalet. On May 8–9 Operation Maccabi was launched to occupy and destroy the remaining villages in the central plain between Ramleh and Latrun. On May 11–12 the town of Safed was conquered; its inhabitants fled to Syria and Lebanon. The town of Beisan met the same fate on May 12; its inhabitants fled to Transjordan and Syria. On the same day Operation Barak was launched in the south to occupy and destroy the villages leading to the Negev. The inhabitants of these villages were driven into the Hebron hills.

Not until May 12 did Egypt, the strongest Arab country, agree to military intervention. Finally, its prime minister, bowing to Muslim and Arab public opinion, secured parliamentary approval for Egypt's intervention. The other Arab countries that had already agreed to intervene were Iraq, Syria, Lebanon, and Transjordan.

But the Arab countries' decision to intervene came too late if it was meant to prevent the destruction of the Palestinian community. It was also too late to prevent the establishment of the Jewish state.

On May 13 Chaim Weizmann wrote President Truman a letter asking for recognition of the Jewish state. On May 14 the British high commissioner left his official residence in Jerusalem on his way home to peaceful retirement in England. The new state came into existence at one minute after midnight Palestine time, or 6:01 P.M. Washington time. By 6:11 P.M. President Truman had recognized Israel.

Thus were sown the seeds of the Palestinian diaspora and the Arab-Israeli conflict.

PREFACE[2]

The major source for this book is my own recollections of what we have endured and my own conviction that ours is a just cause, a cause long forgotten by the Western world (self-righteous in its overly easy conscience) and long mutilated by the Arab world (self-satisfied in its mercenary games).

Consequently this is not a objective work. It is however a sincere narration of a phase in the history of the Palestinian people and of their response to the challenge of adversity that has confronted them over the past two decades. As I lived that phase and took a part in that response, what I have to say, subjective though it is, may offer some notes toward an understanding of what we are doing now and an insight into the why and the how of it.

I am neither concerned nor qualified to indulge in the game of quote and counter-quote adopted by those whose business or ideology drives them to espouse the position of one or the other. I have discovered that with enough diligence, the historian can present a devastatingly convincing version of the Zionist/Israeli/Jewish (call it what you wish) claim in modern Palestine. Another historian, with equal reserves of diligence and partisan to our own claims and grievances, can come up with a perfectly valid and at the same time diametrically opposite view.

"The vexatious issue," as the problem of my people was called during the Truman and Mandate years, has now expanded and become the "Arab-Israeli" conflict; and it is felt that the solution of it by the big powers is as mandatory now as it was mandatory then.

Mine is not a vexatious issue, nor has it much to do with the conflict now raging between the Arabs and the Zionists. Nor is its solution dependent upon, nor will I allow it to be, the whims of the big powers. Mine is an existential problem having to do with the yearning for my homeland, with being part of a culture, with winning the battle of remain myself, as a Palestinian belonging to a people with a distinctly Palestinian consciousness.

[2]By Fawaz Turki, Palestinian publicist, from his book *The Disinherited: Journal of a Palestinian Exile*, pp.7–14. Copyright © 1972 by Fawaz Turki. Reprinted by permission of Monthly Review Foundation.

If I was not a Palestinian when I left Haifa as a child, I am one now. Living in Beirut as a stateless person for most of my growing-up years, many of them in a refugee camp, I did not feel I was living among my "Arab brothers." I did not feel I was an Arab, a Lebanese, or, as some wretchedly pious writers claimed, a "southern Syrian." I was a Palestinian. And that meant I was an outsider, an alien, a refugee and a burden. To be that, for us, for my generation of Palestinians, meant to look inward, to draw closer, to be part of a minority that had its own way of doing and seeing and feeling and reacting. To be that, for us, meant the addition of a subtler nuance to the cultural makeup of our Palestinianness.

The experience of our growing-up years—blame that experience on the Arab governments, blame it on the UN, blame it on God, for the cabalistic interpretation of political events does not interest me—has decidedly ravished our beings. It ravished the law and the order of the reality that we saw around us. It defeated some of us. It reduced and distorted and alienated others.

The defeated, like myself, took off to go away from the intolerable pressures of the Arab world to India and Europe and Australia, where they wrestled with the problem and hoped to understand. The reduced, like my parents, waited helplessly in a refugee camp for the world, for a miracle, or for some deity to come to their aid. The distorted, like Sirhan Sirhan, turned into assassins. The alienated, like Leila Khaled, hijacked civilian aircraft.

If there are still people around who call us "Arab refugees" or "southern Syrians" or terrorists, who want to subdue us, who want to resettle us, who want to ignore us and who want to play games with our destiny, then they are not tuned in to the vibrations and the tempo of the Third World, of which the Palestinians are a part.

Every writer and speaker wants to win his audience to his point of view, a point of view that is carried along by the weight of its supposed impartiality. I have no point of view to make. And I cannot pretend to begin to be impartial.

When I was a child, a few weeks after we left Palestine in 1948, I used to sit with a crowd of people at the camp, mothers and fathers and aunts and grandparents and young wives and children, to listen to the radio at precisely three o'clock every day. The voice from Radio Israel (or Radio Tel Aviv, or whatever damn name it had) used to come on to announce The Messages. Silence would fill the space around us. Tension would grip even the children. "From Abu Sharef, and Jameela, Samir and Kamal in Haifa," the words would come across the air. "To our Leila and her husband Fouad. Are you in Lebanon? We are all well." A few moments pause, then: "From Abu and Um Shihadi, and Sofia and Osama to Abu Adid and his family. Is Anton with you? We are worried." The dispassionate voice continues: "From Ibrahim Shawki to his wife Zamzam. I have moved to Jaffa. Your father is safe with us."

One whole hour of this. During it an outburst of tears at the knowledge that loved ones are well. Despair that a relative is not yet located. Hope that in tomorrow's broadcast a good word may be heard. Then a trip on the bus to the Beirut station to queue up at the message office to send your own twenty-six words across the ether to the other side. Because you could not go over there yourself to say them. Because an armistice line was drawn as a consequence of a war you did not understand, did not want, did not initiate.

A few years later, we were still in that refugee camp on the outskirts of Beirut where life was becoming harder and existence becoming more futile. The Lebanese authorities, conscious of the image of their capital as a "Western city," made attempts to move our camp, as far away as they could, to avoid offending foreign visitors with the sight of it. Our camp was on the way to the airport.

For bureaucratic or other reasons, the initiative failed. But no one at the Ministry of the Interior, and no one in any editor's office, bothered to consider or write about the hardship we would have endured had we in fact been moved forty miles out of town. Or the disruption this might have caused in the lives of children going to school, men going to work, the sick going to their doctors, and the women going to their shops. Or the indignity to a people already devasted by one uprooting from their homeland.

The story of these years is thus not offered as a point of view. It is not written with objectivity. Nor in the telling do I hope to win adherents to my cause. I merely wish to isolate our problem from the Arab-Israeli dispute, identify it and describe it in its human dimensions, for those who wish to know what it was like, what it will be like.

The relentless and persistent falsification of facts by commentators, and the two-decade-long custody of our problem in the hands of the Arab governments, have created myths around who we were and what we wanted. We were the primitive Bedouins roaming the desert; we were an illiterate and disease-stricken mass of refugees packed in DP camps; we were the hateful, embittered Arabs—indistinguishable from other "Arabs"—who yearned to destory Israel and "drive the Jews into the sea." We were the harmless villains of the piece, turned, at the end, into intractable ones.

Given their noisy pursuit of a commitment to Israel and the Zionist experiment, people in the West often blinded themselves to the truth and accepted these myths. Our problem, dehumanized, distorted, and twisted, was flogged into a state beyond recognition. Conversely, the creation of Israel became an experience and a monument. The Western world, which had long tormented and abused the Jewish people, hastened to bless an event that saw an end to their victims' suffering. A debt was to be paid. Who was to pay it and where it was to be paid were not seen as of the essence, so long as it was not paid by Europeans in Europe. After the pogroms in Czarist Russia and the crimes in Nazi Germany, for example, Great Britain and the United States, two countries that gave whole-hearted support to unrestricted Jewish emigration to Palestine and the creation of a "Jewish Home," were concurrently providing for legislation to control "alien entry" into their green and pleasant lands. This was but a manifestation of the style and vocabulary of the Social Darwinism they had for many years practiced in their rencontre with the "unfit" of the earth.

To illustrate this, I need only indulge in a recollection or two of the time I was in Palestine during the last years of the Mandate, as can any individual who has lived under a colonial system and experienced the "native" consciousness.

In the small township of Balad el-Sheikh, near Haifa, where we lived, I was returning home from school one day when I spotted an old man standing at a street corner peddling bread rolls from a tray on a wooden stand. Peddlers are a way of life in our part of the world, men who make and market their own products, unfettered by the structured patterns of a developed economy. Old men with gray hair, like the peddler in question, trying to make a living in a land that has long been ruled, exploited, oppressed, and manipulated by a succession of foreign occupiers.

A British soldier, a youngster with a machine-gun slung over his shoulder, crossed from the other side of the street, nonchalantly walked up to the peddler, and proceeded to beat him on the face and chest. Blows that he aimed, violently and indiscriminately, first with his fists, then with his weapon. When the old man fell to the ground, the soldier picked up the tray, threw it in the air, and then began to break the stand into pieces, hitting it against the wall and jumping on it. With that accomplished, he walked away. All this was done for no apparent, no warrantable, no explicable, reason.

But our English soldier no doubt felt that since there were only Englishmen and one other species of humans populating the earth, he had carte blanche to act as he wished. If by beating up a "native" he could "feel better," then he was entitled to do it. He was not answerable for his act. Not in Palestine; not in India; not in Africa. If he ran over a child with his army jeep, so long as it was a "native" child he need only reverse his vehicle and finish him off. (It happened to a cousin of mine.) If he was being transported overland from his old base to another one across the country, on a tedious trip of long duration, then he could take his gun, aim it, and shoot to death a "native" riding along on his mule, a "native" working in his fields, a "native" coming out of his hut. When this soldier returned home, to live again among his race of Englishmen, he would be chastised for kicking a dog, convicted in court for libeling a man, ostracized for indecent language. (But the world, the times, the English soldier, and I have changed since those days.)

So when Theodore Herzl, the European from Vienna, spoke of creating "a rampart of Europe, an outpost of civilization" against "Asian barbarism" in Palestine, no one came forth to oppose the concept and its execution. The event was applauded.

And it came about that within a short time after its creation at the cost of much misery to others, Israel began to enjoy and bask in the image of a land transformed from, as is often said, "the deserts and marshes of Palestine into the garden that is the Zionist state." Israel was beyond reproach. It has proved itself for the David that it was, surrounded by a monstrous Goliath dedicated to its destruction. There was no question of the integrity and innocence of Israel. There was no question either of who the villains of the region were. (It was too bad about "the Arab refugees"—who as recently as 1918 had formed 92 percent of the population of the country—but they had left voluntarily, opted to live in refugee camps and, at any rate, they too were the enemy. Resettlement of refugees was a picayune problem that remained unsolved because of Arab intransigence.)

The vast machinery of Zionist propaganda, with a great helping hand from Nasser and his fellow Arab leaders, to whom irresponsible pronunciamentos became a fetish, fostered and enhanced this image of a tiny Israel that deserved to continue its mission and its harmless endeavors in the face of the enemy. Everything with Israel that had been and that was is as it must be. Books with titles like *The Miracle in the Desert, Israel's Struggle for Survival,* and *Hope and Fulfillment* discussed the miracle in the desert, Israel's struggle for survival and hope and fulfillment. The Jewish and the Zionist causes were inextricably tied and seen as one.

The consequences of this blind faith in Israel and Israel's activities and intentions were extensive. The foundations of this image were little shaken when Israel blatantly allied itself with the imperialist powers in the 1956 tripartite aggression against Egypt. The massacre of Kafr Qassem in that same year, that senseless murder of fifty-one men, women, and children who were on their way home from the fields, was hardly reported in the Western press. More than that, little was written on how the Israeli government itself attempted to supress the news of the massacre, or on the fact that when the news did ultimately surface and punishment was meted out in the courts, the convicted soldiers served a total of less than one year in jail (and on release some returned to serve in the government). The way the "niggers of Israel," as Hal Draper called the Palestinians living in Israel, were treated in their own homeland by the authorities and by Israeli society was never considered a subject that warranted debate or reporting.

The faults of Israel are not my problem. Let those who support it ponder them. But it has been a paradox of unfathomable dimensions to me, unable to experience the Western consciousness, to watch the spectable of those commentators and activists who have proved themselves worthy of any liberal cause, any humanitarian endeavor, any opposition to oppression, any support for the liberation of colonized or persecuted minorities, yet who, via-à-vis Israel, remain blind to, or brush aside evidence of, Israeli guilt of the same crimes they are themselves crusading against.

With pressures such as these and with the dividends Arab leaders such as Nasser have derived from co-opting our cause for their own nefarious purposes, the central issue that truly was the origion of the crisis, the Palestinian problem, has been lost to sight and sound.

Why this problem was allowed to come about in the first place is the business of the historian. He has a habit of tracing the development of every conflict, pinpointing where its seeds were planted, and endowing every subsequent event with immanent logic. He should be wished luck. For as I. F. Stone has suggested, if God is now truly dead, as some say he is, he undoubtedly died from trying to untangle the origins of the Middle East conflict.

But when and how this problem will be solved *is* our business. We have picked up our own habits, in this world, in this age of ours.

CONCLUSION[3]

The Palestinian refugee problem was born of war, not by design, Jewish or Arab. It was largely a by-product of Arab and Jewish fears and of the protracted, bitter fighting that characterised the first Israeli-Arab war; in smaller part, it was the deliberate creation of Jewish and Arab military commanders and politicians.

The creation of the problem was almost inevitable, given the geographical intermixing of the Arab and Jewish populations, the history of Arab-Jewish hostility over 1917–47, the resistance on both sides to a binational state, the outbreak and prolongation of the war for Israel's birth and survival, the major structural weaknesses of Palestinian Arab society, the depth of Arab animosity towards the Yishuv and Arab fears of falling under Jewish rule, and the Yishuv's fears of what would happen should the Arabs win and what would be the fate of a Jewish State born with a very large, potentially or actively hostile Arab minority.

[3]By Benny Morris, historian, from his book *The Birth of the Palestinian Refugee Problem, 1947–1949*, pp. 286–296. Copyright © 1987 Cambridge University Press. Reprinted with permission of Cambridge University Press.

The Palestinian Arab exodus began in December 1947–March 1948, with the departure of many of the country's upper and middle class families, especially from Haifa and Jaffa, towns destined to be in, or at the mercy of, the Jewish-State-to-be, and from Jewish-dominated districts of western Jerusalem. Flight proved infectious. Household followed household, neighbour followed neighbour, street, street and neighbourhood, neighbourhood (as, later, village was to follow neighbouring village). The prosperous and educated feared death or injury in the ever-spreading hostilities, the anarchy that attended the gradual withdrawal of the British administration and security forces, the brigandage and intimidation of the Arab militias and irregulars and, more vaguely but generally, the unknown, probably dark future that awaited them under Jewish or, indeed, Husayni rule. Some of these considerations, as well as a variety of direct and indirect military pressures, also caused during these months the almost complete evacuation of the Arab rural communities of the Coastal Plain, which was predominantly Jewish and which was to be the core of the Jewish State.

Most of the upper and middle class families, who moved from Jaffa, Haifa, Jerusalem, Ramle, Acre and Tiberias to Nablus, Amman, Beirut, Gaza and Cairo, probably thought their exile would be temporary. These families had the financial wherewithal to tide them over; many had wealthy relatives and accomodation outside the country. The urban masses and the *fellahin*, however, had nowhere to go, certainly not in comfort. For them, flight meant instant desitution; it was not a course readily adopted. But the daily spectacle of abandonment by their "betters," the middle and upper classes, with its concomitant progressive closure of businesses, schools, law offices and medical clinics, and abandonment of civil service and municipal posts, led to a steady attrition of morale, a cumulative sapping of faith and trust in the world around them: their leaders were going or had gone; the British were packing. They had been left "alone" to face the Zionist enemy.

Daily, week in, week out, over December 1947, January, February and March 1948, there were clashes along the "seams" between the two communities in the mixed towns, ambushes in the fields and on the roads, sniping, machine gun fire, bomb attacks and occasional mortaring. Problems of movement and communication, unemployment and food distribution intensified, especially in the towns, as the hostilities drew out.

There is probably no accounting for the mass exodus that followed without understanding the prevalence and depth of the general sense of collapse, of "falling apart," that permeated Arab Palestine, especially the towns, by April 1948. In many places, it would take very little to induce the inhabitants to pack up and flee.

Come the Haganah (and IZL-LHI) offensives of April–May, the cumulative effect of the fears, deprivations, abandonment and depredations of the previous months, in both towns and villages, overcame the natural, basic reluctance to abandon home and property and go into exile. As Palestinian military power was swiftly and dramatically demolished and the Haganah demonstrated almost unchallenged superiority in successive conquests, Arab morale cracked, giving way to general, blind, panic or a "psychosis of flight," as one IDF intelligence report put it.

Town fell first—Tiberias, Haifa, Jaffa, Beisan, Safad—and their populations fled. The panic then affected the surrounding rural hinterlands: after Haifa, came the flight from Balad ash Sheikh and Hawassa; after Jaffa, Salama, Al Kheiriya and Yazur; after Safad, Dhahiriya Tahta, Sammu'i and Meirun. For decades the villagers had looked to the towns for leadership; they followed the townspeople into exile.

If Jewish attack directly and indirectly triggered most of the Arab exodus up to June 1948, a small but significant proportion of that flight was due to direct Jewish expulsion orders issued after the conquest of a site and to Jewish psychological warfare ploys ("whispering propaganda") designed to intimidate inhabitants into leaving. More than a dozen villages were ordered by the Haganah to evacuate during April–June. The expulsions were usually from areas considered strategically vital and in conformity with Plan D, which called for clear main lines of communications and border areas. As well, it was standard Haganah and IDF practice to round up and expel the remaining villagers (usually old people, widows, cripples) from sites already evacuated by most of their inhabitants, mainly because the occupying force wanted to avoid having to leave behind a garrison.

Moreover, for military and political reasons, Arab local commanders and the AHC issued orders to evacuate close to two dozen villages during this period, as well as more general orders to local National Committees and villages to remove their womenfolk and children to safer areas. This included the Arab Legion

order of 13 May for the temporary evacuation of villages north
and east of Jerusalem for strategic reasons—to clear the prospec-
tive battle area. Military reasons also underlay the orders issued
in the various localities to evacuate women and children. Arab irregulars' commanders later in May intimidated villagers into
leaving seven sites in the Lower Galilee, apparently because they
feared the villagers would acquiesce in Israeli rule.

In April–May, and indeed, again in October, the "atrocity
factor" played a major role in certain areas of the country in encouraging flight. Arab villagers and townspeople, prompted by
the fear that the Jews, if victorious, would do to them what, in the
reverse circumstances, victorious Arab fighters would have done
(and did, occasionally, as in the Etzion Bloc in May) to defeated
Jews, took to their heels. The actual atrocities committed by the
Jewish forces (primarily at Deir Yassin) reinforced such fears considerably, especially when amplified and magnified loudly and
persistently in the Arab media, particularly by AHC spokesmen,
for weeks thereafter.

To what extent was the Arab exodus up to June a product of
Yishuv or Arab policy? The answer is as complex as was the situation on the ground. Up to the beginning of April 1948, there was
no Yishuv plan or policy to expel the Arab inhabitants of Palestine, either from the area destined for Jewish statehood or those
lying outside it. The Haganah adopted a forceful retaliatory strategy against suspected bases of Arab irregular bands which
triggered a certain amount of flight. But it was not a strategy designed to precipitate civilian flight.

The prospect and need to prepare for the invasion gave birth
to Plan D, prepared in early March. It gave the Haganah brigade
and battalion-level commanders *carte blanche* to completely clear
vital areas; it allowed the expulsion of hostile or potentially hostile Arab villages. Many villages were bases for bands of irregulars; most villages had armed militias and could serve as bases for
hostile bands. During April and May, the local Haganah units,
sometimes with specific instruction from the Haganah General
Staff, carried out elements of Plan D, each interpreting and implementing the plan in his area as he saw fit and in relation to the
prevailing local circumstances. In general, the commanders saw
fit to completely clear the vital roads and border areas of Arab
communities—Allon in Eastern Galilee, Carmel around Haifa
and Western Galilee, Avidan in the south. Most of the villagers

fled before or during the fighting. Those who stayed put were almost invariably expelled.

There was never, during April–June, any political or General Staff decision to expel "the Arabs" from the Jewish State's areas. There was no "plan" or policy decision. The matter was never discussed in the supreme, political, decision-making bodies, but it was understood by all concerned that, militarily, in the struggle to survive, the less Arabs remaining behind and along the front lines, the better and, politically, the less Arabs remaining in the Jewish State, the better. At each level of command and execution, Haganah officers in those April–June days when the fate of the State hung in the balance, simply "understood" what the military and political exigencies of survival required. Even most Mapam officers—ideologically committed to coexistence with the Arabs—failed to "adhere" to the party line: conditions in the field, tactically and strategically, gave precedence to immediate survival-mindedness over the long-term desirability of coexistence.

The Arab leadership inside and outside Palestine probably helped precipitate the exodus in the sense that it was disunited, had decided on no fixed, uniform policy *vis-à-vis* the civilian evacuation and gave the Palestinians no consistent, hard-and-fast guidelines and instructions about how to act and what to do, especially during the crucial month of April. The records are incomplete, but they show overwhelming confusion and disparate purpose, "policy" changing from week to week and area to area. No guiding hand or central control is evident.

During the first months, the flight of the middle and upper classes from the towns provoked little Arab interest, except at the affected, local level: the rich families arrived in Nablus, Amman, Beirut, in a trickle and were not needy. It seemed to be merely a repeat of the similar exodus of 1936–9. The Husaynis were probably happy that many of these wealthy, Opposition-linked families were leaving. No Arab government closed it borders or otherwise tried to stem the exodus. The AHC, its members already dispersed around the Arab world, issued no blanket condemnation of the flight though, according to IDF intelligence, it tried during these early months to halt the flow out of Palestine, specially of army-age males. At the local level, some of the National Committees (in Haifa, Jerusalem, for example) and local irregulars' commanders tried to fight the exodus, even setting up people's courts to try offenders and threatening confiscation of the property of the departees. However, enforcement seems to have been weak and haphazard; the measures proved largely unavailing. The irregulars often had an interest in encouraging flight as money was to be made out of it.

As to April and the start of the main exodus, I have found no evidence to show that the AHC issued blanket instructions, by radio or otherwise, to Palestine's Arabs to flee. However, AHC and Husayni supporters in certain areas may have ordered or encouraged flight out of various calculations and may have done so, on occasion, in the belief that they were doing what the AHC wanted or would have wanted them to do. Haifa affords illustration of this. While it is unlikely that Husayni or the AHC from outside Palestine instructed the Haifa Arab leadership of 22 April to opt for evacuation rather than surrender, Husayni's local supporters, led by Sheikh Murad, did so. The lack of AHC and Husayni orders, appeals or broadcasts *against* the departure during the following week-long Haifa exodus indicates that Husayni and the AHC did not dissent from their supporters' decision. Silence was consent. The absence of clear, public instructions and broadcasts for or against the Haifa exodus over 23–30 April is supremely instructive concerning the ambivalence of Husayni and the AHC at this stage towards the exodus.

The Arab states, apart from appealing to the British to halt the Haganah offensives and charging that the Haganah was expelling Palestine's Arabs, seem to have taken weeks to digest and understand what was happening. They did not appeal to the Palestinian masses to leave, but neither, in April, did they demand that the Palestinians stay put. Perhaps the politicians in Damascus, Cairo and Amman, like Husayni, understood that they would need a good reason to justify armed intervention in Palestine on the morrow of the British departure—and the mass exodus, presented as a planned Zionist expulsion, afforded such a reason.

But the dimensions and burden of the problem created by the exodus, falling necessarily and initially upon the shoulders of the host countries, quickly persuaded the Arab states—primarily Transjordan—that it were best to halt the flood tide. The AHC, too, was apparently shocked by the ease and completeness of the uprooting of the Arabs from Palestine. Hence the spate of appeals in early May by Transjordan, the AHC and various Arab leaders to the Arabs of Palestine to stay put or, if already in exile, to return to their homes. But the appeals, given the war conditions along the fronts, had little effect: the refugees, who had just left an active or potential combat zone, were hardly minded to return to it, and especially not on the eve of the expected pan-Arab invasion. Besides, in most areas the Haganah physically barred a return. Later, the Arab invasion of 15 May made any thought of a refugee return impracticable. And the invasion substantially increased the readiness of Haganah commanders to clear border areas of Arab communities.

Already in April–May, on the local and national levels, the Yishuv's military and political leaders began to contemplate the problem of a refugee return: should they be allowed back? The approach of the First Truce in early June raised the problem as one of the major political and strategic issues to be faced by the new State. The Arab states, on the local level on each front and in international forums, had begun pressing for Israel to allow the refugees back. And the United Nations' Mediator for Palestine, Bernadotte, had vigorously taken up the cause.

However, politically and militarily it was clear to most "Israelis" that a return would be disastrous. Militarily—and the war, all understood, was far from over—it would mean the introduction of a large, potential Fifth Column; politically, it would mean the reintroduction of a large, disruptive, Arab minority. The military commanders argued against a return; so did political common sense. Both were reinforced by strident anti-return lobbying by Jewish settlements around the country.

The mainstream national leaders, led by Ben-Gurion, had to confront the issue within two problematic political contexts—the international context of future Israeli-Arab relations, Israeli-United Nations relations and Israeli–United States relations, and the local political context of a coalition government, in which the Mapam ministers advocated future Jewish-Arab coexistence and a return of "peace-minded" refugees after the war. Hence the Cabinet consensus of 16 June was that there would be no return during the war and that the matter could be reconsidered after the hostilities. This left Israel's diplomats with room for manoeuvre and was sufficiently flexible to allow Mapam to stay in the government, leaving national unity intact.

On the practical level, from the spring of 1948, a series of developments on the ground growingly precluded any possibility of a future refugee return. The developments were an admixture of incidental, "natural" processes and steps specifically designed

to assure the impossibility of a return, which included the gradual
destruction of the abandoned Arab villages, the destruction or
cultivation and long-term take-over of Arab fields, the establishment of new settlements on Arab lands and the settlement of
Jewish immigrants in abandoned Arab villages and urban neigh-
bourhoods.

The second half of the war, between the end of the First
Truce (8 July) and the signing of the Israeli-Arab armistice agreements in the spring and summer of 1949, was characterised by
short, sharp Israeli offensives interspersed with periods of cease-
fire. In these offensives, the IDF beat the Transjordanian and
Egyptian armies and the ALA in the Galilee, and conquered large
parts of the territory earmarked in 1947 by the United Nations
for a Palestine Arab state. During and after these battles in July,
October and December 1948–January 1949, something like
300,000 more Palestinians became refugees.

Again, there was no Cabinet or IDF General Staff-level decision to expel. Indeed, the July fighting (the "Ten Days") was preceded by an explicit IDF General Staff order to all units and corps
to avoid destruction of Arab villages and expulsion of Arab communities without prior authorisation by the Defense Minister.
That order was issued as a result of the cumulative political pressure during the summer by the Mapam ministers and Shitrit on
Ben-Gurion.

But from July onwards, there was a growing readiness in the
IDF units to expel. This was a least partly due to the political feeling, encouraged by the mass exodus from Jewish-held areas to
date, than an almost completely Jewish State was a realistic possibility. There were also powerful vengeful urges at play—revenge
for Jewish losses and punishment for having forced upon the
Yishuv and its able-bodied young men the protracted, bitter battle. Generally, all that needed in each succesive newly-conquered
area, was a little nudging.

The tendency of IDF units to expel Arab civilians increased
just as the pressures on the remaining Arabs by leaders inside and
outside Palestine to stay put grew and just as their motivation to
stay put increased. During the summer, the Arab governments
intermittently tried to bar the entry of new refugees into their
territory. The Palestinians were encouraged to stay put in Palestine or to return to their homes. At the same time, those Palestinians still in their villages, hearing of the misery that was the lot of

their exiled brethren and despairing of salvation and reconquest of Palestine by the Arab armies, generally preferred to stay put, even though facing the prospect of Israeli rule. Staying put was to be preferred to flight. Arab resistance to flight in the second half of 1948 was far greater than in the pre-July days. Hence, there was much less "spontaneous" flight: villagers tended either to stay put or to leave under duress.

Ben-Gurion clearly wanted as few Arabs as possible to remain in the Jewish State. He hoped to see them flee. He said as much to his colleagues and aides in meetings in August, September and October. But no expulsion policy was ever enunciated and Ben-Gurion always refrained from issuing clear or written expulsion orders; he preferred that his generals "understand" what he wanted done. He wished to avoid going down in history as the "great expeller" and he did not want the Israeli government to be implicated in a morally questionable policy. And he sought to preserve national unity in wartime.

But while there was no "expulsion policy," the July and October offensives were characterised by far more expulsions and, indeed, brutality towards Arab civilians than the first half of the war. Yet events varied from place to place. In July, Ben-Gurion approved the largest expulsion of the war, from Lydda and Ramle, but, at the same time, IDF Northern Front, with Ben-Gurion's agreement if not at his behest, left Nazareth's population, which was mostly Christian, in place; the "Christian factor" was allowed to determine policy. And, in the centre of the country, three Arab villages—Al Fureidis and Khirbet Jisr az Zarka (along the Haifa–Tel Aviv road), and Abu Ghosh (near Jerusalem)—were allowed to stay.

Again, the IDF offensives of October in the Galilee and the south were marked by ambivalance concerning the troops' attitude to the overrun civilian population. In the south, where Allon was in command, almost no Arab civilians remained anywhere. Allon tended to expel and let his subordinates know what he wanted. In the north, where Carmel was in charge, the picture was varied. Many Upper Galilee Arabs, overrun in Operation Hiram, did not flee, contrary to Ben-Gurion's expectations. This was probably due in part to the fact that before October, the villagers had hardly been touched by the war or its privations. The varied religious make-up of the population contributed to the mixed picture. The IDF generally related far more benignly to

Christians and Druse than to Muslims. Most Christian and Druse villagers stayed put and were allowed to do so. Many of the Muslim villagers fled; others were expelled. But many other Muslim villagers—in Deir Hanna, Arraba, Sakhnin, Majd al Kurum—stayed put, and were allowed to stay. Much depended on specific local factors.

During the following months, with the Cabinet in Tel Aviv probably convinced that Israeli-Arab enmity would remain a central feature of the Middle East for many years, the IDF was authorised to clear Arab communities from Israel's long, winding and highly penetrable borders to a depth of 5–15 kilometres. One of the aims was to prevent infiltration of refugees back to their homes. The IDF was also afraid of sabotage and spying. Early November saw a wave of IDF expulsions or transfers of villagers inland along the northern border. Some villagers, ordered out, were "saved" by last-minute intervention by Israeli politicians. The following months and years saw other border areas cleared or partially cleared of Arab inhabitants.

In examining the causes of the Arab exodus from Palestine over 1947–9, accurate quantification is impossbile. I have tried to show that the exodus occurred in stages and that causation was multi-layered: a Haifa merchant did not leave only because of the weeks or months of sniping and bombings; or because business was getting bad; or because of intimidation and extortion by irregulars; or because he feared the collapse of law and order when the British left; or because he feared for his prospects and livelihood under Jewish rule. He left because of the accumulation of all these factors.

The situation was somewhat more clearcut in the countryside. But there, too, multiple causation often applied. Take Qaluniya, near Jerusalem. There were months of hostilities in the area, intermittent shortages of supplies, severance of communications with Jerusalem, lack of leadership or clear instruction about what to do or expect, rumours of impending Jewish attacks on neighbouring villages and reports of Jewish atrocities, and, finally, a Jewish attack on Qaluniya itself (after most of the inhabitants had left). Again, evacuation was the end-product of a cumulative process.

Even in the case of a Haganah or IDF expulsion order, the actual departure was often the result of a process rather than of that one act. Take Lydda, largely untouched by battle before July

1948. During the first months of the war, there was unemployment and skyrocketing prices, and the burden of armed irregulars. In April, thousands of refugees from Jaffa and its hinterland arrived in the town, camping out in courtyards and on the town's periphery. They brought demoralisation and sickness. Some wealthy families left. There was uncertainly about Abdullah's commitment to the town's defence. In June, there was a feeling that Lydda's "turn" was imminent. Then came the attack, with bombings and shelling, Arab Legion pull-out, collapse of resistance, sniping, massacre—and expulsion orders.

What happened in Palestine/Israel over 1947–9 was so complex and varied, the situation radically changing from date to date and place to place, that a single-cause explanation of the exodus from most sites is untenable. At most, one can say that certain causes were important in certain areas at certain times, with a general shift in the spring of 1948 from precedence of cumulative internal Arab factors—lack of leadership, economic problems, breakdown of law and order, to a primacy of external, compulsive causes—Haganah/IDF attacks and expulsions, fear of Jewish attacks and atrocities, lack of help from the Arab world and AHC and a feeling of impotence and abandonment, orders from Arab institutions and commanders to leave. In general, in most cases the final and decisive precipitant to flight was Haganah, IZL, LHI or IDF attack or the inhabitants' fear of such attack.

During the second half of 1948, international concern mounted with regard to the refugee problem. Concern translated into pressures. These pressures, launched by Bernadotte and the Arab states in the summer of 1948, increased as the months passed, as the number of refugees swelled and as their plight became physically more acute. The problem moved to the forefront of every treatment of the Middle East conflict and the Arabs made their agreement to a settlement with Israel contingent on a solution of the refugee problem by repatriation.

From the summer of 1948, Bernadotte, and from the autumn, the United States, pressed Israel to agree to a substantial measure of repatriation as part of a comprehensive solution to the refugee problem and to the general conflict. In December 1948, the United Nations General Assembly upheld the refugees' "right to return." But, as the abandoned villages fell into decrepitude or were bulldozed or settled, and as more Jewish immigrants poured into the country and were accommodated in abandoned Arab houses, the physical possibility of substantial repatriation grew more remote. Allowing back Arab refugees, Israel argued, would commensurately reduce Israel's ability to absorb Jewish refugees from Europe and the Middle East. Time worked against a repatriation of the Arab refugees. Bernadotte and the United States wanted Israel to make a "gesture" in the coin of repatriation, to get the efforts for a comprehensive settlement off the ground. In the spring of 1949, the thinking about a "gesture" matured into the United States' demand that Israel agree to take back 250,000, with the remaining refugees to be resettled in the neighbouring Arab countries. America threatened and cajoled, but never with sufficient force or conviction to persuade Tel Aviv to relent.

In the spring, in a final major effort, the United Nations and United States engineered the Lausanne Peace Conference. Weeks and months of haggling over agenda and secondary problems led nowhere. The Arabs made all progress contingent on Israeli agreement to mass repatriation. Under American pressure, Tel Aviv reluctantly agreed in July to take back 65,000–70,000 refugees (the "100,000 offer") as part of a comprehensive peace settlement. But by summer 1949, public and party political opinion in Israel—in part, due to government propaganda—had so hardened against a return that even this minimal offer was greeted by a storm of public protest and howls within Mapai. In any case, sincerity of the Israeli offer was never tested: the Arabs rejected it out of hand. The United States, too, regarded it as acutely insufficient, as too little, too late.

The insufficiency of the "100,000 offer," the Arab states' growing rejectionism, their unwillingness to accept and concede defeat and their inability to publicly agree to absorb and resettle most of the refugees if Israel agreed to repatriation of the rest, the expiry of the "Gaza Plan," and America's unwillingness or inability to apply persuasive pressures on Israel and the Arab states to compromise—all meant that the Arab-Israeli impasse would remain and that Palestine's exiled Arabs would remain refugees, to be utilised during the following years by the Arab states as a powerful political and propaganda pawn against Israel. The memory or vicarious memory of 1948 and the subsequent decades of humiliation and deprivation in the refugee camps would ultimately turn generations of Palestinians into potential or active terrorists and the "Palestinian problem" into one of the world's most intractable.

ISRAEL'S ARAB MINORITY: THE BEGINNING OF A TRAGEDY[4]

Tell it not in Gath, publish it not in the streets of Askelon; lest the daughters of the Philistines rejoice, lest the daughters of the uncircumcised triumph. (Samuel 1:20)

All well-wishers of Israel, including the official Zionists themselves, are accustomed to the platitude that its peace and security depend upon normal relations with the Arab world which surrounds it. Instead, there has been increasing hostility, in a vicious circle of reciprocal hatred, which threatens to embroil the region, perhaps the world, in war. It is to be feared that the outcome of the Zionist "fulfillment," so far from being the solution to the Jewish problem that was heralded by Zionism, may mean a new act in the tragedy of the Jewish people.

To break out of the vicious circle requires an attempt to win the support and friendship of the Arab masses away from and *against* the Arab rulers, from below, toward the goal of a binational state. For Israel this program begins at home: Israel will never be at peace with the surrounding Arab world, even if it makes a deal with the Colonel Nassers, as long as it is at war with its own Arab minority. This is the place to start.

The very existence of an Arab minority is shadowy in the minds of most Americans—some say, also in the minds of most Israelis—in spite of the fact that it is over one-tenth of the nation, like the Negro minority in the United States.

When the Israeli Arabs are not ignored, they are often labeled *en bloc* as "fifth-columnists" and suspect agents of the foreign Arabs who are foes of Israel; for they are all Arabs, aren't they? They are spoken of as the "remnant of the enemy defeated in 1948" in spite of the fact that they were not defeated in 1948 since they did not fight against Israel.

---

[4]By Hal Draper, historian, socialist, and publicist, from Hal Draper, ed., *Zionism, Israel, & the Arabs: The Historical Background of the Middle East Tragedy*, pp. 58–78. Copyright © 1967 Hal Draper. Reprinted by permission.

Israel's Arab problem, of course, goes back to the beginnings of Zionist colonization. It is not true that the Zionists came into Palestine as "agents of British imperialism" with the creation of the Mandate after the First World War. What is true is that they came as conscious junior partners of British imperialism: they would ensure continued British domination of the country, they proposed, if they were in turn given a free hand to take it over from the indigenous Arabs. Chaim Weizmann, who became Zionism's world leader and later first president of Israel as the shrewd architect of this symbiotic relationship, is quite candid about this in his autobiography. It was not his fault, or that of the Zionists, if this policy foundered after 1945, when the British government under Bevin made a sharp turn to the Arabs.

The Zionist infiltration into Palestine, therefore, took place before Arab eyes as the entrance of an alien and hostile force, under the umbrella of another alien and hostile force. Unfortunately the Zionist movement and the Israel government, despite frequent bows to the ideal of Jewish-Arab friendship, have never ceased to give nourishment to this feeling.

At least ever since Dr. Weizmann blurted out in 1919 that Zionism aimed to make Palestine "as Jewish as England is English," the Arabs have feared that this aim could not be achieved without driving out or otherwise getting rid of the population that was in the way. The Zionists countered with arguments supplemented by promises and pledges. Deeds are always more important.

Today we find that, in truth, the setting up of the Zionist state coincided with a process whereby the large majority of the Palestinian Arabs found themselves separated from their land and homes. How did this happen?

1

And it shall be, when the Lord thy God shall have brought thee into the land which he sware unto thy fathers . . . to give thee great and goodly cities, which thou buildedst not, and houses full of good things, which thou filledst not, and wells digged, which thou diggedst not, vineyards and olive trees, which thou plantedst not . . . (Deuteronomy 6: 10–11)

This is the nearest good starting point for an investigation of the current situation of the Arabs in Israel, as well as of the Arab refugees around Israel. It is a story enveloped in a fog of propaganda on both sides.

On November 29, 1947 the UN General Assembly adopted its resolution for the partition of Palestine. When the British Mandate ended next May, the Zionists declared the establishment of the State of Israel, and the Arab states invaded Palestine to forcibly annul the partition by aggression.

When the fighting broke out in 1948, even before May, there began a great flight and displacement of the Palestinian Arab population, a veritable exodus from their homes and farms. Out of 700,000 Arabs, there were only about 170–180,000 left within the enlarged borders of Israel when it was over.

The official Zionist version is that this flight took place in co-operation with the invading armies of the foreign Arab states. The official Israel government pamphlet *The Arabs in Israel* asserts:

It began on the express orders of the Arab commanders and political leaders, who assured the [Palestinian Arab] people that their evacuation to the neighboring Arab countries would only be of short duration and that they would soon return in the wake of the victorious Arab armies and receive a handsome share of the booty.

In addition, according to the same official version, the Palestinian Arabs had thought the invasion would be a walkaway, but when the Arab armies were defeated, "they panicked and stampeded across the frontiers. . . . Knowing what they had intended to do to their neighbors, they now expected the victorious Jews to mete out similar treatment to them." A mass guilty conscience. The Jews, on the other hand, according to this same account, vainly tried to convince these Arabs to stay and keep the peace.

This official version, therefore, provides the moral and even juridical justification for three aspects of Israel policy:

(1) Israel claims little responsibility for or to the hundreds of thousands of Arab refugees from its territory who are now living across its borders in misery and seething hatred.

(2) The government used the Arab flight to justify a series of laws which have stripped these refugees, as well as many Arabs who never left Israel, or are still in Israel, of their lands, groves and property.

(3) This version of the Arab flight, with its accompanying view of Arab disloyalty, is also the justification for the maintenance, up to today and for the indefinite future, of military-government rule over the large majority of Arabs still in Israel. Eighty-five per cent of the Arab minority in Israel live under po-

litical conditions which often resemble that of a conquered enemy under army occupation by its foe. This is not exactly a help
to Jewish-Arab friendship.

How important this version of the Arab flight is to the Zionists can be realized only by indicating its economic meaning. In
the following summary, the legal terms "absentee property" or
"abandoned" property refer to property seized from Arabs who
had left their homes during the fighting for any reason:

Of the 370 new Jewish settlements established between 1948 and the beginning of 1953, 350 were on absentee property. In 1954 more than one-
third of Israel's Jewish population lived on absentee property and nearly
a third of the new immigrants (250,000 people) settled in urban areas
abandoned by Arabs. . . . Most of the Arab groves were taken over by
the Israel Custodian of Absentee Property. . . . In 1951–52, former
Arab groves produced one and a quarter million boxes of fruit, of which
400,000 were exported. Arab fruit sent abroad provided nearly 10 per
cent of the country's foreign currency earnings from exports in 1951. In
1949 the olive produce from abandoned Arab groves was Israel's third
largest export ranking after citrus and diamonds. . . .
The CCP [UN's Conciliation Commission for Palestine] estimated that
the amount of Isarel's cultivable abandoned Arab land was nearly two and
a half times the total area of Jewish-owned property at the end of the mandate [1948]. . . .
In 1951 abandoned cultivable land included nearly 95 per cent of all Israel's olive groves. . . .

The government's Custodian of Absentee Property was in
1953 "one of the largest employers in Israel, and perhaps the
largest single landlord, renting over 65,000 housing and business
units of Arab absentee property. . . . "

This will give a preliminary idea of the role played by the
flight of the Palestinian Arabs in the establishment of the State
of Israel. Much is at stake when the Zionists insist that the flight
represented an act of hostility to the State of Israel.

But suppose it was only the normal reaction of people trying
to get out of the way of flying bullets? Suppose it was not in cooperation with the Arab invaders, but out of fear of them? Suppose
it was also out of fear of Israeli atrocities? Suppose it was also due
in part to the ouster of peaceful Arabs by Israeli troops?

Let us investigate three forces at work in precipitating the
flight: the Arab states' invasion; the Zionist forces, regular and
irregular troops; and the British who were departing the country
in bitterness in the twilight of their power.

2

Two nations are in thy womb, and two manner of people shall be separated from thy bowels . . . (Genesis 25: 23)

A couple of things about the social structure of the Arab community in Palestine should be mentioned for background.

When the British ended the mandate and withdrew, the Jewish communities had a whole quasi-government, or shadow government, ready to take its place and carry on all essential government functions and social services. Not so the Arabs.

When the British administration evacuated . . . there was no organized Arab body to manage the services of government essential for communal organization. With the breakdown of all functions of government necessary to maintain public law, order, and well-being—water, electricity, posts, police, education, health, sanitation, and the like—Arab morale collapsed.

This provided the context, not the cause, for the flight.

Besides, mass flight was not uncommon in the history of the Middle East, in similar cases where a population had reason to fear the waging of a war over their soil.

It was not only governmental services that collapsed, but also the social structure. As we shall see, it was the Arab upper class which fled first.

The upper class consists, as a rule, of a few great families whose members occupy key positions in the economic, professional and other occupational fields in the country. . . .
It was this small but extremely wealthy and influential class which represented Arab Palestine in practically every manifestation of social, civic, economic and political life. . . . It was common knowledge that their interests were often diametrically opposed to those of the fellahin who constituted three-quarters of the Arab population of Palestine but were illiterate, inarticulate and unable to voice any opinion.

This thin upper-class layer was highly nationalistic but also socially and politically reactionary. Though it did not represent the interests of the peasant masses, yet when it fled, the whole Arab community became structurally unstable. This was even more true in the Arab urban communities, like Jaffa and Haifa.

According to the official Zionist and Israeli version (for example, the government propaganda pamphlet *Arabs in Israel*) not only did the Palestine Arabs support the invasion by the foreign Arab states but, even before the May invasion, Palestine Arabs formed the majority of the bands of Arab irregulars who harassed Jewish settlements in the first months of 1948. This may or may not be so, but how many such Palestine Arabs were there? On the other hand, what was the attitude of the mass of Palestine Arabs?

Arthur Koestler, a lifelong Zionist (Revisionist) who was then in Palestine as a correspondent, writing of this early-1948 period, reports:

Ragged strangers kept appearing in increasing numbers in Arab villages and towns. . . . As the Palestine Arabs showed little willingness to fight, most of the sniping, ambushing and guerilla warfare was done by the foreign volunteers. . . . after the first serious clashes had occurred between Arabs and Jews in Tiberias . . . the heads of the two communities arranged a truce, the Arab delegates stating that the attackers of the Jewish quarter were "strangers who had forced their way into the town."

The Jewish ethnologist Raphael Patai writes:

The majority of the Israeli Moslem Arabs, however, chose not to become involved in the Arab-Jewish fights. On the Jewish side there was never any pressure exercised on them to take up arms against their own brethren; and they themselves tried hard to escape the demands of the Arab armies and guerillas for active help or financial support.

David Ben-Gurion himself, in a magazine article published at the beginning of 1948, testified that

Indeed, the vast majority of the Palestinian Arabs still refuse to join in this war despite the combined pressure of the Mufti and his gangs, of the Arab rulers and potentates who support him and of the Mandatory Power [Britain] whose policy aids and abets Arab aggression.
. . . the Arab villages have in their overwhelming majority kept aloof from the struggle. Were it not for the terrorization by the Arab bands and the incitement of their British supporters, the Arab people of Palestine would have soon resumed peaceful relations with their Jewish neighbors.

This was written before the land-grab had begun. It was only later that Israeli propagandists started putting forth a different version—i.e., *after* the land-grab was under way.

In the same issue of the same Zionist organ from which we have quoted Ben-Gurion, the same picture was drawn by another Arab expert of the Zionists, Yaakov Shimoni. Among other things he stresses that

the fact remains that the bulk of the Arab population has so far kept aloof from attacks on the Jews. Up to the present, the instigators of the disorders have been unable to enlist the mass of either the fellahin or the urban Arabs. . . .

And after a detailed account of the people's reaction, he concludes:

The hopes of the Mufti and the AHE [Arab Higher Executive] have thus far been disappointed because although they instigated and initiated the attack, they have been unable to deliver the goods: the mass of the Arab people of Palestine have failed to rise at their orders and have proved reluctant and incapable of fighting the Jews.

The interested reader can find testimony to the same effect in several other Zionist sources.

Now, as mentioned, the Zionist story is that the Arab Higher Executive called on the Palestine Arabs to flee their homes, come over the border, and wait till they could return in triumph to a conquered land. Now, if we assume for the sake of argument that it was indeed the policy of the AHE to issue this call, it still does not tell us whether or not Palestinian Arabs did in fact heed the call. For that, the testimony we have just cited is more relevant.

3

What mean ye that ye beat my people to pieces, and grind the faces of the poor? (Isaiah 3: 15)

What is agreed upon by virtually all sides, however, is the *class differentiation* in the flight. This may also serve to explain a kernel of truth in the Zionist version of the flight.

It is to the well-to-do Arab upper class (a small minority) that part of the Zionist story *does* apply, not to the Arab masses. In the first phase of the flight—i.e., before the start of heavy fighting, also before the start of heavy fighting, also before the Deir Yassin massacre, for example—it was these elements, the rich leaders of Arab society, who fled of their own free will.

Even the Israel government propaganda pamphlet takes note of the class distinction:

During the earlier phases of the fighting, the movement [of mass exodus] was on a small scale. Approximately 30,000 Arabs, mostly of the well-to-do classes, left for the neighboring states to await the outcome of the struggle, as they had done during the troubles of 1936–39.

But this is relatively grudging admission compared to the abundant evidence on this point from Zionist sources. The *Israel Digest* in April 1949 said that "The well-to-do ones departed before May 14th in pursuance of a deliberate plan" (the plan being the AHE strategy previously quoted from the Zionist story, but the significant thing to note is that *it is here ascribed only to the few rich Arabs* but "The poorer classes did not flee until the first month of Israel's existence. . . ." According to this, the "poorer classes" did not join in the flight until *after* the Deir Yassin massacre and many other things had happened. What then happens to the now-official Zionist story of an AHE plot for a mass exodus as the justification for Israel's refugee policy, land policy, and military government over the Arab minority?

Exactly the same statement is made in the January 1949 issue of the Tel Aviv journal *Israel & Middle East.*

Yaakov Shimoni wrote a few months later that "the educated and wealthier people . . . were among the first to run away, in contrast to the poorer strata of the community. . . ." As early as February 4, 1948, the British High Commissioner reported that "panic continues to increase . . . throughout the Arab middle classes, and there is a steady exodus of those who can afford to leave the country."

A Zionist writier reported: "In the town it was the workers and the poor who remained, together with a thin layer of middleclass families." The well-known journalist Hal Lehrman, writing in *Commentary* for December 1949, summed up:

The imams fled from the mosques, the kadis from the courts, the doctors, the teachers, practically all the intellectuals. Only workers and peasants remained.

A great understanding can be gained if one remembers that the Israeli Arab minority problem as we know it today concerns the treatment of *these workers and peasants who remained,* in spite of all.

4

For they fled from the swords, from the drawn sword, and from the bent bow, and from the grievousness of war. (Isaiah 21: 15)

"In spite of all" covers a great deal. Even if the Arab invaders' contribution to the flight was not that given in the Zionist version (the call to an exodus, etc.), still it played a big role. This role, however, was usually just the opposite of that which is commonly used to justify Israeli policy.

The Palestine Arab population did not flee out of sympathy with and in cooperation with the Arab invaders, but *out of fear of them and of the war.* This is easy to understand, but for the Zionists to admit this is to stamp their subsequent Arab minority policy with a certain brand.

Yet it creeps into even the Israel propaganda pamphlet which puts forward the official story; there we learn incidentally that time and again the foreign Arab commanders had to use force to prevent the local Arabs from making truces with the Israel forces. It creeps into the book by the Revisionist leader Schechtman where, as a matter of fact, we get the theory (by Schechtman) that the very reason why the AHE called for a mass exodus was "to prevent the possibility of establishing normal relations between the Jewish authorities and the Arab minority; for once this occurred, it might lead to Jewish-Arab cooperation and ultimately to Arab acquiescence in the existence of Israel." For a chauvinist like Schechtman, this already confesses a great deal.

Pierre van Paassen, a well-known pro-Zionist of the Christian-mystic fellow-traveling type, is anxious to prove in his book that the Arabs did not flee out of fear of *Israeli* atrocities. No, he argues, they fled out of fear of being murdered by the Mufti's henchmen if they stayed and refused to cooperate. He seems quite unaware that he is giving the lie to the official Zionist version and condemning its policy.

The ardent Zionist historian Harry Sacher likewise gives us this truth: he remarks that "the Arab commandants *ordered*" the Arabs on the fringes to evacuate their villages" (italics added).

An Israeli writer told in 1949 of the village of Tarshiha, whose Arabs did not flee. The villagers described how Kaukji, the Syrian leader of the Arab irregulars who had undertaken guerrilla operations even before the formal invasion,

ruled this district for several months and quickly brought it towards destruction and death. . . . One hears the same story throughout the whole of Western Galilee, in dozens of villages along the Lebanese frontier, the same tale of the despotic rule of Kaukji's brigands. They would carry people from their homes in the darkness of the night—never any questions asked. It was enough to "be on the list" on the slightest suspicion, a single word from one of the brigands. They removed them from their families to places outside the village, a few shots were heard in the darkness, and once more the population was reduced by a couple of villagers.

This is hardly the description of a population which was so sympathetic to the invader that it deserves, today, to be robbed, discriminated against, and slandered as "fifth columnists" en masse.

Chaim Weizmann, speaking to U.S. Ambassador McDonald in 1948, talked "of the flight of the Arab population from Israel—a flight at times so panicky that coins were left on the tables of huts in the Arab villages. . . . " This also scarcely fits the official story about a planned exodus at the call of the foreign Arabs.

5

But this is a people robbed and spoiled; but they are all of them snared in holes, and they are hid in prison houses: they are for a prey, and none delivereth; for a spoil, and none saith, Restore. Who among you will give ear to this? who will hearken and hear for the time to come? (Isaiah 42: 22-23)

A similar picture emerges from war-news items of the time in the *Palestine Post*, semi-official Zionist English-language daily in Jerusalem. When Iraqi invading forces took over the Ramallah area, which was and is Arab, they had to proclaim martial law and a curfew—

and the population was warned that violators would be shot at by the Iraqis. . . . Houses of Arabs who try to run away in the future will be blown up, the P.B.S. [radio] announced. Mukhtars and elders of villages in the Ramallah area were . . . threatened with severe punishment in the event of panic or chaos. (May 7, 1948)

This is a population under foreign occupation, not a population cooperating with invaders. Or take the report on Tiberias, quoting a Jewish Agency spokesman, which appeared in the *Palestine Post* on April 21, 1948: The local Arab leaders there had always been friendly, opposed to the anti-Jewish policies of the AHE; Kaukji's irregulars had occupied their houses "against the wishes of the inhabitants"—

A number of clashes occurred between the local and foreign Arabs, and local Arabs asked the British authorities for help to get rid of the invaders, but none was given.

Then, when the invaders were defeated by Jewish forces, they forced the local Arab families to evacuate. "This measure was meant to rouse the neighboring Arab States and induce them to send help."

In the same issue, the Zionist daily editorializes on the fact that the entire Arab population of Tiberias "were forced to leave by the Arab command. . . . In fact, the gangs were resisted as far as possible by those whose interests they had come to 'protect.'"

The nearly five months of fighting in Palestine has proved that the Arabs of the country—the ordinary townsmen,the fellahin and the Bedu [Bedouins] of the South—have no heart in the struggle. They did not want it to begin and they have no wish for it to continue.

But many of thes Arabs, forced to abandon their land, were later robbed of it through the "abandoned land" and "absentee property" laws rigged up for the purpose by the Israelis.

Or if they wound up across the border in refugee camps, they became willy-nilly part of the hapless hundreds of thousands who were reviled as "enemies" and "fifth-columnists" while their property was being stolen.

How could non-hostile Arabs wind up across the border? Read, for example, a feature article in the *Palestine Post* of May 12, 1948, written sympathetically by Dorothy Bar-Adon: she describes how

the "displaced" Arabs seeking refuge in the Emek unburden their hearts to the Jews whom they meet at roadblocks or in the fields. It is the familiar, time-worn complaint—"they," the outsiders. are responsible for all this.

And she describes how "The refugees are driven from pillar to post. There is simply no room and no food." They go to Nazareth; then despairingly have to move on to Jenin; to Beisan; nowhere can they be provided for.

So the refugee crosses to Trans-Jordan. From here he may be deported back again. And where does one go then?

Dorothy Bar-Adon prefaces this account with the appealing remark: *"And who can understand this bewildered running better than the Jew who has been doing it on and off for a few thousand years?"*

A Revisionist-Zionist writer who minces no words about his aim of squeezing all the Arabs out of Palestine—even this chauvinist found it possible to report honestly in 1950:

I truly sympathize with the great pain of those tens of thousands of Arabs who fled from Israel under pressure of the Mufti's bands, although they themselves wished to continue to live in neighborliness with the Jews and find work and their livelihood among them. I know of villages which defended themselves with arms against the forced entry of hired Mufti soldiers, and subsequently "evacuated" the villages for fear of military courts which threatened them.

He mentions about a dozen that he knows of "personally."

Or take the case of the Jawarish (or Arab el-Guarish) tribe, as it came to light after they were finally resettled. This tribe had been such firm allies of the Zionist colonizers that they had been trusted to guard the Jewish settlements at Gedera; they had helped Jews get around British regulations and Arab hostility against Jewish purchase of land by lending their own names for the deals. Yet, when the fighting began, they had to flee simply to live, winding up in one of the refugee camps of the Gaza strip. They were not repatriated until years later—even these Arabs, who were quislings from the point of view of the nationalists—and even they never got their own land back, but were resettled on new land provided by the state with a well-publicized ceremony in 1953.

Perhaps the most notable case of a tribe that was friendly to and supported the Jews, but which fled across the border during the fighting, was that of the village of Abu Gosh, which we will not document here since it is a longer and more important story which will fit better into a subsequent article on Israel's Arabs since 1948.

But in most cases it did not matter whether Arabs were friendly or hostile; it did not matter why they had to flee; it did not matter whether their flight was due to fear of the foreign Arab "liberators" or of Israeli atrocities like Deir Yassin; many were impartially stripped of their land and property, or relegated to the miserable refugee camps if that was where they landed, or subjected to military rule inside Israel—on the pretext that they had fled in order to answer the call of Israel's enemies!

6

Thou makest us a byword among the heathen, a shaking of the head among the people. (Psalms 44: 14)

If the foreign Arab invaders are the first force to be considered that precipitated the flight, then the second that must be taken up is the British.

The attitude of the British imperial power in giving up the mandate was a vicious snarl of spite: "We wash our hands of this mess, and may you all bog down in it. . . . " And if the resulting disordered tangle were to become bad enough, who knows but that the British might be called back? They were not sorry to see themselves followed by chaos. And more than one observer has charged that they helped chaos along a bit.

The sharpest indictment of the British role as a precipitant of the Arab flight was made by E. N. Koussa, a prominent Israeli Arab attorney, in a letter to the *Palestine Post* of February 2, 1949. Koussa testifies how the British authorities, before departure, encouraged and often initiated Arab evacuation, worked "to create an atmosphere permeated with fear and alarm," etc. "When conditions in Tiberias, where the friendly relations between Arabs and Jews formed a bright illustration of the possibility of the two communities cooperating, became acute, the British authorities forcibly transported the Arab inhabitants en masse to Transjordan," he charged (as quoted by Schechtman).

The Greek Catholic bishop of Haifa, Msgr. Hakim, also ascribed much responsibility to the British. A World Jewish Congress leader, N. Barou, wrote that the British helped the flight along "by spreading atrocity stories. . . . They also provided transport, convoys, etc." and he repeats the accusation about Tiberias. When British authorities told Arabs (in Haifa, for example) that the Jews would cut them to pieces if they stayed, some may really have thought so or they may have been motivated by guile, but in either case our own investigation has only the following question before it:

Insofar as the British role was a factor in causing the flight, how can one justify the draconic punishments imposed by Israel on the Arab minority as well as the refugees for what was not their own doing? How in good conscience can even the paid Israeli propagandists claim that the harsh refugee policy, or the landgrab, or the military government, is justified because these Arabs who were displaced were "enemies of Israel"?

7

Now go and smite Amalek, and utterly destroy all that they have, and spare them; but slay both man and woman, infant and suckling, ox and sheep, camel and ass. (1 Samuel 15: 3)

All this might be enough in itself to confute the Zionist version; but when we find further that Zionist-Israeli forces themselves played a prominent role in causing and intensifying the flight, then a darker and more sinister shadow falls over the harsh penalties which they later imposed on the Arab victims of their own actions.

The first sector of this question concerns the Zionist terrorist group, the Irgun Zvei Leumi, the military outgrowth of the Revisionist wing of Zionism—i.e., the most chauvinistic, most anti-Arab, most reactionary wing, which shaded into fascist tendencies (today organized in Israel in the Herut party, now the second strongest in the country). These extreme chauvinists always had, as compared with the other Zionists, the most consistent perspective of a Palestine which would not only be "as Jewish as England is English," but which would also be as *Araberrein* as Hitler wanted Germany to be *Judenrein*.

From early in the fighting, it seems clear, the Irgun oriented toward utilizing the war to achieve this objective, well in advance of the official Zionists' uneasy drift toward this same end. They struck their big blow on April 9, 1948 against Deir Yassin, an Arab village near Jerusalem on the highway to Tel-Aviv.

Why against Deir Yassin? The distinguished British Zionist editor Jon Kimche writes:

Dir Yassin was one of the few Arab villages whose inhabitants had refused permission for foreign Arab volunteers to use it as a base of operations against the Jewish life-line into Jerusalem; they had on occasions collaborated with the Jewish Agency.

Deir Yassin had to be the victim *because* its Arabs were friendly with the Jews. In *Labor Action* Al and Ed Findley gave more details called from the Jewish press:

It was the only village in the Jerusalem area that had not appealed to any Arab authority as being in danger from the Jews. The villagers lived under an agreement of non-agression with Jewish settlements surrounding it. In the winter of 1947 (long before the Dir Yassin massacre in April 1948) Abba Hushi, Jewish labor leader, cited a number of Arab villages in which the villagers had fought off Arab bands attempting to infiltrate and occupy them as positions against the Jews. Dir Yassin was prominently noted. Its villagers had successfully repelled an armed Arab band which attempted to entrench itself in the village mill. These Arab villagers . . . faithfully carried out their obligation to exclude strangers and to maintain peaceful relations, despite the partition fighting. . . .

This was the village chosen by the Irgun for their planned massacre of (writes Kimche) "some 250 innocent Arabs, among them more than a hundred women and children." The International Red Cross representative who visited the scene of the outrage, Jacques de Reynier, reported that the bodies of some 150 men, women and children had been thrown down a cistern while some 90 other bodies were scattered about. The houses were destroyed. The few villagers who were not slaughtered were paraded by the Irgun through the streets of Jerusalem—in triumph.

Deir Yassin resounded through the land, indeed through the world, and with the desired effect. Even a record of friendship for the Jews was no protection, no insurance. It was after this that the Arab flight became general.

There is no question about the fact that there were also atrocities committed by the Kaukji and Mufti armed forces against Jews; the invaders had their Deir Yassins too, even if on a smaller scale. There is an abundance of testimony on this. But this would be relevant only in a debate on a subject which is not ours: namely, which side was worse in the Palestine war?

8

Such is the way of an adulterous woman; she eateth, and wipeth her mouth, and saith, I have done no wickedness. (Proverbs 30: 20)

But didn't the Jewish Agency condemn the Deir Yassin massacre and apologize for it? It did. Even if that were the whole story, few people would wonder why the mass of Arabs, already confused and panicked by Arab invaders and British, decided that flight held greater safety than trusting in the regrets of Ben-Gurion. But there are two other facets to this story.

(1) The official-Zionist army, Haganah, repudiated the massacre, undoubtedly sincerely, but also went on to claim that the Irgun had attacked Deir Yassin without any military justification and without the agreement of the official forces. The Irgun countered by releasing the exact text of the letter from the regional Haganah commander agreeing to the attack (not to a massacre, of course). This has not really been refuted. The friendly village was not supposed to be turned into an abattoir, naturally, but it *was* supposed to be assaulted and invested as a military operation, in cynical violation of any non-aggression obligation to it.

(2) The official-Zionists righteously deplored and condemned—but did absolutely nothing to take any effective steps against the repetition of Irgun atrocities. On the contrary, the relations between the official Zionists and the Irgun were now closer than ever.

Only seven months before, on September 18, 1947, the Haganah had raked the Irgun and Sternists with the denunciation: "these organizations gain their livelihood by gangsterism, smuggling, large-scale drug traffic, armed robbery, organizing the black market, and thefts"; and announced measures to root out terrorism. But partition changed all that in Novermber. By December the Haganah had overcome its moral sensibilities and was negotiating with Irgun for an agreement on cooperation. *Such an agreement was reached in April, the very month of the Deir Yassin massacre.*

The prominent Zionist historian Harry Sacher uneasily limits his comment on this to:

> . . . much is still obscure as to the relations between the Haganah or the Government and the Irgun. For comprehensible reasons the Government does not think the time yet come to tell its story fully and frankly. . . .

Among the obscure relations is undoubtedly the role of the other official-Zionist armed force, the Palmach. The *Palestine Post* reported four days after the massacre:

> The Haganah statement denied IZL [Irgun] claims that Palmach units had cooperated in the attack, and pointed out that it was only after urgent appeals for help that the Palmach had provided covering fire, to enable the administration of first aid to the wounded dissidents [Irgunists] in the village. (April 13, 1948)

It is not easy to see what, according to the official story, the Palmach was doing there in the first place.

So it is not quite true that the Deir Yassin massacre was *simply* the uncontrollable act of mavericks for whom the official Zionists were not responsible, as it is represented by all good Zionist writers who duly express their horror at it. They do not express any horror at the idea that the government and Haganah at this time made their alliance with these perpetrators of this "Lidice," and continued it. (It was not Arab-exterminationism which moved them to break with the terrorists; it was the assassination five months later of the UN mediator, Count Bernadotte, by Sternists.)

9

Is there yet any portion or inheritance for us in our father's house?
(Genesis 31: 14)

The Deir Yassin massacre "was a turning point," says Sacher quite accurately. The foreign Arab invaders trumpeted its horror far and wide, no doubt with the aim of stimulating anti-Israel militancy on the part of the anti-war Palestine population; the actual result of their propaganda was to convince all strata, poor as well as rich Arabs, that the best thing to do was to get out of the war zone—to flee until the hostilities were over.

The massive effect of Deir Yassin on the flight is testified to from all sides. The flight for the first time became general. The matter of chronology is very important; for it proves that the flight cannot be explained away as due to some previous call by the Arab invaders, as is done by Zionist party-liners and the official history-rewriters of Israel.

Another thing has to be noted about the impact of Deir Yassin. Like others we have used the term "official Zionists" as distinct from the terrorists. But this was the month *before* the establishment of the state. As far as the Arab people knew, was the Irgun really less "official" than the Haganah?

Jon Kimche's book provides an important bit of background here. He explains at length how the Irgun set about convincing the British, the world press and the Arabs that it, not Haganah, was the decisive power in the Zionist community, that it was "taking over," etc. The British passed this on to the Arab governments.

It had the desired effect among the Arabs. It swayed many who had been hesitating on the brink of decision, whether to flout the United Nations and go to war against the Palestine Zionists or not. For though it has become a habit among Israelis and pro-Zionists to assume that there was nothing but evil hatred behind the Arab decision to go to war against Israel, and that the Arab explanation that they came to save their brethren from attack by the terrorists was a cheap excuse for the benefit of those who cared to believe it, it must be stressed that there was great and very real Arab concern for the fate of the Palestine Arabs. This concern reached fever-heat when the British information was passed on that the terrorists were becoming the decisive factor in the Jewish armed forces.

Kimche notes that this belief was reinforced when the Irgun took it upon itself in April to attack Jaffa, the Arab twin city to Tel-Aviv.

10

Woe to him that buildeth a town with blood, and establisheth a city by iniquity! (Habakkuk 2: 12)

Deir Yassin was fresh in the minds of all when later in April the Zionist forces got ready to attack the Arab city and port of Haifa in anticipation of the withdrawal of the British troops. The Haifa situation requires special attention because it is the big show-piece for the Zionist contention that, far from pushing the Arabs out, the Jews pleaded with them to stay. As in some other cases, there is a kernel of truth here which the Zionist apologists pretend is the whole story.

Menachem Begin, the Irgun commander, stresses in his book that the effect of Deir Yassin was decisive for the flight from Haifa:

The legend of Dir Yassin helped us in particular in the saving of Tiberias and the conquest of Haifa. . . . [And after describing the assault on Haifa:], All the Jewish forces proceeded to advance through Haifa like a knife through butter. The Arabs began fleeing in panic, shouting: "Dir Yassin!"

In this period there were indeed cases where official Zionists tried to persuade the Arabs not to flee. Haifa was one of these; in this commercial city Jewish-Arab relations had been particularly friendly. It was the terrorists and their chauvinist ilk who realized earlier than the others that the Zionists had an exceptional opportunity to "solve the Arab problem" within the Jewish state-to-be by the expedient of getting rid of the Arabs themselves. Friendly relations stood in the way of this aim. Hence the year before, in this very port city, the Irgun had tried out a "Deir Yassin" on a small scale:

The Irgun picked an area in Haifa that was known for friendly Jewish-Arab relations and threw a bomb at the entrance of a factory employing 1800 Arabs and 400 Jews, killing six Arabs and three British workers. Their provocative act resulted in the massacre of 42 Jews.

As we have seen the Arab Higher Executive too reserved its choicest hatred for those Arabs who tried to maintain friendly relations with the Jews. In the middle was the Arab leadership of the Haifa community, who opposed the AHE and wanted to make a truce with the Zionist authorities.

If there was an Arab community in Palestine that had no sympathy at all for the war against Israel, it was the Haifa Arabs, who stood to lose—were indeed losing—their whole livelihood and existence. Their evacuation of the city was due to threats from the Arab invaders and panic fear evoked by the Irgun atrocity, reinforced and encouraged by the British.

This feeling of panic was also reinforced by the tactics of the beleaguering Haganah, in spite of the fact that Zionist authorities urged the populace to stay. This was a species of psychological warfare waged against the population with the intention of producing demoralization. Koestler insists that this demoralization was an important reason for the Haifa flight, and furthermore:

By that time Haganah was using not only its radio station, but also loudspeaker vans which blared their sinister news from the vicinity of th Arab shuks. They warned the Arab population to keep clear of the billets of the foreign mercenaries who had infiltrated into the town, *warned them to send their women and children away* before the new contingents of savage Iraqis arrived, promised them safe conducts and escorts to Arab territory, and hinted at terrible consequences if their warnings were disregarded. [Italics added.]

Kimche, who was there, also describes the "psychological blitz" launched on the Arab quarters, and concludes: "The Arab nerve broke shortly after dark, and the flight from the town assumed panic proportions even before general fighting had started." (He does not say anything about a warning to send away the women and children.) It was particularly after this that the Jews tried to persuade the remaining Arabs to stay. The latter were anxious to agree and come to a truce, but, according to Kimche's personal account, it was the threats of the Arab League authorities which finally conviced the Haifa Arabs that flight would be safer. Only 5000 remained out of about 65,000.

But though they had left in a panic, there was a strangely unpanicky atmosphere in the port area. The departing Arabs meekly allowed themselves to be searched by the Haganah. They exchanged greetings and farewells with Jewish port workers, with many of whom they had worked for years.

These are among the Arabs whose flight, according to the latter-day Zionist hack version, was due to sinister enmity against the Jews.

Whatever weight anyone chooses to give to the various cruel pressures on these Arabs pushing them toward flight, not one of the real reasons for the flight justifies the later merciless Israeli punishment of these victims, for the "crime" of fleeing.

Moreover, in the case of Jaffa, there were two additional factors: (1) As mentioned, this attack was launched by the Irgun itself, the very perpetrators of Deir Yassin; and (2) "The desire to get out of the range of Arab bombs which were soon to fall on Tel-Aviv was as potent an incentive as the fear of the Jews," explains a Zionist writer.

11

By little and little I will drive them out before thee, until thou be increased, and inherit the land . . . for I will deliver the inhabitants of the land into your hand; and thou shalt drive them out before thee. . . . They shall not dwell in thy land. . . . (Exodus 23: 30-33)

But the blackest part of the true story is still to come. It was only in the first period that it was official Zionist policy to frown on the flight. They were still under the influence of the lip-service which they had been used to giving to idea of Jewish-Arab friendship; the flight had been unexpected; but they were not too slow in reorienting. Within three months after Deir Yassin, the official Haganah forces themselves were driving the Palestine Arab population out of their native villages, towns and cities, like cattle.

Referring to the flight, "Dr. Weizmann . . . spoke to me emotionally of this 'miraculous simplification of Israel's tasks' . . . " reported U. S. Ambassador McDonald (an active Zionist propagandist) in his book. The flight was greeted as a "miracle" by more than Weizmann; and like other pious people, they had no objection to helping the miracle along.

By August 1, Foreign Minister Sharett was saying that "the Palestinian Arab exodus of 1948 is one of those cataclysmic phenomena which, according to the experience of other countries, changes the course of history." While Israeli soldiers were driving innocent Arabs out of their homes, the government was already making clear that it would be a long while before any of the refugees were allowed back.

The New York *Herald Tribune*'s war correspondent Kenneth Bilby, in a book remarkable for the general impartiality of its tone, says, after relating that at Haifa the Zionists urged the people to stay:

Not until the war had swung noticeably in favor of the Jews and the pressure of the Jewish immigrant inflow had begun to exert itself did Israeli government policy change. Then those civilian Arabs who fell into the army net were not only permitted to depart: they were encouraged. And the borders of Israel closed to the refugees, except for a few family categories.

Likewise Jon Kimche, in the British Zionist organ which he edits:

But after the first period of fighting, the Palestine Arabs were no longer encouraged to stay; on the contrary: they were "encouraged" to leave Lydda and Ramleh, and later, towns like Beersheba.

The quote-marks around "encouraged" give way to a franker formulation in Kimche's book:

Ramleh and Lydda fell on the 13th [July]; and a flood of 60,000 panicky Arabs were compelled to take the road to the nearby Arab lines. This was no Haifa. The Jews no longer hoped the Arabs would stay. They had tasted the benefits which the earlier Arab policy of evacuation had bestowed upon them.

Which means that the 60,000 people were expelled. There had not even been a pitched battle with Arab forces (let alone the civilians), because the Arab Legion had withdrawn without a fight. The people were simply driven out, to make the towns *Araberrein* and provide property for incoming Jews to expand into. Among the people expelled were refugees from Haifa and Jaffa. This was done by the Haganah, not by Irgun.

But although the Arab Legion had already withdrawn, here is Bilby's description of how the Israeli troops entered Lydda. It is the only such passage in Bilby's book, which has been favorably cited by Zionists as source to disprove *other* Arab charges of atrocities:

The ring around the twin cities [Lydda and Ramleh] was now complete. At dusk one evening an Israeli jeep column took off from the Lydda airport and raced into Lydda, with rifles, Stens, and submachine guns blazing. It coursed through the main streets, blasting at everything that moved. The town toppled in panic. I went into Lydda the following day with Major Yeruham Cohen, brigade intelligence officer, and the corpses of Arab men, women, and even children were strewn about the streets in the wake of this ruthlessly brilliant charge. Civilians who had been trapped by the Jewish encirclement cowered behind shuttered windows; white flags were draped from every home.

The reader must keep in mind that many Arab inhabitants who survived the submachine guns, and were merely driven out onto the open road, are among those who were punished for becoming "absentees" by laws which stripped them of their "abandoned" property.

In 1949 Hal Lehrman wrote in *Commentary* (December):

Now that I've traveled every corner of this country [Israel], it has become clear that the Israeli troops must have been decidedly tough even with non-combatant Arab during the war. There are, for instance, too many dynamited, desolated native villages where little or no fighting ever occurred. The Jews simply came in and smashed the place, often sparing only the mosques . . . it is obvious, too, that the Israelis—themselves surprised by the scope and speed of the Arab exodus—did an extra-thorough job of destruction to make sure that the Arabs would have noth-

ing to come back to. There is no evidence that this was official
government policy, but it certainly must have been in the minds of many
local commanders. . . . Looting was not too zealously repressed either.
No less an authority than the present Speaker of the Knesset, Joseph
Sprintzak, has been quoted as saying that the looting of Arab homes and
shops was a major defeat for the new government of Israel.

Then, after referring to the Deir Yassin massacre, Lehrman
asks " Were there other outrages?" and quotes a UN observer as
saying yes. And he continues:

I am more shaken by the expressions of grief and shame I have privately
received from non-political but prominent Israelis whose personal integrity is beyond question. "The Israeli soldier has looted, burned, and
slaughtered," I have been told, "and it is no comfort for us that soldiers
of every other army do likewise." It is even hinted that certain officers actually ordered their troops to let themselves go. The best evidence that
there were atrocities—and, I suppose, the best apology for them, if such
things can be apologized for—came to me from a high-ranking veteran
of the Jerusalem siege. "Our soldiers," he said, "were no worse than the
Americans or British. They were even better. . . . "

But the question we are interested in here is not the moral superiority of the Haganah looters and perpetrators of atrocities
over Americans or British, or vice versa, but in a far simpler one:
Many Arab peasants against whom the looting and atrocities were
committed, and who were driven out or who fled in fright, were
later robbed of property and land and had a military government
imposed over them *because* they fled or were driven out—i.e., because they left their habitations as a result of or in fear of such
atrocities—and this was done not by Haganah soldiers but by the
parliament and government of Israel. This was the real atrocity.

12

**My father made your yoke heavy, and I will add to your yoke: my father
also chastised you with whips, but I will chastise you with scorpions.**
(1 Kings 12: 14)

Besides, the looting was not mere looting for its own sake; at
least in part it was committed in the Zionist cause; that is, as a
means of driving out the Arabs. Jon Kimche explains with heavy
heart, in his book, speaking of the Haganah and the Jewish Agency:

. . . . the Irgun practice of looting Arab homes and shops was soon explained away and later justified as ministering to the needs of Jewish evac-
uees who had lost their homes and their all as a result of the four months

of attack from Jaffa. It was perhaps natural, though it was certainly detestable, that before long the rest of the Jewish soldiers of the Haganah and the Palmach should join in the orgy of looting and wanton destruction which hangs like a black pall over almost all the Jewish military successes. It could have been stopped by firm action at the outset. But it soon became a practice for which there was always a material incentive, a sophisticated justification, and an excuse.

The fact that the "detestable" practice was initiated by the Irgun is significant. Irgun was the arm of a movement which consciously and systematically aimed at making Palestine *Araberrein*. Looting and *"wanton* destruction" was a political means. As in so many other cases, the Revisionist-Irgun-Herut movement showed the way to consistent Zionist practice, and the official Zionists followed with more or less reluctance, consistency and heartburning.

But it would be a mistake to think that the ousting of Arabs by official Israeli forces was a matter only of massacres or unofficial looting. The strange thing about the official-Zionist version of the flight is that one of the most important contributions of the Israelis to the ousting of Arab peasants was—in 1948—public, overt, and reported in the Zionist press as military news. This was the dynamiting of villages, and evacuation of their population, on grounds or pretext of military necessity, when foreign Arab invaders had used or might use them for a base. There is also involved the barbarous practice, introduced by the British, of collective punishments for a whole village in case of sniping.

Thus Arthur Koestler recorded in his diary on June 6, 1948 as he drove along the road from Haifa to Tel-Aviv, observing some peaceful Arabs still tilling their fields:

But not for long. A few weeks later some Arab lads will start sniping from these villages at Jewish trucks on the road; the Jewish army will herd the villagers together, dynamite their houses, and put the young men into concentration camps; while the old ones will tie a mattress and a brass coffeepot on the donkey, the old women will walk ahead leading the donkey by the rein and the old man will ride on it. . . .

At this point, the official Zionist apologist will inform us that this is military necessity, and cannot be helped. Before commenting, let us see some more military necessities. We quote from the military news published as a matter of course by the *Palestine Post* in 1948:

. . . Kolonia village overlooking Motza was destroyed by a Haganah striking force. . . . Most of the houses in Kolonia, occupied by Arab gangs [Kaukji's foreign Arab guerrillas] that had been attacking Castel, were blown up on Saturday night, and in a short but sharp fight the Arab unit in the village was wiped out. . . . *Yesterday, Haganah men completed the destruction of the village by blowing up the remaining houses.* . . . The village had been evacuated by most of its residents during the past week. . . . (April 12, 1948. Italics added.)

The next day the paper reported, in a similar news item, that three villages had been "pounded into desolation" and "reduced to rubble" after being deserted by their residents and occupied by "Arab gangs." It adds matter-of-factly:

Abu Shusha village . . . was recaptured by the Haganah this morning, and is being blown up. (April 13, 1948)

The fact is then, that Arab villages were systematically dynamited and razed not, or not merely, in the course of fighting but *after capture.* The military necessity was presumably to prevent their use by hostile forces. No doubt, the system of destroying these villages down to their foundation stones had a real convenience for the Israeli forces from this point of view, though other civilized armies seem to have gotten along in various wars without this practice. For present purposes we will also assume for a moment that the Zionist authorities never gave a moment's thought to the fact that this convenient custom had the additional advantage of scorching the earth for the Arab inhabitants and contributing to the "purity" of an *Araberrein* Palestine. We only ask readers to remember, once again, that even if we accept the plea of military necessity at face value, the question which is at issue in this study is the subsequent fate of the innocent Arab peasants who were driven out and despoiled out of this alleged military necessity, and not because of their alleged offense in taking flight at the call of the Arab invaders.

But it would take great willpower to convince oneself that military necessity was the answer. Kenneth Bilby wrote, for example, summing up the 1949 picture:

Israel ruled three-quarters of Palestine, and scores of Arab villages deemed uninhabitable had been razed *as insurance against their owners' return.* (Italics added.)

Harry Sacher, a prominent British Zionist leader, is very delicate in the following remarks:

. . . for strategic purposes the Jews began to blow up the Arab villages, which they occupied. . . . The massacre at Deir Yassin by the Irgun on the 9th April, 1948, was a turning point. . . . It became the rule that, when the Jewish forces advanced, the Arab inhabitants of the occupied territory fled; *nor was the flight always without stimulation or encouragement from the Jews.* (Italics added.)

An internationally known professor and author at Hebrew University, Norman Bentwich, remarks regarding the injustice of the later Absentee Property Law:

Many [Arab residents of Israel] were driven out for a time from their villages by the Jewish military forces in the course of the campaign, and are now living in adjacent villages, and are prevented from recovering their properties which are vested in the Custodian.

Hal Lehrman—writing about an entirely different topic, the widespread prejudice by Israeli Jews against the new immigrant Oriental Jews—quotes an Israeli friend who complained to him, "not entirely in sour jest, that 'we drove out our good Arabs, and now look at what we have in their place!'" The alleged half-jest is about the Oriental Jews; the remark which slips out incidentally about having driven out the Arabs is *not* part of the sour jest.

13

And it came to pass, when Joram saw Jehu, that he said, Is it peace, Jehu? And he answered, What peace, so long as the whoredoms of thy mother Jezebel and her witchcrafts are so many? (2 Kings 9: 22)

As a matter of fact, the infamous land-grab, which after the war was carried through systematically by special laws and ordinances, got started during the war itself under the umbrella of military operations. Dr. Don Peretz writes:

When Israel's military and paramilitary forces first occupied abandoned Arab areas military field commanders improvised policy on the spot, often turning property over to the secretaries of Jewish agricultural settlements or local security officers.

In a series of articles on Israel's Arabs which appeared in the leading Israeli paper *Haaretz*, we read that

Every piece of land which had been abandoned for any reason whatever—whether in the whirl of war, or during the truces, or soon after the Israeli occupation—was at once seized by the nearby [Jewish] settlement or settlements and attached to their estates.

This grab was not a matter of individual lawlessness merely; it was organized and stimulated by Zionist authorities for Zionist aims. Dr. Don Peretz describes it for this period:

Squatters [on seized Arab property] often received semi-official sanction for their occupation of empty buildings. Even before the status of the abandoned Arab areas was determined, the Jewish Agency was directing the flow of new immigrants toward the vacant Arab settlements. The military also participated in this unauthorized mass-requisitioning. In one instance, a group of army officers supported by tanks seized large areas of absentee [Arab] property in Jaffa. [Peretz's footnote here refers to the January 9, 1949 issue of *Haaretz*.]
When the first Custodian of Abandoned Property was appointed, in July 1948, all of Jaffa had been occupied. . . .
In one of his early reports the Custodian claimed that nearly all absentee houses had been occupied and that their seizure by the Jewish Agency for the use of new immigrants would be recognized. Nearly all movables in these houses, which had not been looted or destroyed, were sold to the army before the Custodian arrived.

The role of the Jewish Agency in this grab was attested to in November 1949 when Finance Minister Kaplan (the cabinet member in charge) made a Knesset speech replying to charges of government laxness. He "accused institutions like the Jewish Agency, which were responsible for the settlement of new immigrants, of causing the greatest difficulties in management of absentee property."

At this time, the callous robbery of the Arabs was not yet being justified officially by reference to the needs of the new immigrants. The conception had not yet taken root in all circles that the injustices and crimes committed against European Jewry by bestial anti-Semites were sufficient reason for the wronged Jews in turn to commit injustices and crimes against the native Palestinian Arab population. It was being *done*, but only officially-unofficially. When the first Custodian made his report to the Knesset, such robbery was condemned at least in words, though nothing whatsoever was done against it. The government washed its hands; so did Haganah.

In his April 18, 1949 report to the Knesset Finance Committee, the Custodian maintained that the "moral feelings" of the Jewish community had "prevented the despoliation of the enemy," but he did admit this much:

Feelings of revenge, moral justification and material temptation did, however, overcome many.
In such conditions, only extreme measures by the military, civil and legal authorities could have saved, not only the property, but many individuals and institutions from moral degeneration.
Such action was not forthcoming and was, perhaps, impossible in the prevailing conditions, and affairs in many areas degenerated without restraint.

Note that this official lists "material temptation"—i.e., looting for the sake of the loot—only third; and note his reference not only to individuals but to "institutions," which means the Zionist agencies and organizations.

The leading newspaper *Haaretz*—then, as now, a Zionist voice that was deeply conscience-stricken over it all—spoke out. Its columnist, the Hebrew author Moshe Smilanski (of the Ichud), agreed with the Custodian's report that a large part of the public was responsible for the theft of Arab property. "Towns, villages and agricultural property were robbed without shame, and lawless individuals of the masses as well as the intelligentsia enriched themselves from occupied property." He called for measures against those responsible, but that was naive.

Smilanski also wrote: "Some time we will have to account for its theft and despoliation not only to our consciences but also to the law." There he was quite wrong. The same people who tolerated the robbery devised a whole series of laws which not only legalized the grab but permitted its systematic extension; but that is for another article on the story of the Israeli Arab minority.

14

Now ye may see this, as we have declared, not so much by ancient histories, as ye may if ye search what hath been wickedly done of late through the pestilent behavior of them that are unworthily placed in authority. (Esther [Apocrypha] 16: 7)

While the robbery could always be reconciled with law, given the power of a state, it could not be reconciled with conscience by those Israelis who hold out against the tide of chauvinism in the little country. The intellectuals of Ichud or *Haaretz* are wont to lament the moral degeneration exhibited when a people, themselves so recently persecuted and despoiled in Europe, visit such wrongs upon a minority which is under their own newly acquired power.

Without in the least derogating this moral indignation at the treatment of the Arab minority, which is richly justified, one aspect of the denunciation misses the mark. The moral indignation should not be visited in the first place against the miserable, harassed, driven Jewish DPs from Europe who, in their fear and need, were used as pawns to grab the land and property of the dispossessed Arabs. They were steered and pushed into this position by those who knew what they were doing—Zionist arms like the Jewish Agency, Zionist authorities in the armed forces and government, both by design and by toleration.

Zionism—the ideology of Jewish chauvinism—showed that it was and is one of the deeply reactionary conceptions of the political world. The child of anti-Semitism, it became the father of another form of ethnic oppression; if genocide means the murder of a people as such, then there should be a word for the robbery of a people as such.

What Zionism created in Palestine in 1948 was the first act of a tragedy.

A SMALL PEACEFUL VILLAGE[5]

On Sunday morning, April 11, 1948, I flinched when I read the headlines in New York: "Jews attack village of Deir Yassin. Massacre of civilians reported. *Irgun* and Sternists accused." I read the article fast. The way the *New York Times* described it, Deir Yassin was a"peaceful village" and its "civilian population" had been "massacred by terrorists."

I remembered Deir Yassin well from the late twenties and the last thing I would have called it was a "peaceful village." Way back in 1929, Arab marauders out of the village of Kalandia had attacked Motza, a Jewish setlement since 1894. Bands out of Deir Yassin and Lifta then cut off the Jewish relief force that tried to reach Motza. The Makleff family, one of the oldest, most respected families, was massacred in their home. One of my father's old friends, Broza, lay critically wounded, hovering between life and death for weeks.

In 1936, when I was in charge of an *Irgun* defense position in Givat Shaul, one of the Jewish Jerusalem's outlying suburbs, we continually faced attempted forays into our homes from Deir Yassin. We dug our "illegal" weapons every night and waited, while the Jewish supplementary police repulsed the infiltrators

[5]By Yitshaq Ben-Ami, former Irgun fighter, from his book of memoirs, *Years of Wrath, Days of Glory: Memoirs from the Irgun*, pp. 439–448. Copyright © 1982 by Y. Ben-Ami. Reprinted by permission of Robert Speller & Sons, Publishers Inc.

again and again. Months later, we had a defense position in near-by Motza commanded by Hillel Kook, and he often asked my help to transport men to their night duties in Motza. Driving back and forth to Motza from Jerusalem, I spent many hours lying in road-side ditches after ambushes out of Deir Yassin. The "peaceful lit-tle village" the *Times* now spoke of, earned itself quite a reputation over the years as a nest for terrorist attacks on the highway and the outlying settlements. Together with Lifta, the Arab village lying to the left of it entering Jerusalem, its "civilian population" tried to choke off traffic to and from Jewish Jerusa-lem whenever trouble was brewing.

Reading the newspaper I knew something had been "lost in translation." It took me a long stretch of time and many conversa-tions with Mordechai Raanan, *Irgun* Commander in Jerusalem, with Nathan Yalin Mor, the key *Lehi* commander, and with men out of the ranks who had participated in the operation before I was able to put together all the pieces.

It was a far more involved story than the one the *Times* had printed. The first week in April, the Hebrew forces in Jerusalem had learned that Iraqi and Jordanian soldiers, as well as a number of Europeans of various origins, had installed themselves in the surrounding Arab villages. The night of April 2nd, Deir Yassin opened intense fire on the Jewish suburbs of Beit Hakerem and Bait Vegan. The firing lasted all night. For the next several nights running, *Haganah* and *Irgun* troops reconnoitered Deir Yassin; by the seventh of April, the *Irgun* and *Lehi* commanders had decided to attack and occupy the village. This would discourage further night attacks, help secure the highway to Tel-Aviv and consoli-date Hebrew control of the western area of Jerusalem.

Because of limited coordination and cooperation between *Irgun-Lehi* and the *Haganah*, the *Haganah* was not asked to join in the operation. When their commander, David Shaltiel, learned about the plans on April 7, he wrote to the *Irgun-Lehi* command-ers that he had no objections to the occupation of the village. However, he warned against destroying it, "since this may lead to the occupation of the ruins by foreign forces." He added that to prevent such foreign occupation, "the *Irgun-Lehi* must stay on and occupy the village."

Some one hundred and twenty men and women were mobi-lized for the attack, but only one hundred went out to do battle because of a lack of weapons. They had thirty-three rifles, thirty-five *Irgun*-made Sten guns, three Bren guns, pistols, grenades (homemade by the *Lehi*) and only forty rounds of ammunition for the riflemen and one hundred rounds for the Sten guns. The *Irgun* units were led by Ben-Zion Cohen (Ghiora). Yehoshua Goldsmit, fittingly enough a native of Givat Shaul, Deir Yassin's usual target, assisted in the briefing of the combatants. He explained the plan of attack, gave the soldiers the password, then issued his final instructions. No one was to fire unless absolutely necessary; no unarmed people were to be shot at; no property was to be destroyed. The goal was not to kill or pillage, but to occupy the village and secure the highway. All prisoners would be transported towards the Arab lines to the East.

On Friday, the attackers slowly and quietly made their way toward the village in the predawn darkness. By the first light of dawn, somewhat behind schedule, they approached the entrance of the village, preceded by an armored car atop which a loudspeaker began repeating warnings in Arabic to the inhabitants: "The forces of the *Irgun* and *Lehi* are attacking you. Run towards Ein Karem or seek shelter below the village. We come to chase the foreign forces in your villages." The element of surprise had been sacrificed in an attempt to save civilian lives.

Suddenly, the Arab positions opened fire, and the armored car struck an anti-tank ditch and capsized. Hundreds of villagers obeyed instructions and fled for their lives but many stayed behind.

Murderous fire fights ensued. Every house and every stone wall served as a defensive position for the Arabs, while the attackers, exposed, had to charge each individual structure to secure it. The houses were entered by blowing down the doors. If the defenders gave up, they were sent to a stockade behind the fighting lines; if they did not, the house was belabored with hand grenades.

As the attackers gained ground, they found a number of surprises: among the prisoners were a Moslem Colonel from Yugoslavia, a British sergeant, two Iraqi soldiers and other Britons." A store of weapons was discovered: eighteen German rifles, forty pistols and ammunition. More surprises—many of the Arab women who were captured turned out to be men—disguised in peasant women's garb. Eventually thirty such armed "women" were identified.

The battle continued, house after house, courtyard after courtyard, and by 10 A.M. the number of wounded reached forty, though the count was imprecise because the dead lay among the wounded. The stalled armored car turned into a first aid station, and men were wounded and lost their lives carrying their comrades to the medics. The battle was much fiercer than expected, and it took the attackers time before they could orient themselves. For many it was the first exposure to open battle. Some were veterans of guerrilla warfare, but this was totally different and some were as young as seventeen.

The battle heated up fiercely when the *Irgun* commander was shot by an Arab who emerged from a house carrying a white flag. Angrily the attackers advanced, slowly occupying one house at a time, always warning "Give up! Come out with your hands high!" And usually being answered with heavy fire. After about a dozen houses were dynamited, the inhabitants started coming out more freely. First women, then children, then old men, followed by young men wearing khakis.

By two in the afternoon, most of the houses had been taken, though to the end, the defenders tried different deceptions. Men came out with hands high and then suddenly drew out guns and started firing. These ruses only made things bloodier and more tragic for both sides.

The seizure of the houses continued through Friday, up until the following morning, when at last the house of the village head was taken. It had been fortified and stubbornly defended. The attackers raised the Hebrew flag over the house.

David Shaltiel, the *Haganah* commander, had met with the *Irgun* commander, Mordechai Raanan on Friday afternoon, and they agreed that the village would be taken over by the *Haganah* on Sunday morning. Raanan was anxious to disperse his men back to their bases as soon as it was safe, since the British were quartered in the environs and might take advantage of the concentration of *Irgun-Lehi* forces to settle old accounts. One intelligence report said they might bomb the village from the air. The *Irgun-Lehi* units had suffered excessive casualties, but had no available replacements.

Sunday, the *Lehi* took over the occupation duty. By midnight, the *Haganah* surrounded the village. On Monday morning, a unit of *Gadna*, the paramilitary youth branch of the *Haganah*, marched into the village and faced the bedraggled *Lehi* soldiers.

"We came here," the *Gadna* commander announced "to take in our hands a village that the bandits of the *Irgun-Lehi* desecrated with their barbarous acts . . . to cleanse it from the shame they brought on the Jewish population . . . ." The youngsters, fifteen or sixteen years of age were then ordered to train their guns on the *Lehi* men.

Only the intervention of the *Irgun-Lehi* city commanders prevented an ugly, bloody incident. The *Lehi* unit simply marched out, shocked by the betrayals. The Hebrew soldiers had lost five men, and forty-four had been wounded. The Arabs had lost two hundred and twenty people.

By Sunday morning, rumors had already started circulating in town that the "renegades" had committed atrocities in Deir Yassin. A Red Cross representative asked permission to visit the village and the *Lehi* commander unhesitatingly approved his request. The representative roamed through the village unmonitored, accompanied by two Jewish doctors. His final comment was, "As we see, some people were killed by explosives, others by gun shots." He made no mention of atrocities and promised the *Lehi* commander a written confirmation that he had seen nothing untoward. One of the Jewish doctors, Dr. Avigdori, told the *Lehi*: "Come into my office in a day or two and I'll give you a copy of the report on behalf of the three of us." A discussion followed on how to dispose of the dead bodies to avoid an epidemic. The Red Cross man suggested covering the corpses with lye or burning them.

There was no lye. Nothing was done for another day.

The promised document was never produced. When Dr. Avigdori was approached during the following weeks, he finally blurted out: "There is pressure." When asked "from whom?" he answered: "I cannot tell you."

Once the battle for Deir Yassin was over, David Shaltiel launched a wide propaganda attack against the *Irgun-Lehi*. He heralded the offensive with a statement issued on the 12th, which he posted on the walls of Jewish Jerusalem:

This morning, the men of *Lehi-Irgun* ran away from Deir Yassin and our forces entered the village. . . . We were forced to assume this responsibility because the renegades brought about, through their their shameful action, the creation of a new front in western Jerusalem. They chose as their target one of the most peaceful villages . . . during an entire day, they were engaged in the slaughter of women and children simply for murder and pillage. . . . When they finished their deeds, they ran away.

These were the words of the same man who, five days earlier, had delivered a written message to the commander of the *Irgun-Lehi* stating: "I have no objection to your carrying out the action on Deir Yassin." The same man who, three days later, when the attack was over, made no complaint about "shameful" acts, but simply agreed that the *Haganah* would take over the occupation and policing of the village. The only condition he had made was that *Irgun-Lehi* should bury the dead. Raanan had refused, stating that his men did not have the means to dispose of the bodies and that they were exhausted and had to be relieved.

One of the worst "horror propaganda" campaigns in history was launched against the "renegades." The Arab and British press jumped at the opportunity and soon far surpassed the smear efforts of the Jewish Establishment. One immediate effect was that all hope was dashed of compromise with those Palestinian Arabs who might have hoped for coexistence with the Hebrew population. For a long while after Deir Yassin, when Arab settlements were attacked, panic broke out and the inhabitants fled generally behind the lines of the Arab Legion. Gradually, their land and deserted homes were taken over by some eight hundred thousand Jews who had also fled their homes in Arab countries where they had resided before Islam conquered the Middle East.

After the Deir Yassin incident, negotiations with the *Haganah* were rougher. Since December, 1947, the *Irgun* had been holding discussions with representatives of the Jewish Agency, working out possible collaboration. The discussions continued despite verbal and physical attacks by the *Haganah* and the Agency on the *Irgun*. There were repeated confrontations and incidents between the *Haganah* and the *Irgun* around the country, including a wave of kidnapping and counter-kidnapping. In early 1948, a *Haganah* unit tossed hand grenades into a crowd in Tel-Aviv which had gathered to hear an *Irgun* fund-raising broadcast in Moghrabi Square.

When *Irgun* officer Yedidiah Segal was kidnapped by the *Haganah*, and then found dead near an Arab village, negotiations temporarily broke down, and just as the *Yishuv* was on the verge of independence, it was once again faced with the specter of a civil war. Yedidiah's mother then told the *Irgun*: "I do not want the shedding of my son's blood to cause a civil war."

On April 15, Begin wrote to us in New York:

I know that you have made supreme efforts . . . and thanks to you we made progress . . . but there is no limit to our needs, as there is no limit to the dangers threatening us. . . . it is absolutely excluded for us to form a government at our own initiative. . . . the [Jewish] Agency promises . . . that in one month—only one month—it will form a government!

. . . once again—if the Agency yields and a government is not formed—then a government will be formed by us! You in the diaspora must have confidence in us. For years we walked a tightrope. We have not fallen. We shall not fall!

Finally, on April 15th, the secret agreement between the *Haganah* and the *Irgun* was approved by the Zionist Executive with thirty-nine voting for and thirty-two (Labor and "new immigrants") voting against. Ben-Gurion steadfastly opposed any agreement with "the renegades." The agreement was patterned somewhat on the old United Resistance Movement accord, and gave the *Haganah* sector commanders overall authority. It required prior agreement of the *Haganah* for proposed action by the *Irgun* and accepted the principle of reprisals against British forces which committed violence against the population. It included the *Irgun*'s repeated statement that if and when a government would be established, the *Irgun* would dissolve itself.

One important clause for us in the diaspora was the one that formally authorized the *Irgun* to continue to raise its funds independently from the Agency and *Haganah*. However, to the end the *Haganah* men in the diaspora denied the existence of this clause.

Although arms and funds were still meager, and though only a handful of men were on full-time pay with the *Irgun*, the command decided, early in April, on its largest single operation—the capture of Jaffa. The idea was first of all to stop Arab sniping from the Menshia Quarter which was endangering life in many parts of Tel-Aviv. Secondly, it was to prevent Egyptian forces from landing in Jaffa and attempting to reach Jerusalem, splitting the country and cutting off the Negev. Tel-Aviv was the heart of the *Yishuv* and Egyptians in Jaffa would pose a grave danger. Finally, the British still maintained a great number of tanks in Jaffa, which also represented a great threat to Tel-Aviv. All these factors taken together made the capture of Jaffa top priority. And it appeared to be within the realm of possibility. Two successful attacks on a British camp in Pardess Hanna on April 4th, and on an ammunition train five days later, had provided the strike force with the minimum arms necessary for the assault.

On April 25th, six hundred *Irgun* men moved out from their staging area, and began a battle that eventually involved some fifteen hundred of their men and women.

The ruined buildings of Jaffa's Menshia Quarter were an excellent defense, fortified and honeycombed with tunnels. British tanks and cannons were positioned behind the Arab lines, while the heaviest weapons the *Irgun* possessed were two two-inch mortars.

It appeared that the British, for their own reasons, were determined to hold on to Jaffa up to the 15th, their projected departure day in May. When the *Irgun* men broke through the Arab lines to the sea and isolated the Menshia Quarter, the British counterattacked. They found more resistance than they anticipated, and flew in reinforcements from Cyprus and Malta. But still they managed to hold the inner city of Jaffa, now mostly deserted, only for a few more days. On May 13th, the city was fully occupied by *Haganah* and *Irgun* units. The *Irgun* had lost forty-two men and four hundred more had been wounded.

The British at last pulled out. No Egyptian landings were made in Jaffa as they were earlier in Gaza and Tel-Aviv was not cut off from the southern part of the country.

By the 11th of May, the leaders of the Agency gathered all their courage and decided to proclaim a Provisional Hebrew Government. In a six to four vote, the "responsible" leaders at long last voted for independence. At 8 o'clock in the morning of May 14th, the British lowered their Union Jack in Jerusalem. By noon, the Declaration of Independence of the State of Israel was broadcast over the radio by Ben-Gurion, the man who only twenty years earlier had taught me that neither a Hebrew majority nor a Hebrew State were our ideal, and that nothing would ever be won by the might of arms.

Begin had promised Ben-Gurion earlier, "if the official leaders set it up (a new government) . . . we shall support it with all our strength."

On Saturday night, May 15th, on the radio station of the *Irgun*, Begin made his announcement to the people of Israel:

The Hebrew Revolt of these last four years has been blessed with success—first Hebrew revolt since the Hasmonean insurrection that has ended in victory. . . .
The State of Israel has arisen. . . . the words of your *Irgun* fighters were not vain words: it is Hebrew arms which decide the boundaries of the He-

brew State. . . . so it is now, so it will be in the future. . . .
You, brother of our fighting family . . . alone and persecuted, rejected, despised . . . tortured . . . cast into prison . . . driven to the gallows, but went forth with a song. You have written a glorious page in history!

III. ENTRENCHED POSITIONS:
ISRAELI EXPANSIONISM
VS. PALESTINIAN REVANCHISM

EDITOR'S INTRODUCTION

Israelis were called upon to fight for their new state during the course of four wars (1948, 1967, 1973, and 1982). Despite the state's gaining control over much additional territory and its success in pushing to the sidelines after 1982 its most implacable enemy, the Palestine Liberation Organization, no progress was made in addressing the central issue in Israel's dilemma: genuine Israeli security is impossible without resolving the Palestinian problem. Palestinians' grievances have not dissolved in all the bloodshed, nor have they grown attenuated with the passing years; Palestinians' determination to have back their land, with or without the dubious assistance of their nominal friends in the Arab states, remained as strong as ever. They regarded the failure of the 1978 Camp David accords—which never seriously addressed their needs or aspirations—as yet another international betrayal. Their bitterness has never slackened. The worldwide growth of nationalism as a focus of popular political energy has merely underlined for the Palestinians the continuing desperate urgency of their situation.

This section examines the ways in which the positions of both sides have grown ever more rigid from the 1950s through the late 1980s. In the first article W. Thomas Mallison, an American professor of international and comparative law, succinctly states the position of the vast majority of United Nations member states, that a way must be found within international law to accord full international rights under that law to both the Israeli and Palestinian peoples. The next article examines the Israeli and Palestinian cases with regard to well-known U.N. measures. Michael Adams, a British Middle East expert and former journalist, summarizes the violations of the U.N.'s 1948 Universal Declaration of Human Rights suffered by the Palestinians in the occupied territories and elsewhere. Edward W. Said, a Palestinian-American professor of literature, considers in the third article the ways in which the majority of the U.S. news media have consistently taken the Israeli side in the conflict to the constant detriment of Palestinian civil and national rights. In the fourth article Rabbi Meir Kahane, an American-Israeli member of the Knesset (who was officially forbidden in October 1988 to stand again for parliament on the grounds that his ultranationalist Kach Party was "racist and undemocratic"), offers a vivid example of how far the hard right in Israel has come in its demands and in its plans. He outlines his scheme to remove all non-Jews from Israel—all except those who are willing to go on living there without any political rights, and even they could do so only on the basis of a yearly renewable permission to stay. This is the only way, Kahane and his many followers believe, to achieve "peace in the region." In the fifth article Noam Chomsky, an American linguistics expert and political writer, describes the new credence given in Israeli society to religious and chauvinist fanaticism, which he sees as exemplary of the extreme divisions caused by chronically unresolved political tensions and of a cycle of occupation, resistance, repression, and moral degeneration.

THE UNITED NATIONS AND THE NATIONAL RIGHTS OF THE PEOPLE OF PALESTINE[1]

I. Introduction to the Recognition of National Rights

A juridical consideration of national rights should start with two basic premises. The first is that national rights do not arise until there is first a community of people with a national identity. The second is that the right of self-determination is the preemi-

[1]By W. Thomas Mallison, professor of law and director of the International and Comparative Law Program at George Washington University, Washington, D.C. From *The United Nations and the Question of Palestine: A Compilation of Essays, 1980–1982*, pp. 38–52. (This is a paper presented at the Second United Nations Conference On the Question of Palestine, held at Vienna, August 25–29, 1980.) Copyright, United Nations, 1983. Reproduced by permission.

nent national right. Without self-determination, free from external coercion or interference, the people have no meaningful political choices. Any other national rights such as independence and sovereignty follow from the successful exercise of the right of self-determination.

It is important that a people seeking self-determination have a strong sense of national identity. In addition, the world community of states must manifest acceptance and accord recognition to the claimed national identity. Before the establishment of the United Nations as the preeminent international organization, states could only express such acceptance and recognition on an individual basis. While this is still important, the existence of the United Nations General Assembly as the committee of the whole of the world community allows states to act collectively with an efficiency which was not previously possible. It is a universally accepted legal principle that the individual acts of states create or make customary international law and general principles of law. When states act through the General Assembly it is clear that they do not lose their authority to make a law. The extent to which a General Assembly resolution is based on the historic competency of states to make law as opposed to powers granted under the United Nations Charter is an interesting question of legal theory. The crucial point is that combining both sources of authority, states may now make law in a relatively rapid and efficient manner. Resolutions of the General Assembly adopted by overwhelming majorities have particularly persuasive lawmaking authority. Whether such resolutions are deemed to be law themselves, or merely evidence of law, it is clear that, either way, they provide an authoritative legal basis for subsequent actions.

The United Nations Charter pertains to peoples as well as to states. Among the purposes of the organization specified in the first article of the Charter is:

To develop friendly relations among nations based on respect for the principle of equal rights and self-determination of peoples . . .

This marks a significant departure from the old legal theory that international law accords rights only to states and governments and not to groups or individuals.

II. The Recognition of the Palestinians as a People with a National Identity

The Palestinians, without distinction as to religion, were a people *de facto* as the inhabitants of the country named Palestine long before the 20th century, and they had close connections with their fellow-Arabs in adjoining Syria and Lebanon. The Palestinians, Syrians and Lebanese, along with other Arab peoples, were under the rule of the Ottoman Empire until the First World War. Following that conflict, Great Britain was designated as the Mandatory Power under the League of Nations Mandate for Palestine. The Covenant of the League of Nations itself recognized "provisionally" the "existence as independent nations" of the communities which were formerly parts of the Turkish Empire and this included provisional recognition of the Palestinians. Because the Mandate, consistent with the requirements of article 22 of the Covenant, was designed to lead the people of the country to independence, it contained an implicit recognition of Palestinian national identity. The United Nations accorded the Palestinians *de jure* recognition of their status as a people with national rights in the provisions of the Palestine Partition Resolution authorizing them to establish "the Arab State." From the time of that resolution in 1947 until 1969, however, the United Nations emphasized the Palestinians' *de facto* role as individuals who were refugees and war victims. The United Nations actions of that period were designed to implement their individual right of return and achieve their elementary human rights.

In 1969 the General Assembly shifted its perspective to acknowledge the Palestinians as a people having rights under the United Nations Charter. The first preambular paragraph of General Assembly resolution 2535B (XXIV) of 10 December 1969 recognizes "that the problem of the Palestine Arab refugees has arisen from the denial of their inalienable rights under the Charter of the United Nations and the Universal Declaration of Human Rights." The first operative paragraph provides recognition by the United Nations of the Palestinians as a people with a national identity by reaffirming "the inalienable rights of the people of Palestine." This recognition of juridical status has been reaffirmed by all subsequent resolutions of the General Assembly which deal with the subject.

General Assembly resolution 2672C (XXV) of 8 December 1970 follows the pattern of the resolution just considered. A preambular paragraph reaffirms the inalienable right of "the people of Palestine" and the first operative paragraph uses the same words in referring to the people's national rights. The second operative paragraph repeats the identical words in declaring that full respect for the people's inalienable rights is indispensable for the achievement of a just and lasting peace. General Assembly resolution 3210 (XXIX) concerns the status of the people by providing that "the Palestinian people is a principal party to the question of Palestine." It also concerns the status of its representative by inviting the Palestine Liberation Organization as "the representative of the Palestinian people" to participate in plenary meetings of the General Assembly concerning the question of Palestine. This status is further augmented by the seventh operative paragraph of resolution 3236 which "*Requests* the Secretary-General to establish contacts with the Palestine Liberation Organization on all matters concerning the question of Palestine." In resolution 3237 (XXIX) of 22 November 1974 the General Assembly invites the Palestine Liberation Organization to participate in the sessions and work of the General Assembly and of all international conferences convened under the auspices of the General Assembly in the capacity of observer. The people of Palestine have a relationship to the Palestine Liberation Organization similar to the French people's relationship to the Free French organization (later known as the Fighting French) when France was under military occupation.

It provides useful clarification to contrast the Palestinian people with "the Jewish people" entity claimed by the State of Israel. The Zionist "Jewish people" concept was developed by the Zionist Organization/Jewish Agency prior to the establishment of the State of Israel. Before the rise of Zionist nationalism, "the Jewish people" referred simply to voluntary adherents of the religion of Judaism, the oldest of the monotheistic religions of universal moral values. The Zionists have impressed their own secular meaning upon the term and have given it a more precise juridical definition through various Israeli statutes. "The Jewish people" concept within the State of Israel accords its members certain privileges and rights on a discriminatory basis which are denied to other Israelis. The same concept applied to persons outside the State of Israel imposes upon them a juridical link with the State of Israel whether they desire it or not. For example, in the *Eichmann Case* the Israeli District Court stated that "the connection between the Jewish people and the State of Israel constitutes an intergral part of the law of nations." Because of the discriminatory characteristics of "the Jewish people" concept, it would constitute a violation of articles 55 and 56 of the Charter of the United Nations if the General Assembly recognized it. The United State Government has explicitly rejected "the Jewish people" concept as a valid concept of international law in a letter from Assistant Secretary of State Phillips Talbot addressed to Rabbi Elmer Berger.

The United Nations Charter provides that "the United Nations shall promote, *inter alia:*

universal respect for, and observance of, human rights and fundamental freedoms for all without distinction as to race, sex, language, or religion.

Consistent with this requirement, "the Palestinian people" must comprise all Palestinians on a non-discriminatory basis. If it did not do so, it could not be recognized by the General Assembly without violation of the Charter provisions concerning human rights. In summary, "the Palestinian people" includes individuals of diverse religious identification today as it did before the rise of Zionist nationalism. It also will be essential to maintain this characteristic in the establishment of the Palestinian state in order to comply with the human rights requirements for each of the two states authorized by the Palestine Partition Resolution as well as with the human rights provisions of the United Nations Charter.

III. The Right of Self-Determination in International Law

The practice of self-determination preceded the development of the principle or right of self-determination in international law. The American Revolution and the subsequent Latin American revolutions against European colonialism provide pre-eminent historic examples. The idea of self-determination was present in President Woodrow Wilson's Fourteen Points. Professor Kissinger has accurately described the situation as it existed at the post–First World War peace settlement:

In 1919, the Austro-Hungarian Empire disintegrated not so much from the impact of the war as from the nature of the peace, because its continued existence was incompatible with national self-determination, the legitimizing principle of the new international order.

It is important to note that the principle of self-determination was reflected in the provisions of the League of Nations Covenant through the mandates system with the mandatory powers assuming "a sacred trust" to promote "the well being and development of such peoples." At the present time the only examples of peoples who were placed under the mandates system who have not achieved self-determination are the people of Palestine and the people of Namibia (Southwest Africa). The widespread implementation of self-determination since the end of the Second World War is reflected directly in the membership of the United Nations.

One of the major purposes of the United Nations, which has been set forth above, is the development of friendly relations based upon respect for "the principle of equal rights and self-determination of peoples . . . " It is sometimes contended by those who oppose self-determination for others that the Charter only states that self-determination is a principle and not a right. This view lacks merit since the carefully drafted and equally authentic French text states, "du principe de l'égalité de droits des peuples et de leur droit à disposer d'eux-mêmes . . . . " By using the word "droit" in connection with self-determination, the French text removes any possible ambiguity. Article 55 of the Charter emphasizes the importance of self-determination by stating that peaceful and friendly relations are based on respect for it. Article 73 of Chapter XI concerning non-self-governing territories provides that members assuming responsibility for such territories are required to "develop self-government, to take due account of the political aspirations of the people, and to assist them in the progressive development of their free political institutions. . . . "

The General Assembly has performed the task of interpreting and developing these principles from the early history of the organization to the present time. It should be recalled that the Palestine Partition Resolution 181 provides authority for two distinct national self-determinations in Palestine. General Assembly resolutions 1514 (XV) of 14 December 1960, entitled "Declaration on the Granting of Independence to Colonial Countries and Territories," is an important statement of basic principles and rights. The first two operative paragraphs of this resolution provide:

1. The subjection of peoples to alien subjugation, domination and exploitation constitutes a denial of fundamental human rights, is contrary to the Charter of the United Nations and is an impediment to the promotion of world peace and co-operation.
2. All peoples have the right to self-determination; by virtue of that right they freely determine their political status and freely pursue their economic, social and cultural development.

The vote on this resolution was 90 votes in favor to none opposed, with 9 abstentions. Since there were no opposing votes, this resolution must be interpreted as reflecting the stated legal views of the then full membership of the United Nations. In view of the increasing implementation of self-determination since 1960, the present membership of the General Assembly provides strong support for the views expressed in the 1960 resolution. Subsequent applications of the self-determination principle of resolution 1514 to Algeria, Angola, and to Zimbabwe (Rhodesia) indicate the view of the General Assembly resolution that a right to self-determination is established in 12. The entire course of action taken by the United Nations and the overwhelming majority of its members since 1960 is consistent with this basic self-determination resolution.

General Assembly resolution 2625 (XXV) of 24 October 1970, entitled "Declaration on Principles of International Law Concerning Friendly Relations and Cooperation Among States in Accordance with the Charter of the United Nations," provides further development of the right of self-determination. It considers a number of principles and under the heading of the "principle of equal rights and self-determination of peoples," the first paragraph states:

By virtue of the principle of equal rights and self-determination of peoples enshrined in the Charter of the United Nations, all peoples have the right freely to determine, without external interference, their political status and to pursue their economic, social and cultural development, and every state has the duty to respect this right in accordance with the provisions of the Charter.

This statement of law has a highly authoritative character since the General Assembly adopted it by consensus, that is, with not a single state in opposition.

IV. The Application
of the Right of Self-Determination
to the People of Palestine

The provisions of the Palestine Partition Resolution which provide authority for the establishment of "the Arab State" constitute the first direct recognition of the Palestinian national right of self-determination by the General Assembly. The second such recognition is provided by General Assembly resolution 2649 of 30 November 1970. This resolution expresses concern that, because of alien domination, many peoples were being denied the right to self-determination. It then condemns those governments which deny the right to peoples "recognized as being entitled to it, especially the peoples of southern Africa and Palestine." The legal effect of this significant resolution is that the prior resolutions setting forth the basic right of self-determination, resolutions 1514 and 2625 considered above, are now specifically applicable to the Palestinian people.

With the adoption of resolution 2672C on 8 December 1970, the General Assembly moved toward acknowledging the correlation between the right of self-determination and other inalienable rights. The second preambular paragraph recalls resolution 2535B and the first such paragraph reiterates the language contained in that resolution providing that the Palestine Arab refugee problem had arisen from the denial of their inalienable rights. The two operative paragraphs of resolution 2672C state that the General Assembly:

1. *Recognizes* that the people of Palestine are entitled to equal rights and self-determination, in accordance with the Charter of the United Nations;
2. *Declares* that full respect for the inalienable rights of the people of Palestine is an indispensable element in the establishment of a just and lasting peace in the Middle East.

In addition to reiterating the specific Palestinian national right of self-determination, this resolution links the achievement of Palestinian inalienable rights to the achievement of peace in the Middle East. It should be recalled that article 1 of the Charter requires the United Nations to bring about peace "in conformity with the principles of justice and international law." It should be clear that neither of these principles is honored unless Palestinian rights are implemented.

General Assembly resolution 3089D of 7 December 1973 enunciates the relationship between the rights of self-determination and return by providing in its third operative paragraph that the General Assembly:

Declares that full respect for and realization of the inalienable rights of the people of Palestine, particularly its right to self-determination, are indispensable for the establishment of a just and lasting peace in the Middle East, and that the enjoyment by the Palestine Arab refugees of their right to return to their homes and property . . . is indispensable . . . for the exercise by the people of Palestine of its right to self-determination.

The necessary legal linkage of return and self-determination is designed to assure Palestinians the practical exercise of national self-determination as a "people." It is based on the common sense conception that there can be no self-determination without return to the areas where self-determination may be exercised.

An analysis of operative paragraph 3 reveals that while the General Assembly understandably views the achievement of return as a necessary prerequisite to the effective exercise of self-determination, the right of self-determination of Palestinians as a national group was apparently not intended to follow invariably from the return of individual Palestinians. The pertinent wording provides that the "Palestine Arab refugees" are entitled to enjoy "their right to return to their homes and property," while the "people of Palestine" is entitled to exercise "its right to self-determination." The use of "Palestine Arab refugees" when referring to return is apparently meant to stand in contradistinction to the use of "people of Palestine" when reference is made to self-determination.

General Assembly resolution 3236 of 22 November 1974 concerns the right of return and it also has preeminent importance concerning the right of self-determination. Its fifth preambular paragraph recognizes that "the Palestinian people is entitled to self-determination is accordance with the Charter of the United Nations." The first operative paragraph provides that the General Assembly:

Reaffirms the inalienable rights of the Palestinian people in Palestine, including:
(a) The right to self-determination without external interference;
(B) The right to national independence and sovereignty.

The exact boundaries of the area in Palestine in which these inalienable rights apply must be settled *de jure*. The language of the resolution quoted above includes the "right to national independence and sovereignty" as a particularization of the self-determination right.

In operative paragraph 5, resolution 3236 prefers to methods by which rights may be regained. It provides that the General Assembly:

Also reaffirms the legitimacy of the peoples struggle for liberation from . . . alien subjugation by all means including armed struggle."

Since the American Revolution relied upon armed struggle to achieve self-determination abut a century and a third before the principle of self-determination was used in the post–World War I peace settlement, it is not surprising that the General Assembly specifies it as a permissible method today. Its permissibility is legally significant as an authoritative General Assembly assertion that armed struggle for self-determination is consistent with the purposes and principle of the United Nations Charter. In a situation such as Palestine where the people has been denied its right of self-determination by armed force, the right to regain it by armed struggle is considered permissible under article 51 of the Charter concerning self-defense.

V. The Geographical Area in which Palestinian Self-Determination Applies

Where "in Palestine," to use the wording of resolution 3236, may Palestinian national self-determination including independence and sovereignty be exercised? General Assembly resolution 2625 (XXV) dealing with "Principles of International Law Concerning Friendly Relations," which has been considered concerning the right of self-determination, also provides basic legal interpretation concerning areas where self-determination may be exercised. Under the heading of the "principle of equal rights and self-determination of peoples" the penultimate paragraph provides:

Nothing in the foregoing paragraphs shall be construed as authorizing or encouraging any action which would dismember or impair, totally or in part, the territorial integrity or political unity of sovereign and independent states conducting themselves in compliance with the principle of equal rights and self-determination of peoples as described above and thus possessed of a government representing the whole people belonging to the territory without distinction as to race, creed or colour.

The quoted wording is of particular importance since it is designed to preserve the territorial integrity or political unity of non-discriminatory states which have a government "representing the whole people belonging to the territory." The State of Israel cannot qualify as such a state as long as its discriminatory Zionist features, including the denial of the right of return of Palestinians to their homes and property, are maintained in municipal law and practice. Pursuant to this provision of resolution 2625, the General Assembly may provide for lawful *de jure* boundaries for the State of Israel which do not preserve its "territorial integrity or political unity" as they may exist *de facto* at a particular time as a result of military conquest and of illegal annexation. The prohibition on the acquisition of territory by military conquest is regarded as fundamental in the United Nations Charter and in resolutions of both the General Assembly and the Security Council.

The only *de jure* boundaries which the State of Israel has ever had are those which were specified for "the Jewish State" in the Palestine Partition Resolution. Following the Armistice Agreements of 1949, which did not fix *de jure* boundaries, the State of Israel existed within *de facto* boundaries until June 1967. It is possible that those pre-1967 boundaries may have received some international assent. Security Council resolution 242 of 22 November 1967, after emphasizing "the inadmissibility of the acquisition of territory by war, refers in the first operative paragraph to the principle of "withdrawal of Israel armed forces from territories occupied in the recent conflict." Since there is no statement of withdrawal from territories occupied at a time before 1967, this may amount to an indirect recognition of the pre–June 1967 boundaries. Operative paragraph 1 also refers to the principle of the "territorial integrity and political independence of every State in the area and their right to live in peace withing secure and recognized boundaries."

It is clear that two different national exercises of the right of self-determination cannot take place simultaneously upon precisely the same territory, and the careful wording of resolution 3236 is consistent with this reality. Consequently, those Palestinians who choose to exercise their individual right of return within the State of Israel cannot exercise Palestinian nation self-determination within that state. Since resolution 181 established the principle of two states in the area and subsequent resolutions have not departed from this concept, it is clear that it is not the intent of the General Assembly to authorize Palestinian self-determination within the State of Israel. The Palestinian national right of self-determination as recognized in General Assembly resolutions may be exercised "in Palestine" within the de jure boundaries of the Palestinian state which are yet to be determined, and outside the de jure boundaries of the State of Israel as ultimately determined.

*VI. Conclusion: Two National States
in Palestine with Rights and Obligations
for Each*

In the Palestine Partition Resolution, the General Assembly acted to resolve a situation of conflict and crisis by authorizing the establishment of two democratic states in the territory of the Palestine Mandate. The rights to establish the States were balanced by concomitant obligations to do so in accordance with the United Nations Charter and the terms of the Partition Resolution including its crucial human rights provisions. The ensuing resolutions of the General Assembly adhere to the basic elements of the Partition Resolution.

On July 22, 1980 the United Nations General Assembly met in its Seventh Emergency Special Session following the negative vote of the United States at the 2220th meeting of the Security Council on 30 April 1980 which prevented that body from acting on Palestinian national rights. The General Assembly adopted a resolution on this subject on July 29, 1980. It specifically recalled and reaffirmed resolutions 3236 and 3237 of 22 November 1974 "and all other relevant resolutions pertinent to the question of Palestine." A key paragraph of the resolution provides that the General Assembly:

REAFFIRMS the inalienable rights in Palestine of the Palestinian people, including:
(a) The right to self-determination without external interference and to national independence and sovereignty;
(b) The right to establish its own independent sovereign state.

Another key paragraph provides that the General Assembly:

CALLS UPON Israel to withdraw completely and unconditionally from all the Palestinian and other Arab territories occupied since June 1967, including Jerusalem, with all property and services intact, and urges that such withdrawal from all the occupied territories should start before 15 November 1980.

The roll-call vote on this resolution was 112 in favor 7 against and 24 abstentions. The five states which joined the United States and Israel in negative voting were Australia, Canada, Dominican Republic, Guatemala and Norway. Although the vote was considerably short of unanimity, it demonstrated substantial world-wide support, which went far beyond the requirement of the United Nations Charter for a two-thirds vote on important matters, for the national rights of the Palestinian people. This is the first time that the majority of Western European states has abstained rather than voting negatively on such a resolution.

This resolution, like other General Assembly resolutions on the same subject, does nothing to infringe upon legitimate Israeli national interests. The last paragraph quoted above appears to accord at least *de facto* recognition to the boundaries of Israel as they existed prior to the massive Israeli attack of June 5, 1967.

Security Council resolution 242 of 22 November 1967 concerning "a just and lasting peace in the Middle East" is widely regarded as having been accepted by each of the states which are directly affected by it. The State of Israel, nevertheless, has been engaged in a systematic policy of "creating facts" through the imposition of civilian settlements in the territories occupied since June, 1967 which is entirely inconsistent with the territorial provisions of resolution 242. This Security Council resolution has been supplemented by the resolutions of the General Assembly which have been considered here. In particular, resolution 242's undefined "just settlement of the refugee problem" is made specific by the General Assembly's recognition of the right of return for individual Palestinians. In addition, the General Assembly has recognized the national rights of the Palestinian people in carefully formulated terms which do not infringe upon the legitimate rights of the State of Israel. These Israeli national rights which remain inviolate include, among others, the rights to self-determination and to national independence and sovereign equality with other States consistent with international law including the pertinent United Nations resolutions. The Israeli rights do not include, among others, supposed rights to deny self-determination and independence to the Palestinian people and a supposed right to establish Israeli borders on the basis of military conquest and illegal annexations.

The outcome of the United Nations resolutions is that there is continuing authority for the establishment of two States in Palestine. The authority to provide for a state carries with it the authority to impose limitations including those based upon the human rights provisions of the Charter. A limitation which is inherent in the authorization of the two states is that each may exercise its national rights conditioned on, at the least, the requirement of non-obstruction of the national rights of the other.

The Palestinian right to self-determination, including national independence and sovereignty, has been established unequivocally as a matter of law. It is too well known to require elaboration that it has not yet been achieved as a matter of fact. The most urgent contemporary need is for a comprehensive sanctioning process to enforce the existing law. This process should start with the economic sanctions provided for in the United Nations Charter and, if they are unsuccessful, the military sanctions should be invoked.

THE UNIVERSAL DECLARATION OF HUMAN RIGHTS AND THE ISRAELI OCCUPATION OF THE WEST BANK AND GAZA[2]

The search for peace in Palestine has been complicated and frustrated over the past half-century by all kinds of factors which are irrelevant to Palestine itself. Among them have been the intervention of the Great Powers in pursuit of their own strategic interests; the rival ambitions of the surrounding Arab governments; the competition for vital oil supplies; the sympathy aroused by the persecution of the Jews in Europe; and the need felt by American presidential candidates to win the support of the influential Jewish community in the United States.

All of these factors have been important in shaping the course of events in Palestine—and yet none of them has any bearing on

[2]By Michael Adams, senior fellow of the Centre for Arab Gulf studies, Exeter University, from Ibrahim Abu-Lughod, ed., *Palestinian Rights: Affirmation and Denial*, pp. 67–78. Copyright © 1982, Medina Press. Reprinted by permission.

the question of what is right and what is wrong as far as the *people* of Palestine are concerned. What is more remarkable—and discreditable—is that until very recently those who took it upon themselves to try to decide the future of Palestine did so without paying any attention to the rights of the Palestinians themselves.

That situation is changing. During recent years the phrase "the legitimate rights of the Palestinian people" has gained acceptance as expressing one of the fundamental requirements for a peaceful settlement in the Middle East. It found a place in the joint statement on the Middle East published by the U.S. and Soviet governments in October 1977. It has been emphasized in various statements published by the nine Western European governments that cooperate within the European Economic Community (EEC). The latest of these statements, published after the heads of government of the EEC met in Venice in June 1980, spoke of the need to recognize *and to implement* two principles universally accepted by the international community. The first of these was the right to existence and security of all states in the region, including Israel; and the second was justice for all the peoples, which implied, in the words of the Venice statement, "recognition of the legitimate rights of the Palestinians." Even the agreement signed at Camp David by President Sadat and Mr. Begin in September 1978, which aroused such violent hostility throughout the Arab world, stated that any solution resulting from the proposed Arab-Israeli negotiations must "recognize the legitimate rights of the Palestinian people and their just requirements."

So the principle has been accepted, even by those most widely accused of neglecting the Palestinian element of the Arab-Israeli conflict. But no one has yet answered the question that must immediately follow: What are those "legitimate rights" and those "just requirements" to which the Palestinians are entitled?

The answer to that question must closely affect the nature of any political settlement emerging in the Middle East. But while the debate goes endlessly on about the *political* rights that the Palestinians should enjoy, the world loses sight of the other rights, the ordinary, everyday, human rights, to which in theory the Palestinians, like any other people in the world, are entitled, and of which they have been unjustly deprived for so long. That this should be so—that while the politicians argue about concepts like autonomy and self-determination the Palestinians should be living in a kind of limbo in which they are denied not only the right to political self-expression but even the most elementary protection against oppression and discrimination—is a scandal for which there can be no possible justification.

Consider the situation of the Palestinians living in the West Bank and the Gaza Strip. For more than thirteen years they have been subjected to an alien dominion against which they have no protection. In every detail, the pattern of their daily lives is dictated by the occupation regime. Walking and sleeping, they are at the mercy of a military authority which has the power—and uses it freely—to invade their homes, to arrest them, to detain them without trial, to deport them, to demolish their homes, and to impose collective punishments on whole communities. Their publications are censored, they may not engage in political activities, their right to assemble together for any purpose is rigorously controlled. Their schools and universities are subjected to arbitrary interference. Their lands are confiscated without warning and under the specious pretext of military "security," only to be handed over to Israeli settlers as part of barefaced program of colonization that has been repeatedly condemned as illegal by the highest international authority. Even the water supplies on which the Palestinian farmers depend are being diverted by the Israeli authorities to serve the interests of Israeli settlers at the expense of the indigenous owners of the land.

These are evil practices, illustrating in detail the wider evil of a military occupation. Like the occupation itself, they constitute a kind of moral pollution, whose effect, as the more far-sighted Israelis are coming to realize, is to corrupt the occupiers as it injuries the occupied. A regime that depends upon this kind of injustice and discrimination requires from those who administer it a disregard for moral and humanitarian principles that is deeply degrading. The fact that the occupation regime has been in existence for thirteen years does much to explain the internal crisis and the decline in moral standards so evident in Israel today. One of the many similar warnings from prominent Israelis concerning the dangers involved comes from Meron Benvenisti, who served for a time after the 1967 June War as deputy mayor of Jerusalem. In the Israeli newspaper *Ha'aretz* of June 27, 1979, Benvenisti wrote:

Occupation by its very nature corrupts the occupier. The harm that twelve years of occupation has caused to Israel's moral fabric is nothing to the damage it will cause in the coming period when protest and its suppression, violence and counterviolence, are intensified in the [occupied] territories and the situation deteriorates to the point to civil rebellion which will be answered by severe repression. The Military Government and the Defense Establishment will have to pay the price of the annexationist policy, with thousands of Israeli soldiers becoming embroiled in brutal confrontations.

There were those who thought that Benvenisti was exaggerating; but events on the West Bank in the summer of 1980 suggest that his forecast is likely to prove an accurate one if action is not taken soon to remedy the shocking state of affairs in the occupied territories.

We might add to Benvenisti's comments that when a situation like this continues unchecked, and when the world knows about it but lacks the will or the power to put a stop to it, all attempts to bring justice and order into international affairs are undermined. Cynicism above the value of the United Nations and of such bodies as Amnesty International is encouraged, and it becomes harder than ever to win support for the unending fight against tyranny and injustice and discrimination in the world.

It was in a concerted attempt to combat these evils that the General Assembly of the United Nations adopted, in December 1948, the Universal Declaration of Human Rights. The preamble to the declaration spoke of "the equal and inalienable rights of all members of the human family" and declared it to be "essential, if man is not to be compelled to have recourse, as a last resort, to rebellion against tyranny and oppression, that human rights should be protected by the rule of law." That idea, echoed in the article quoted above from the Israeli press, has the closest possible relevance to the situation in the Arab territories occupied by Israel today. No less than fifteen of the thirty articles of the declaration refer to rights that at present are denied to Palestinians living in the West Bank and Gaza Strip. In other words, exactly one-half of the *Universal* Declaration of *Human Rights*, which was designed to give equal protection to all members of the human family, gives no protection to the inhabitants of the territories occupied by Israel.

Article 3 states: *"Everyone has right to life, liberty and security of person."* But in the occupied territories, where thousands of Palestinians are in prison or under administrative detention for supposed offenses against the occupation regime, no one enjoys "security of person" against the military government, which is able at will to invade homes and to arrest or detain or deport individuals by simple administrative order. A horribly vivid demonstration of this state of insecurity occurred in June 1980, when the Arab mayors of the West Bank towns of Nablus and Ramallah were the victims of car-bomb attacks that left them both maimed, while a third mayor was saved from a similar fate by a timely warning. Whether or not the Israeli authorities were themselves implicated in these attacks (as many Israelis suggested), they certainly afforded the Palestinian leaders no protection against them; nor have the perpetrators of the outrage, members of the Jewish terrorist organization "Terror Against Terror," been brought to justice.

Article 5 states: *"No one shall be subjected to torture or to cruel, inhuman or degrading treatment or punishment."* The subject of torture in the occupied territories has been exhaustively treated by various bodies, including the U.N. Special Committee to Investigate Israeli Practices Affecting the Human Rights of the Population of the Occupied Territories. In its report to the General Assembly in November 1978, the special committee referred to evidence which "confirms the allegations that persons under interrogation are ill-treated and that no adequate remedies exist to safeguard such persons from abuse."

It is proper to observe here that the most abundant evidence of torture and other violations of the human rights of the Palestinians in the occupied territories has been regularly put forward by the Israeli League of Human and Civil Rights over a period of more than ten years. Also, in recent years the Israeli press has drawn attention to numerous examples, not only of torture, but also of various forms of "inhuman or degrading treatment" exercised by the Israeli occupation authorities against the inhabitants of the West Bank and the Gaza Strip.

For a long time the press in the Western world was extremely cautious in the coverage it gave to human rights violations in the occupied territories. It is difficult to find an adequate explanation for this reticence on the part of the press—and, indeed, of Western governments as well—when the evidence of such violations was so comprehensive and had for the most part been supplied by Israeli witnesses. In recent years, however, the international press has begun to overcome its reluctance to criticize the government of Israel over so important an issue and has shown a growing concern about the evidence of widespread ill-treatment, including torture, of Arabs in the occupied territories. The most exhaustive coverage of the subject was provided, after an inquiry extending over six months, by the Sunday *Times* (London) in June 1977. On the basis of its findings, this leading British newspaper voiced the conclusion that the torture of Arab prisoners was "widespread and systematic" and that "it appears to be sanctioned as deliberate policy."

The report in the *Times* did much to open to public debate this important issue of human rights. The Israeli government took issue with the newspaper, and in Israel itself there was concern as well as indignation over accusations so far-reaching and so carefully documented. The National Lawyers Guild in the United States instituted its own inquiry into the subject and in November 1978 published a 121-page report which concluded that torture was one of a number of oppressive measures adopted by the Israeli authorities as part of a program whose objective was to encourage the emigration of the Palestinian inhabitants of the occupied territories.

Three months after the publication of the report by the National Lawyers Guild, the American State Department, in its annual review of human rights practices in countries receiving American aid, also took up the question of torture in Israel. Referring to the persistent allegations of the systematic ill-treatment of Arab prisoners, the State Department expressed the view—a very guarded view but one that received widespread attention because of the American government's generally protective attitude toward the government of Israel—that "the accumulation of reports, some from credible sources, makes it appear that instances of mistreatment have occurred."

The Sundary *Times* and the National Lawyers Guild called for an impartial investigation to examine the question of the ill-treatment of Arab prisoners in the occupied territories. The call was taken up by other bodies and was echoed inside Israel, where a writer in the *Jerusalem Post* said that "a well-investigated report by a high-level commission, headed if possible by a judge of the Supreme Court, would be welcome, whatever its verdict." That was in February 1979, but no such public investigation has yet been conducted.

Article 7 states: *"All are equal before the law and are entitled without any discrimination to equal protection of the law."* It is not necessary to spend much time in demonstrating that this article does not apply to the inhabitants of the occupied territories. The only law to which they are subject is the arbitrary "law" of the military government, reinforced by the 1945 Emergency Regulations inehrited from the British mandatory government and applied in military courts or by simple administrative orders from the military governor. Military law is enforced only against them, not against the Israeli settlers who have been imposed upon the occupied territories. Indeed, it is a complaint frequently voiced by responsible Israelis that the Israeli settlers act in defiance of the law and often even enjoy the protection of the military government for their illegal actions against the Arab population.

After the series of car-bomb attacks on the Palestinian mayors, the French newspaper *Le Monde* carried an interview, on June 19, 1980, with Israeli General of the Reserve Mattitiyahu Peled, a leading figure in the Sheli party. The following is an extract from that interview:

Speaking of the future of democracy in Israel, Mr. Peled showed himself very pessimistic "not simply because of the emergence of the phenomenon of Jewish terrorism, but because this terrorism has the official support of the government. The members of Gush Emunim [an extremist group of Jewish settlers in Israel] are organized on a military basis and the army supplies them with arms, ammunition and explosives. Their acts remain unpunished and I will go so far as to say no one dreams of seeking out the guilty parties, who seem to act with the blessing of the authorities. . . . This state of affairs represents, without any doubt, the beginning of the collapse of the whole democratic system in Israel, for it is a matter of public knowledge that the extremists are supported by the army's Chief of Staff and by the Prime Minister personally."

So the Israeli authorities, which react very violently against even the most minor infringements of the law by the Arabs in the occupied territories, react in a completely different way to far more serious infringements of the law when these are committed by Jews. Indeed, on the evidence of Reserve General Peled, the authorities actually support and encourage and arm these Jewish lawbreakers in their assaults on the unarmed Arab population.

In other words, the law in the occupied territories has one meaning for Jews and quite a different one for Arabs. This is a conclusion from which no Israeli that I know would dissent (and of which many Israelis would approve). Discrimination in legal matters, as in every other aspect of life, is indeed a natural and logical consequence of military occupation, where the law becomes an instrument to enforce the will of the occupier against the interests of the occupied.

International law, which in theory should protect the inhabitants of the occupied territories against victimization and discrimination by the military government, is in this instance powerless, since the government of Israel has refused to recognize that the provisions of the Fourth Geneva Convention (for the Protection of Civilians in Time of War) are applicable to the occupied territories. In this, as in many other respects, the government of Israel is at odds with the rest of the international community and is defying the will of the United Nations. That such a situation should be allowed to persist and that the Palestinians in the occupied territories should remain, after more than thirteen years, the victims of sustained and legalized discrimination, is a grave reproach to all the governments that have signed the Geneva Conventions and voted for the resolutions of the United Natons calling on Israel to respect the conventions in its treatment of the population of the West Bank and Gaza Strip.

Article 9 states: *"No one shall be subjected to arbitrary arrest, detention or exile."* No one disputes the fact that all inhabitants of the occupied territories (except, of course, the Jewish settlers) are liable at any time to arbitrary arrest or to administrative detention (which may last for several years), even if they have not been convicted, or even accused, of any crime. I myself know a number of Palestinians from the West Bank who have been arrested without any accusation being made against them, held in prison without trial for as long as three years, and eventually released without explanation or apology. The State Department report that I have referred to stated that at the time of its publication there were 2,149 Arabs in prison for security offenses, of whom 30 were under administrative detention (meaning that they had not been charged with any offense), and that a further 360 Arab suspects were awaiting trial. So much for freedom from arbitrary arrest or detention.

Article 9 also states that no one should be subjected to *exile*, and the word has of course a particularly tragic significance for the Palestinians. More than two million Palestinians living outside Palestine regard themselves as exiles from their homeland; their bitterest grievance is the refusal of the Israeli authorities to allow them to live in the land where they or their parents were born and brought up. That dimension of the Palestinian problem is outside the scope of this paper. What does concern us here is that since 1967 the Israeli military government has deported from the occupied territories well over a thousand Palestinians against whom they had no legal complaint (if they had had any evidence of any criminal offense, they would presumably have put them on trial) but whom they did not wish to remain in the territory under their control. In many instances, the Israelis selected these people for deportation clearly because they were the leaders of the Palestinian community in the West Bank and the Gaza Strip and therefore likely to encourage a spirit of resistance to the occupation regime. In other words, they sent them into exile because they were patriots, whose example and leadership might prove infectious and whose removal would render the remaining population more tractable and submissive.

The most recent and conspicuous example of this practice on the part of the Israeli authorities concerns the mayors of the West Bank towns of Hebron and Halhoul. On May 2, 1980 these two men, Fahad Qawasmeh and Mohammed Milhem, were seized together with the *qadi* (Islamic judge) of Hebron, Sheikh Rajab Tamimi, put into a helicopter with black bags over their heads, and dumped across the border in south Lebanon. There was no pretense of any legal process against them, and their deportation was condemned by the Security Council of the United Nations. But this did not save them from the fate which has overtaken hundreds of others whose qualities of leadership and courage in resisting oppression have made them undesirable in the eyes of the Israeli authorities. Among those personally known to me who have suffered this particularly cruel fate are Rouhi al-Khatib, the mayor of Arab Jerusalem; Dr. Walid Kamhawi of Nablus; Abdel-Jawad Saleh, who at the time of his deportation was mayor of El-Bireh; and Dr. Hanna Nasir, president of Bir Zeit University and perhaps the most distinguished educationist of his generation in Palestine.

Article 10 states: *"Everyone is entitled in full equality to a fair and public hearing by an independent and impartial tribunal, in the determination of his rights and obligations and of any criminal charge against him."* Those I have just mentioned were of course given no "fair and public hearing"; on the contrary, they and many others were bundled across the de facto border into Jordan, surreptitiously, in the wee hours of the morning, often in conditions of considerable physical hardship, without the opportunity to communicate with their families or to settle their domestic affairs, and without any legal process at all. Thousands of others have testified in Is-

raeli military courts that the confessions on the basis of which
they were sentenced to long prison terms had been extorted from
them by torture. The Israeli lawyer Felicia Langer, who has defended countless Palestinian political prisoners in the Israeli
courts (and made herself very unpopular in Israel as a result) has
published, in a book entitled *With My Own Eyes*, details of many
such cases in which no humanitarian considerations were allowed
to influence the decisions of the military courts. No one could tes-
tify with more authority than this brave and experienced lawyer
to the fact that these courts can in no sense be considered the
"independent and impartial tribunal" specified in Article 10 of
the Declaration.

Article 12 states: *"No one shall be subjected to arbitrary interference with his privacy, family, home or correspondence,"* but that, on the
contrary, *"everyone has the right to the protection of the law against such
interference or attack."* Even those who have never visited the occupied territories, and who are too young to remember the German
occupation of most of Europe, should have no difficulty in understanding how absurd such a right becomes in the context of a military occupation. The occupier, with the army behind him as the
only effective authority, arrogates to himself the absolute right
to interfere, at any moment and on any pretext, with the privacy
of the citizens under occupation. He may do so in the pursuit of
"security," a concept which can be stretched to justify every form
of oppression. He may do so with the simple purpose of intimidation, and it is my own conviction, based on a great deal of personal experience in the occupied territories, that this is often the
purpose of the Israelis when they invade the homes or the refugee camps where the Palestinians live. But, whatever the pretext,
there can be no doubt about the fact that the Palestinians in the
West Bank and Gaza enjoy no freedom, by day or by night, from
the threat that their privacy may at any moment be interfered
with by the occupation forces. As for the law—which means simply the authority of the military government itself—it is used, not
to protect them against such interference, but to enforce it.

Article 13 states: *"Everyone has the right to freedom of movement . . . [including] the right to leave any country, including his own,
and to return to his country."* What a bitter irony this article must
have in the eyes of any Palestinian! The right to leave his own
country: there is no difficulty for him in that—indeed, the Israelis afford him every opportunity to do so. But to return to his

country—that is another matter. If that right could be enforced, how many thousands of Palestinians would flock back to the homes and even the refugee camps which they were "encouraged" to leave in 1967 or from which they have been deported since them?

Even the right to freedom of movement within the occupied territories is subject to the arbitrary will of the occupation authorities. Any Palestinian's movements may be restricted by administrative order confining him to his house or his village. The lives of whole communities may be affected by the curfews which have been a feature of the Israeli occupation of the West Bank, sometimes to prevent and at other times to punish any signs of a spirit of resistance. I have witnessed several of these punitive curfews, sometimes enforced for one or even two weeks and imposing grievous hardship especially on the most vulnerable members of the community—the aged, the infirm, mothers with small children. Even without such overtones of physical intimidation, it is evident that the concept of freedom of movement is irreconcilable with that of a military occupation.

Article 15 states: *"Everyone has the right to a nationality,"* and that *"no one shall be arbitrarily deprived of his nationality."* It is perhaps difficult for us whose national identity is not in dispute, who need not fear that anyone will attempt to question our right to call ourselves Englishmen or Italians or Frenchmen, to appreciate just how poignant is the longing, or how strong the will, of Palestinians to achieve the same unquestioning acceptance. When we are critical, as we must be, of the injustice and the brutality which characterize the Israeli occupation today, we should not forget that the struggle for Palestinian independence began more than half a century ago, when Britain was the occupying power. Palestinian nationalism is not something new or artificial, although—paradoxically—it has become much stronger and more clearly articulated with the dismemberment of the old Palestine. Both governments, the British in the 1930s and the Israeli today, have behaved and are behaving in a way this is not merely brutal and unjust, but that is self-defeating. For they have stimulated the desire of the Palestinians to exercise the right which the Universal Declaration holds out as a promise to all peoples: the right to a nationality. I look forward to the day when they will enjoy it in full freedom.

Article 17 states: *"No one shall be arbitrarily deprived of his property."* That sounds straightforward enough and so self-evident as to be hardly worth including in an international charter of human rights. But for the Palestinians, whose situation in this as in so many other respects is exceptional, there is nothing straightforward about it. There is no guarantee for any inhabitant of the occupied territories has his property—especially the property that is most valuable to him, his land—will not be taken from him without warning and without redress.

Israel's relentless colonization of the occupied territories by the establishment of Jewish settlements on Arab land has often been described as a policy of "creeping annexation." Its political implications are clear—and they have become even more clear since the signing of the Camp David agreement. Hardly a week now passes without the announcement by the Israeli government of fresh plans to establish Jewish settlements, especially in the West Bank—and this despite the repeated rulings of the United Nations and even of the government of the United States that such settlements are illegal. Besides their damaging effect on the search for peace, these Israeli settlements clearly contravene Article 17 of the Universal Declaration in that they arbitrarily deprive Palestinian landowners of their property.

Here it is proper to mention the role of the United States in facilitating and encouraging the Israeli government's program of colonization throughout the occupied territories. The president of the United State has repeatedly said that his government regards the Israeli settlements in the occupied territories as illegal and that they represent a set of obstacles in the way of the search for peace. Yet it is the enormous financial assitance that the United States provides which enables the Israeli government to go ahead, at a time of great economic stringency, with this very costly program. The absurdity of the American position in the matter is self-evident. It is with justification that the Palestinians hold the American government ultimately responsible for this violation of one of their most fundamental rights: the right to retain possession of the land that has been theirs since time immemorial.

Article 19 states: *"Everyone has the right to freedom of opinion and expression: this right includes freedom to hold opinions without interference and to seek, receive and impart information and ideas through any media and regardless of frontiers."* Here again it is not necessary to waste many words in explaining that the Palestinians in the occupied territories cannot enjoy this freedom. Freedom of opinion and expression is quite simply incompatible with a situation where one people is under military occupation by another. The opinions held by the Palestinians in the occupied territories, whose overriding ambition is to regain their freedom, are inevitably distasteful to the Israelis, who use every means to prevent their free expression.

The occupation authorities seek to achieve this by imposing a strict censorship on all publications circulating in the occupied territories and by preventing the circulation of other publications freely available to Israeli citizens, including the Israeli settlers in the West Bank. The censorship also applies to books, with no concession made to the principle of academic freedom. The Arab universities in the West Bank are particularly affected and are strictly controlled in the matter of the textbooks available to their students. In particular, of course, any publication that gives expression to the political and national aspirations of the Palestinians is subjected to close scrutiny and frequent censorship by the occupation authorities.

Article 20 states: *"Everyone has the right to freedom of peaceful assembly and association."* The occupation authorities would be illogical if they neglected, in their control of ideas and their expression, to restrict also the right of the Palestinians under occupation to meet for the free exchange of ideas and to form political associations. The free exchange of ideas is anathema to any regime of military occupation, and the Israeli regime is no different from other occupation regimes. Its regulations strictly forbid the formation of any political association in the occupied territories and any assembly of three or more persons for the purpose of political discussion. The military government has on many occasions enforced this regulation.

Article 21 states: *"Everyone has the right to take part in the Government of his country, directly or through freely chosen representatives."* Here we come to the heart of the matter. This is the fundamental issue where the rights of the Palestinians are concerned. If the Palestinians enjoyed the right to take part, through freely chosen representatives, in the government of their country, they would not be subject to all the other disabilities in this sad catalog. They would then have no need to resort to violence in pursuit of rights which we all take for granted.

There is, of course, no question but the Palestinians under occupation are denied this right. It is indeed their chief grievance. For thirteen years they have been under the arbitrary rule of an alien regime whose authority they totally reject. If they are to regain the right to take a proper share in choosing a government acceptable to themselves, the first and inevitable step must be the ending of the regime of military occupation. From that, everything else could follow. But so long as the occupation is maintained, the right enshrined in Article 21 will be denied to the Palestinians.

Article 22 states: *"Everyone, as a member of society, . . . is entitled to the realization . . . of the economic, social and cultural rights indispensable for his dignity and the free development of his personality."* To secure this right, in all its aspects, is not easy for anyone, even in a free society. It is patently impossible for a people living under an occupation regime whose central objective, whether in economic, social, or cultural affairs, is to restrict the free development of its identity. So long as it remains the purpose of the government of Israel to impose its rule on the occupied territories, the inhabitants of those territories will be denied the dignity and freedom that are their birthright.

Finally, Article 28 proclaims: *"Everyone is entitled to a social and international order in which the rights and freedoms set forth in this Declaration can be fully realized."* Here it is not only the Palestinians who have a legitimate complaint. As we have seen, the Palestinians are deprived of many of the rights and freedoms proclaimed in the Declaration of Human Rights adopted by the General Assembly of the United Nations more than thirty years ago. But we who believe that these rights ought to be enjoyed by the Palestinians, so long as we are unable to implement this article of the declaration, are likewise deprived of the right to "a social and international order" in which these rights and freedoms can be fully realized by all. We have the right, as well as the duty, to urge our own governments to adopt policies that will enable us, not merely to pursue our own national objectives, but to see that this same freedom is extended to others.

In his inaugural address President Carter declared: "Our commitment to human rights must be absolute. . . . Because we are free we can never be indifferent to the fate of freedom elsewhere." This should be the basis of our approach to the present situation in Palestine. It is because we are free ourselves that we cannot be indifferent to the fact that the Palestinians in the occupied territories are denied the same freedom. That is why we must do all we can do insure that the disgraceful state of affairs in the territories now occupied by Israel is brought to an end.

THE FORMATION OF AMERICAN PUBLIC OPINION ON THE QUESTION OF PALESTINE[3]

In Western Eurupe generally speaking, public attitudes toward the the Palestinians, which on the whole only grudgingly and very recently have begun to show some improvement, are considerably in advance of the United States. In America the situation has genuinely improved over the past five or six years, although judging from recent talk about the Middle East by various presidential candidates, the low level of talk and of quick public acceptability of such talk are depressingly evident.

I would like therefore to analyze the background of these American attitudes insofar as these public views and attitudes reflect and embody a rarely questioned consensus and an unconscious ideology, both of which derive from certain specific features of American society and history. That will take up the first part of my paper. In the second part I shall give concrete examples of how the consensus and the ideology work with reference to the Palestine question.

American Consensus and Ideology

Because the United States is a complex society made up of many, often incompatible, subcultures, the need to impart a more or less standardized common culture through the media is felt with particular strength. This is not a feature associated only with the mass media in our era but one that holds a special pedigree going back to the founding of the American republic. Beginning with the Puritan "errand in the wilderness," there has existed in

[3]By Edward W. Said, professor of comparative literature at Columbia University, from Ibrahim Abu-Lughod, ed., *Palestinian Rights: Affirmation and Denial*, pp. 215-225. Copyright © 1982, Medina Press. Reprinted by permission.

the United States an institutionalized ideological rhetoric expressing a particular American consciousness, identity, destiny, and role, whose function has always been to incorporate as much of American (and the world's) diversity as possible, and to re-form it in a uniquely American way. (This rhetoric and its institutional presence in American life have been convincingly analyzed by numerous scholars, including Perry Miller and, most recently, Sacvan Bercovitch.) One result of this is the illusion, if not always the actuality, of consensus, and it is as part of this essentially nationalist consensus that the media, acting on behalf of the society they serve, believe themselves to be functioning.

The simplest and, I think, most accurate way of characterizing this consensus is to say that it sets limits and maintains pressures. It does not mechanically dictate content, nor does it mechanically reflect the interest of a certain class or economic group. We must think of it as drawing invisible lines beyond which a reporter or commentator does not feel it necessary go to. Thus the notion that American military power might be used for malevolent purposes is relatively impossible within the consensus, just as the idea that America is a force for good in the world is routine and normal. Similarly, I think, Americans tend to identify with foreign societies or cultures projecting a pioneering, new spirit (e.g., Israel), with those who are wresting the land from ill use or from savages. On the other hand, Americans often mistrust or do not have much interest in traditional cultures, even those in the throes of revolutionary renewal. Americans expect that Communist propaganda is guided by similar cultural and political constraints; but in America's case the media's setting of limits and maintaining of pressures is done with little apparent admission or awareness that this is what in fact is being done. And this too is an aspect of set limits. Let me give two simple examples. First, Palestinians are systematically considered to be terrorists: nothing else about them is as consistently referred to, not even their bare human existence. Second, when the United States hostages were seized and held in Teheran, the consensus immediately came into play, decreeing more or less that only what took place concerning the hostages was important about Iran. The rest of the country, its political processes, its daily life, its personalities, its geography and history, were eminently ignorable. Iran and the Iranian people were defined in terms of whether they were for or against America. But these matters are best understood in practice, and we shall see what this entails when we come to specific analyses.

After World II the United States took over the imperial role formerly played by France and Britain. A set of policies was devised for dealing with the world that suited the peculiarities and the problems of each region of the world affecting (and affected by) U.S. interests. Europe was designed for postwar recovery, for which the Marshall Plan, among other similar U.S. policies, was suited. The Soviet Union, of course, emerged as the United States' most formidable competitor; and, as no one needs to be told, the Cold War produced policies, studies—even a mentality—which still dominate the relationships between one superpower and the other. That left what has come to be called the Third World, an area of competition not only between the United States and the U.S.S.R. but also between the United States and various native powers only recently in possession of their independence from European colonizers.

Almost without exception, the Third World seemed to U.S. policymakers to be "underdeveloped," in the grip of unnecessarily archaic and static "traditional" modes of life, dangerously prone to Communist subversion and internal stagnation. This is the framework into which the Palestinians have fitted. For the Third World, "modernization" became the order of the day as far as the United States was concerned. And, according to James Peck, "modernization theory was the ideological answer to a world of increasing revolutionary upheaval and continued reaction among traditional political elites." Huge sums were poured into Africa and Asia with the aim of stopping communism, promoting U.S. trade, and above all, developing a cadre of native allies whose express *raison d'être* seemed to be the transformation of a backward country into a mini-America. In time the initial investment required additional sums and increased military support to keep it going. And this in turn produced the interventions all over Asia and Latin America that regularly pitted the United States against almost every brand of native nationalism.

The history of U.S. efforts on behalf of modernization and development in the Third World can never be completely understood unless it is also noted how the policy itself produced a style of thought, and a habit of seeing the Third World, which *increased* the political, emotional, and strategic investment in the very idea of modernization. Vietnam is a perfect instance of this. Once it was decided that the country was to be saved from communism—and, indeed, from itself—a whole science of modernization for Vietnam (whose last, and most costly, phase was known as "Vietnamization") came into being. It was not only government specialists who were involved, but university experts as well. In time, the survival of pro-American and anti-Communist regimes in Saigon dominated everything, even when it became clear that, on the one hand, a huge majority of the population viewed those regimes as alien and oppressive, and, on the other, the cost of fighting unsuccessful wars on behalf of these regimes had devastated the whole region and cost Lyndon Johnson the presidency. Still, a very great amount of writing on the virutes of modernizing traditional societies acquired an almost unquestioned social, and certainly cultural, authority in the United States, while in many parts of the Third World "modernization" was connected in the popular mind with foolish U.S. spending, unnecessary gadgetry and armaments, corrupt rulers, and brutal U.S. intervention in the affairs of small, weak countries.

Among the many illusions that persisted in modernization theory was one with special pertinence to the Islamic world: namely, that before the advent of the United States, Islam existed in a kind of timeless childhood, shielded from true development by an archaic set of superstitions, prevented by its strange priests and scribes from moving out of the Middle Ages and into the modern world. The Islamic world seemed indifferent to the blandishments of "Western" ideas altogether. What was especially troubling about its attitude was a fierce unwillingness to accept any style of politics (or, for that matter, of rationality) that was not deliberately its own. Above all, the attachment to Islam seemed especially defiant.

Ironically, few Western commentators on "Islamic" atavism and medieval modes of logic noted that a few miles to the west of Iran, in Begin's Israel, there was a regime fully willing to mandate its actions by religious authority and by a very backward-looking theological doctrine. Whereas Western journalists and intellectuals became expert at derisively quoting various Islamic edicts in Iran (which seemed quite reactionary), no one bothered to point out, for example, that the modern Israeli editon of the Babylonian Talmud (edited by Rabbi Adin Steinzaltz), which is taught in many Israeli and some American schools, has in its Tractate Berachot such passages as the following: "A Jew who sees tombs of Gentiles should say: 'Your mother shall be sore confounded, she that bore you shall be ashamed, behold the end of the Gentiles shall be a wilderness, a dry land and a desert,' Jeremiah 50,12."

Religious intensity was thus ascribed solely to Islam. A retreat into religion became the way most Islamic states could be explained—from Saudi Arabia, which, with a peculiarly Islamic logic refused to ratify the Camp David accords, to Pakistan, Afghanistan, and Algeria. In this way, then, we can see how the Islamic world was differentiated in the Western mind generally, in the United States in particular, from regions of the world to which Cold War analysis could be applied. There seemed to be no way, for example , in which one could speak of Saudi Arabia and Kuwait as parts of "the free world"; even Iran during the shah's regime, despite its overwhelming anti-Soviet commitment, never really belonged to "our side" the way France and Britain do. Nevertheless, U.S. policymakers persisted in speaking of the "loss" of China, Vietnam, and Angola. In this context, it has been the singularly unhappy lot of the Persian Gulf's Islamic states to have been considered by American crisis-managers as places ready for U.S. military occupation. Thus George Ball, in the *New York Times* magazine of June 28, 1970, warned that the "tragedy of Vietnam" might lead to "pacifism and isolation" at home, whereas U.S. interests in the Middle East were so great that the president ought to "educate" Americans about the possibility of military intervention there.

One more thing needs mention here: the role of Israel in mediating Western and particularly American views of the Islamic world since World War II. In the first place, as I have already said, very little about Israel's avowedly religious character is ever mentioned in the press. Only recently have there been overt references to Israeli religious fanaticism in the Western press, and all of these have been to the zealots of Gush Emunim, whose principal activity has been the violent setting up of illegal settlements in the West Bank. Yet most Western accounts of Gush Emunim simply leave out the inconvenient fact that it was the "secular" Labour government that first instituted illegal settlements in occupied Arab territory, not just the religious fanatics now stirring things up. This kind of one-sided reporting is, I think, an effect of how Israel—the Middle East's "only democracy" and "our staunch ally"—has been used as a foil for Islam. All the social and ideological peculiarities that over the years have allied Israel and South Africa tend to get no attention whatever. Instead, Israel has appeared as a bastion of Western civilization hewed (with much approbation and self-congratulation) out of the Islamic darkness.

Secondly, Israel's security has become automatically interchangeable with fending off Islam, perpetuating Western hegemony, and demonstrating the virtues of modernization. At this point, of course, Orientalism and modernization theory dovetail nicely. If Orientalist scholarship traditionally taught that Muslims were no more than fatalistic children tyrannized by their mindset, their *'ulama,* and their wild-eyed political leaders into resisting the West and progress, was it not the case that every political scientist, anthropologist, and sociologist worthy of trust could show that, given a reasonable chance, something resembling the American way of life might be introduced into the Islamic world via consumer goods, anti-Communist propaganda, and "good" leaders? The one main difficulty with the Islamic world, however, was that, unlike India and China, it had never really been pacified or defeated. For reasons which seemed always to defy the understanding of scholars, Islam continued its sway over its adherents, who, it came regularly to be argued, were unwilling to accept reality or at least that part of reality in which the Western superiority was demonstrable.

Efforts at modernization persisted throughout the two decades following World War II. Iran became in effect the modernization success story and its ruler the modernized leader par excellance. As for the rest of the Islamic world—Arab nationalism, Egypt's Gamal Abdel Nasser, Indonesia's Sukarno, the Palestinian national movement, Iranian opposition groups, thousands of Islamic teachers, brotherhoods, orders—all of this was either opposed or not covered by Western scholars with a heavy investment in modernization theory and in American strategic and economic interests in the Islamic world.

During the explosive decade of the 1970s, Islam seemed to give more and more proof of its fundamental intransigence. There was, for example, the Iranian revolution: neither pro-Communist nor promodernization, the people who overthrew the shah were simply not explainable according to the canons of behavior presupposed by modernization theory. They did not seem to be grateful for the quotidian benefits of modernization (cars, an enormous military and security apparatus, a stable regime) and the virtues of modernization. In these ways, therefore, three sets of illusions economically buttress and reproduce each other in the interests of shoring up the Western self-image: the view of Islam, the ideology of modernization, and the affirmations of Zionism.

In addition, to make "our" attitudes to Islam very clear, a whole information and policymaking apparatus in the United States depends on these illusions and diffuses them widely. Large segments of the intelligentsia, allied to the community of geopolitical strategists, deliver themselves of expansive ideas about Islam, oil, the future of Western civilization, and the fight for democracy against both turmoil and terrorism. For reasons that I have discussed elsewhere, the Islamic specialists supply more material, despite the fact that only a fraction of what goes on in academic Islamic studies is directly infected with the cultural and political visions to be found in geopolitics and Cold War ideology. Adding to this are the mass media, which take from the other two units of the apparatus what is most easily compressed into images: hence the caricatures, the frightening mobs, the concentration on "Islamic" punishment, and so on. All of this is presided over by the great power establishments—the oil companies, the mammoth corporations and multinationals, the defense and intelligence communities, the executive branch of the government. When President Carter spent his first New Year's Day in office with the shah in 1978, and said that Iran was "an island of stability," he was speaking with the mobilized force of this formidable apparatus, representing U.S. interests and covering Islam at the same time.

American Public Policy and the Question of Palestine

On September 9, 1979 ABC broadcast a conversation between Barbara Walters and Yasser Arafat. The program was part of the network's "Issues and Answers" series, taped on September 8 in Havana during the last hours of the conference of non-aligned countries. Much of what was said about the conference in the U.S. press focused on tensions between President Tito and Fidel Castro, yet ABC's choice of Arafat for what was to be the only major televison coverage of the conference indicated accurately enough that, even in Havana, the PLO and the Palestine question stood at the center of the issues being discussed. Walters's prominence as a journalistic star gave the interview more gravity, as did the Middle East expertise she had gathered from having interviewed Anwar Sadat, Menachem Begin, and Arafat himself on previous occasions. I do not think it is wrong to assume that viewers were supposed to understand that Walter's "doing" Arafat meant that in some vague, undefined way history was being dramatized before their eyes. In this case the historical event was Arafat's trial for harboring intentions to destroy Israel and kill all the Jews.

Every so often in the interview Walters would ask routine political questions: What did Arafat think of the resolutions (still to be voted on) condemning Egypt and supporting the PLO? What sort of aid was Cuba giving the PLO? Was it correct that Arafat had intervened to forestall a U.N. Security Council vote on Palestinian rights so that Andy Young would not be embarrassed at having to cast a U.S. veto? But the interview's main business consisted in a more and more impassioned Walters asking Arafat questions, not of policy, but of destiny. Isn't it true, she asked three times, that the PLO's charter advocates the destruction of Israel? Each time she asked the question, and each time she rephased it, her insistence declaimed moral partisanship. She was not "just" a reporter doing her job; she was Right asking (perhaps potential) Evil to cease and desist from genocide. She was, in fact, raising the specter of the Holocaust before her audience's eyes, and quite decently exposing Arafat's latent nazism to the world. He, on the other hand, hesitated—his poor English forcing him time and again to counter the question with the wrong question. Have you actually read the charter? And what disreputable translation did you use? he asked, as if the charter guided his every move and as if only a linguistic philosopher could really decode the charter's deep mysteries. How could Walters, scrupulously doing her job know (and how much less likely was it that her viewers could know) that most of the frequent *Palestinian* criticisms of Arafat were that he did not truly observe one or another clause in the charter? But that could not possibly emerge in such an interview anyway. What was astonishing was how quickly and easily a journalist could escalate the rhetoric from politics to the grandiose level of history and destiny, and, perhaps more maddening, how little of the same kind of rhetoric is ever directed against Israeli or Zionist leaders being interviewed.

Consider that as recently as 1969 Golda Meir said that Palestinians do not exist; since then every Israeli prime minister has referred to the four million Palestinians in terms that have been intended dramatically to express doubt about their genuine existence. General Rabin referred to them as "so-called Palestinians" and Menachem Begin calls them "the Arabs of *Eretz Israel*." Israel has no constitution, but in none of its Basic Laws is there a provision made for (much less a reference to) the 650,000 Palestinians who are in fact Israeli citizens. Moreover, in having literally destroyed about 400 of the original 500 Palestinian villages, Israel not only eradicated a society but dispossessed its people and occupied the remainder of its territory. And Israel continues to bomb, strafe, and punish the civilian refugee population without respite. Begin's party, the Likud, states quite explicitly in its constitution that Israel intends to hold on to the West Bank, and even to occupy the East Bank (that is, the sovereign state of Jordan). Yet, in spite of all this, there has never been an occasion when a reporter in the United States has publicly asked an Israeli politician questions about these matters. The great questions about existence, about genocide, about recognition are regularly asked of the Palestinians, who have been turned into metaphysical abstractions all signaling the destruction of the Middle East's most powerful state, the end of the Jewish people, and protracted terror and violence.

In this state of affairs, which is primarily a public information and policy question of very great moment indeed, print and broadcast journalism are seriously implicated. Barbara Walters is no especially culpable figure in this respect: she is, I believe, a well-intentioned reporter who has followed unquestioningly the trend, the rhetorical space opened at least a generation before her. The result is that few people have been prepared to open the Palestinian file as something representing a direct challenge to certain concrete Israeli policies and to concrete aspects of Zionist history. On the one hand, therefore, most things about Israel appeared sacrosanct, since as an idea the country was a once-empty land now filled with those Jews not destroyed by nazism. On the other hand, since the Palestinians did not really "exist," and since their narrative continuity as a people could not easily be ascertained (there are practically no works in English about them, they

belong to the exotic Islamic Orient, not to the West; they were
an essentially backward peasant people whose world silence could
be interpreted as indifference), they came to represent nothing
more than an obstacle to Isareli existence. In time, when it became clear after 1967 that Israel was going to have to deal with
its "non-Jewish" subjects, Palestinians were an immediate flaw in
Israel's actuality: How could Israel be said militarily to occupy
territory not its own? How could mere Arabs unanimously resist
Israeli "preventive detention"? How could an organization such
as the PLO make claims on Israel's hitherto unqualified legitimacy and assert the presence of another people on the same Palestinian soil? All these questions were unilaterally equated with
"terrorism" and a threat "to eliminate Israel," and for politeness'
sake not asked.

What happened, and why did it happen? The answer has in
the end very little to do with a Zionist lobby, although such a lobby obviously played a role of some sort. Let us start charitably
with the understandable explanations first. Zionsim can easily be
said to have achieved remarkable things for Jews. However much
the record may have caused disagreements within the Jewish
community, I think it is true that in the liberal Western world's
eyes the struggle for Palestine was an affirmative thing. Certainly
after World War II the struggle seemed irresistibly important,
and Israel was established—part of the same effort that included
the Marshall Plan, as one historian has recently said. No attention
to speak of was given to what Israel cost the native Palestinians,
whose actual numerical majority was, as late as the spring of
1948, three times greater than that of the ever-augmenting number incoming Jews. Except for the odd U.N. report, neither the
academic experts on the Middle East nor the press provided
much space to the Palestinian side of the story, which was mainly
a story of loss, exile, and dispersal. History seems always to be
written from the victors' standpoint, and the Israelis were the
winners. In addition, Israelis and pro-Zionist Americans provided
the local consumer of news with what was happening: after all,
how many Palestinians spoke or wrote English, and what did it
mean to the average American to be a Palestinian and to suffer
for it? Even today, when the Arab world is full of civilian casualties, how many Arab funerals are shown on American television?
Whereas hundreds of thousands of Palestinians actually lost their
country and became for the most part stateless exiles, no one

could sympathetically name a single Palestinian or identify with a Palestinian story the way readers of *Exodus*, admirers of Moshe Dayan, and students of Martin Buber could.

Into this vast gap about the Palestinians flowed a limited number of clichés, endlessly deployed, repeated, and rephrased almost unthinkingly. In the background lurked a strong Western prejudice against Arabs and Muslims—violent and uncultured terrorists—while in the foreground one could go on about Israeli modernity and democracy, about the *kibbutzim* (all of which programmatically exclude non-Jews), about the marvelous army, and so forth. For journalists and politicians it was de rigueur to be "for Israel," as if that automatically meant being for civilization, against the Holocaust, and with the American way of life. By 1967, when Israel came into possession of approximately a million more Palestinians, to be "for Israel" meant being for life, for values, for civilization itself. The Palestinians were just there in order for Israel's "benign occupation" to be carried out. To be critical of Israel was to fall into the pattern set forth by nazism. In the process, of course, the history of Zionism, which to some extent created today's miltant Palestinian resistance, disappeared: Israel stood alone in the eastern Mediterranean, a virtuous plot of land without time, without any but the history of anti-Semitism, without people except surviving Jews and terroristic "Arabs."

As one watched Barbara Walters, one could begin to understand why neither she nor her colleagues ever asked Begin, for example, where the Palestinians came from anyway, and why Palestinians should feel animosity toward Israel, or why most Africans and Asians identify with them and not with Israel. She did not know—and, what was more important, there was no rhetoric for her to use easily even if she did know. To a very great extent the recent U.S. interest in the PLO is a function both of a renascent Palestinian political struggle and of a backward, novelty-seeking press, as well as of the phenomenon referred to as "the return of Islam." The shortcomings of that interest are equally a function of all three factors. In any case, were Arafat to have spoken naturally about his own life of the lives of his friends and relatives, then the concrete punishments of Zionism for the Palestinian might have emerged. And were Walters to have asked him a personal question—"Why do you and your young men and women willingly endure Israeli bombardment in your camps and still wage the struggle for Palestinian self-determination?—the interview might have been informative. But the journalist could not escape the false positions into which one habitually falls in talking about the Palestinians and the Middle East. From one perspective, too much rhetoric and metaphysics; from another, not enough human detail.

The results of this skewed situation have recently been unimaginable for any other foreign policy question. Consider some recent grotesqueries in which the U.S. media and the politicians have followed along for the most part uncritically.

1. The Camp David events of September 1978. Following much talk about the Palestinian problem, a simple question arises. Why were no Palestinians present or consulted? Even if Carter, Sadat, and Begin were treated by Cronkite, Walters, and Brinkley with the respect normally given to prophets, would it not have been possible for someone to venture out loud that it was a bit peculiar to speak *about* and *for* Palestinians, but not by any means to speak *to* them? And still we are informed every few days that Jimmy Carter, perhaps only to assure his reelection, will, in his best presidential manner, bring Sadat and Begin to the White House to get the autonomy talks off dead-center. Yet, the *New York Times* tells us, there is no chance that Sadat and Begin will agree on the really crucial question governing the colonial settlements: the question—however metaphyical it might seem to ordinary mortals—of Israeli security. No one asks (perhaps because it is too naive a question): Why bother with an autonomy agreement, since none of the major questions except sanitation can be talked about, and since it will not be accepted by anyone—least of all the Israelis, who hold all the power, or the Palestinians, in whose benefit it is supposed to be occurring?

2. The March 1980 U.N. vote, after which the U.S. disavowed its position. We now know that Ambassador McHenry flew to Washington with the text of the resolution in his pocket the night before the vote. What exactly caused the failure to communicate? Did the text drop out of his pocket between the airport and the White House? Or was it that the president, the ambassador, the secretary of state, and the national security adviser, neither singly nor teogether, understood the language of the resolution? Or was it that somebody else—perhaps Robert Strauss—instructed the president that the vote would have to be disavowed if the campaign were to continue successfully?

One cannot know of course, but these are not the really consequential questions. What counts, in my opinion, is that every candidate, including the president himself, has attacked a policy declared to be our policy in the name of that policy. Lewis Carroll could not have dreamed up a nicer conundrum, nor a cleverer logical and political absurdity. And still the U.S. constituency has not been heard from, just as the press—which has been on the wrong side of every argument or prediction in the Middle East— follows along sheepishly, reporting the idiocies with no indication that it is aware that they are in fact idiocies, not to be tolerated by any rational human being.

3. The question of human rights. On this point words fail one; or, if they do not, they ought to be extremely strong words indeed. Let me ventrue a few. It is a scandal that Palestinian rights are assumed to be negligible and that such an assumption has become the common currency of everyday politics and discourse in the United States. When the press and the government can whip up sentiment in America in favor of treating the ex-shah as a charity case, hardly anyone except a courageous Australian journalist, Claudia Wright, has the courage to tell the story of Ziad abu Ein, a Palestinian who is being extradited by the United States at Israel's simple request, in flagrant violation of every decent human sentiment and every known legal precept. Palestinian rights have been trampled on; they have been ripped up, torn to shreds in legal fact and in the bodies or our people. And yet no one says anything. Instead we have Senator Kennedy's fatuous words about Israel's security, as if the mere mention of the word *Israel* were enough to assure him of a place in posterity. One could go on and on.

But in the end the Palestinian problem is *the* Middle East problem. It is about the denial of human rights for "natives." It is about unremitting war waged by Israel against the non-European Arab inhabitants of Palestine, a war that continues today in war-destroyed southern Lebanon and in the occupied territories. It is about unrestrained militarism, destruction, and overspending. Palestine is the human truth hidden beneath propagandistic thought-stopping headlines, like "resurgent Islam," "Middle East crises," and "Israeli democracy." The Palestinians are everywhere in the region: the Gulf is dependent on them, every Islamic movement supports them, every liberation movement sees their struggle as the vanguard struggle. Above all, the independence and democracy of the Palestinian political struggle represents a genuine alternative to superpower maneuvers in outmoded, unacceptable spheres of influence. After all, the Palestinian idea in its essence opposes religious and ethnic exclusivism, which have dispossessed all four million "non-Jews" (as Israel designates them officially), and proposes instead equality of Jews and Arabs alike. This is not an idea to be backed away from, especially at a time when Americans have been fed a diet of ideological hatred for nonwhites and for "Islam," and when no criticism of Israel is the easiest line to take in a country that is less critical of Israeli policies than Israelis themselves.

SEPARATION—ONLY SEPARATION[4]

. . . A policy of liberalism that allows the Arabs a life of material gain and freedom guarantees their remaining in the land and attempting to destroy Israel from within. *They must leave the country for their own lands—that must be Israeli policy*. As part of that policy, life must be made very difficult for them. That is the way to encourage emigration and spare Israel tragedy.

I urge the adoption of a program to deal with the Arab problem in Eretz Yisrael, with its basis the real rational and Jewish relationship of citizen, nation, and state.

I urged the adoption of the following program to clarify the character of the nation, the state, and its citizens and the position of its noncitizens; and to prepare the framework for the transfer of Arabs from the Land of Israel (the state and the territories liberated in 1967):

The land, the state, exists to serve the people. Only tyrants say the opposite. In the beginning there was the family, tribe, clan, people. They have a common origin, history, heritage, destiny. The land has a definite, specific function. It exists to serve the people as a vessel to hold them and to allow them to live their

[4]By Rabbi Meir Kahane, member (1984–1988) of the Israeli Knesset and founder-director of the Kach ("force") Party, from his book *They Must Go*, New York: Grosset & Dunlap, pp. 249–266. Copyright © 1981 by Meir Kahane. Reprinted by permission.

unique way of life, to achieve their national purpose and heritage. The state is a tool to serve that purpose and to enable the people to achieve their fulfillment. Neither state nor land has a will or authority of its own. The identity and character of the land and state are decided upon and granted by the people. The land and state do not command, they obey; they do not order, they serve; the exist only for the purpose of the people whose name is attached to them.

The people are the masters and proprietors of the land, and as such they are the citizens of it. Those who are not members of the family, tribe, clan, people, nation, clearly have no ownership, proprietorship, or legal ties to the land. They cannot be citizens since they are not members of the people, the nation. Strangers can, of course, become part of the people and nation through the process and discipline of Judaism and *halakah*. But that is the only way they can become citizens of the state.

What rationality is there to claim that a piece of land has the will, authority, and power to convey to those who live on it citizenship, regardless of who they are? It is human beings who define the land, not the land that defines the human beings. One does not become an "Israeli" because one lives in the land. For the land itself is defined by the will, ownership, and title to it of the people of Israel. One can be an "Israeli" when belonging to the people of Israel, when joining the nation, the people, not simply by living on the piece of land that is the mere servant and vessel of the people.

And so, the right of non-Jews to live in the Land of Israel is a thing to be decided upon by the owners of the land, its citizens—the Jews, under the Jewish concept of *resident stranger* (*ger toshav*). Residence or removal of noncitizens is decided by the owners of the land according to that concept and what is good and right for the people and nation whose land and state it is. With this as a basis, let it be declared that:

1. The identity between the state and the nation shall be the sole basis of citizenship in the State of Israel. The State of Israel belongs to and exists only for the Jewish nation and is therefore the Jewish state, the home in which the Jewish nation lives. It is therefore only membership in the Jewish nation which gives citizenship in the Jewish state. All members of the Jewish nation—without exception and whoever they may be—are entitled to automatic citizenship in the Jewish state, and no one who is not a member of the Jewish nation can acquire such citizenship. Membership in the

Jewish nation and people can be acquired through the process and discipline of Judaism and halakah. *Non-Jews can live in the land without citizenship and political rights, up to a number whose maximum is limited by the security consideration of the state and Jewish people. No state, no matter what the attitude of the noncitizens, can allow unlimited numbers of them to live in the country. The resident permits of all resident strangers shall be good for one year and shall be reviewed at the end of every year.*
2. Every Arab resident of Eretz Yisrael shall be offered a voluntary transfer to an Arab or, if possible, a non-Arab land. Those who accept shall be given full compensation for property, plus a cash bonus, as well as first priority for visas for the West (with occupational training if necessary). Fair compensation for property shall be fixed by an impartial body with payments to be made in regular, reasonable installments. The body shall include members of the Jewish and Arab communities. Payments to Arabs for their property shall be made with consideration for the debts owed those Jewish communities. Arab oil states shall be asked to contribute the money they received for the property expropriated without compensation from the Jews who were expelled from Arab lands. This offer of compensation and bonus shall be good for two months so as to enable all Arabs in the land to consider it carefully. After that, step 3 of the program will take effect.
3. Arabs who decline the offer shall be asked to make a pledge of their loyalty to the Jewish state in which they accept the Land of Israel as the home of the Jewish people and recognize total Jewish sovereignty over it, as well as the absolute and exclusive right of the Jewish people to it. Those who do so shall remain as residents and noncitizens of Israel with no national sovereignty and no political and voting rights, since they are not members of the Jewish nation. They shall have individual rights to live their own cultural, economic, religious, social, and communal lives, without those government benefits available only to citizens. The state shall limit the number of noncitizens in accordance with security considerations.
4. Those who refuse to accept noncitizen status shall be compensated for property, but not given a bonus, and shall be transferred only to Arab—not Western—lands. The transfer shall be effected peacefully, if possible, but if the Arab still refuses, then forcibly and without compensation. The Arabs who are transferred shall be taken to the Lebanese or Jordanian borders or to the area separating Israel and Egypt.
5. Remaining Arabs who have pledged loyalty to the Jewish state, but who shall subsequently be found guilty of national or security offenses, and all those who knowingly aid such people shall not be imprisoned but shall be deported without compensation.
6. The world Jewish community shall be thoroughly informed on the prob-

lem and especially on the consequences of failing to carry it out. World Jewry shall be asked to mount an emergency campaign to finance the emigration program

7. In the meantime, there shall be a campaign to persuade the Arabs to leave voluntarily. Arabs shall be required to serve for three years in a work corps beginning at the age of eighteen, and for one month every year thereafter. No Arab shall be allowed to study in a university without a declaration of loyalty to the Jewish state.

8. Taxes shall be collected fully from the Arabs of Israel, unlike the present policy which allows a vast amount of tax evasion. Similarly, a firm and vigorous policy will prevent land seizure and illegal building by Arabs.

9. National insurance payments shall be limited to Jews only.

10. There shall be created, within the context of national army service, labor battalions for Jews, which will train them in physical, manual labor and occupational vocations. A campaign to hire Jewish workers shall be given top priority.

The question of the poor and deprived in Israel is one that is loaded with potential for explosion. The desperate problem of young couples unable to find decent housing because of the staggering costs; the pitiful state of education; the lack of schools and centers to impart values and training; the escalating costs of food and all basic items—all add up to a social problem that could erupt into riots and civil war. The *shchunot* ("neighborhoods") are centers of conflict between rich and poor, Sephardim and Ashkenazim. Money is needed for housing, jobs, basic needs. There simply has not been enough money until now.

The transfer of the huge bulk of Arabs from the country will enable the government each year to transfer many billions in funds previously spent on the Arab sector to the impoverished Jewish classes. The left bemoans the fact that there is not enough money for both the poor and the new settlements. Nonsense! The monies that are today spent on Arab national insurance, welfare, schools, health facilities, roads, sanitation, and all the other services can be made available for Jewish needs. Removal of the Arabs will be a giant step toward removal of both enemy and poverty.

There are many benefits. The Arab property—homes, fields, and villages—that will be bought by the government can be made available to young couples under a population-dispersal program, which will be a boon to the country strategically, socially, and economically.

The exodus of the Arabs will put an end to the wholesale seizure of state land, which would then become available for settlements of all kinds.

The exodus of Arab workers, far from being a permanent blow to the economy, will prove a blessing. Because of the availability of plentiful and cheap Arab labor, Jews began to shun manual, physical labor. The result was a sick, unhealthy society in which Jews used and then came to depend on Arabs to do the vital but unsavory tasks without which no society can exist. Not only did the Arabs create a crisis in terms of a dangerous Jewish disdain of physical labor, but as a result Jews stopped working, and this created a critical shortage of Jewish labor. This, in turn, made Arab labor no longer a luxury but a necessity. The reliance on Arab labor is both a national disgrace and a danger. In addition, the hiring of Arab children and women to work for slave wages and in outrageous conditions not only takes jobs from Jews who cannot work for such low wages, but is a moral shame and outrage that corrupts the Jewish character.

In addition, of course, there is the stark fact of growing physical strength on the part of Arabs who do hard manual labor while Jews grow soft. This has led to the attacks on Jews in cities of "mixed" population. And the very fact that factories hire Arabs brings them into the cities, where the incidence of crime and sexual attacks soars.

All this will, of necessity, be changed. When there are no Arab workers, the Jews will be *forced* to work. When there is no choice, Jewish employers will be *forced* to pay decent wages. When there is a national work shortage, the government will be *forced* to adopt an emergency policy of Jewish labor. "Work battalions" will be created within the army or other national service. Every young soldier will be given intensive training in occupational vocations and experience in basic manual labor. No student will be able to graduate high school or enter a university without having spent part of each year giving national service in the form of manual labor.

The removal of the Arabs from the land will throw open the territories as a challenge to world Jewry, especially the young. The opportunity to settle everywhere in the biblical portions of Israel and, thus, truly meet Jewish historic destiny can be presented to them as it has never been until now.

Opponents of Arab emigration call such plans "incitement to revolution." But the truth is that the very existence of the State of Israel already assures that. It is the presence of Jews and Jewish insitutions in East Jerusalem, the government's plans to "Judaize" the Galilee, the very existence of Tel Aviv and an "Israel" in place of a "Palestine," that incite and assure Arab hatred and dreams of revenge.

The idea of transferring Arabs out of Eretz Yisrael is not new. Joseph Weitz of the Jewish National Fund saw the Arab problem clearly and wrote: "It should be clear that there is no room for both peoples to live in the country . . . and in that case there is no alternative to moving the Arabs to the neighboring countries, moving them all, except, perhaps, those living in Bethlehem, Nazareth, and the Old City of Jerusalem. . . . " (Joseph Weitz, *Diaries and Letters to the Children*, Tel Aviv, 1965, p. 181)

Weitz was a strong proponent of the Judaizing of the Galilee and was influenced by veteran Joseph Nahmani of the Jewish National Fund. Nahmani's understanding of the problem is seen in the memorandum sent to Prime Minister Ben-Gurion in January 1953 concerning the problem of the Arabs in the Galilee. "The very existence of a unified Arab group in this part of the country is an invitation to the Arab states to press their claims to the area. . . . When the time comes, it will play the part played by the Germans in Czechoslovakia at the beginning of World War II. . . . "

An angry Professor Ephraim Urbach told a symposium on the Arabs in 1968: "I read an interview with the author Haim Hazaz [one of Israel's most prestigious writers], in which he simplistically suggested solving the problem of the Arabs as follows: the war cost us three billion pounds—let's take three billion more pounds and give them to the Arabs and tell them to get out." (*Midstream*, April 1968) Urbach is a well-known dove. He did not find Hazaz's views, in his words, "edifying." Perhaps not, but Urbach has no answer at all.

In 1937 the British Royal Commission under Lord Peel proposed as a possible solution to the Jewish-Arab conflict the partition of Palestine into a Jewish and an Arab state. As part of this plan the transfer of some 200,000 Arabs from the proposed Jewish state to the Arab one was proposed. A great debate arose in the Zionist movement over this, and especially in the largest of the grounds, the Laborite Mapai. Two of the central figures in the party, who were also among the leading figures in the Zionist movement, came out strongly for the transfer. Berl Katzenelson, ideologician and spokesman, declared: "The question of the transfer of population has aroused controversy: Is it permitted or forbidden? My conscience in this is perfectly clear. A distant neighbor is better than a close enemy. They will not lose by their transfer and we certainly will not. In the last analysis, this is a political reform settlement for the benefit of both sides. For a long time I have felt that this is the best of the solutions, and during the times of trouble I understood even more strongly that one of these days this thing *must* come about. I did not, however, imagine that the transfer 'outside of Eretz Yisrael' would mean to the area of Shechem. I believed and still believe that they will yet move to Syria or Iraq. . . . " (1937)

The other proponent of removal of the Arabs from the proposed Jewish state was the future first prime minister of Israel. On July 29, 1937, David Ben-Gurion said: "If it is possible to move Arabs from village to village to village within the boundaries of the British mandate—it is difficult to find any political or moral reason not to transfer the same Arabs from an area under Jewish rule to one that will be under Arab rule. . . . Even under the maximum moral scruples it is impossible to object to a transfer that guarantees the transferees both satisfactory material conditions and maximum national security. For the Arabs who will be settled in an Arab state, this transfer will be a full and total satisfaction of their national aspirations."

Some of the best-known early Zionist spokesmen discussed the transfer of Arabs. Arthur Ruppin, in May 1911, suggested that the Zionists buy land near Aleppo and Homes in northern Syria for the resettlement of Palestinian Arabs. Both Leo Motzkin and Nahum Sokolow, later to become president of the World Zionist Organization, considered the idea of transfer. The most consistent and persistent advocate of the concept was the Anglo-Jewish writer Israel Zangwill, who sought a state for the Palestine Arabs in Arabia.

There is the beginning of an awakening. In 1972, when I first raised the issue in public in a speech at Haifa University, universal reaction was hotly negative. Prime Minister Golda Meir publicly charged that I had offened the sensibilities of the Arabs, and editorials and columnists vilified me. One of the most bitter attacks was by nationalist "hawk" Moshe Shamir. In 1973 charges of incitement were filed against me when the Jewish Defense League of Israel (Kach) launched a campaign among the Arabs of Israel offering to aid those who wished to emigrate. Not only did Arabs from all over Israel and the territories respond, but an Israeli Arab from the Galilee village of Fasuta, Emanuel Khoury, worked full-time in the region and gathered many names. The lesson to be learned from this is that a sizable number of Arabs would be eager to leave the country for some *Western* state. This should hardly surprise anyone, for are there not many Israeli Jews who happily do the same?

In the years that followed, difficult years for myself and the Kach movement, persistence and determination in the face of arrests and vilification were rewarded. Not only is there a dramatic change in the attitude of the general public vis-à-vis the need to transfer the Arabs, but various personalities have begun to speak out on the subject. To be sure, they have not yet the courage or understanding to call for a compulsory transfer of all Arabs who will not accept conditions of noncitizen residency, and they still speak of "voluntary emigration," but they are beginning to move in the right direction. They are proof of the power of small but determined catalysts.

And so in January 1979 Meir Har-Zion, one of the best-known heroes of the Israeli army, wrote concerning the Arabs: "I do not say we should put them on trucks or kill them. . . . We must create a situation in which for them, it is not worth living here, but rather in Jordan or Saudi or any other Arab state."

Har-Zion was applauded by Israeli's most famous songwriter, Naomi Shemer ("Jerusalem of Gold"), in an article in the Labor newspaper *Davar* (February 9, 1979): "Arab emigration from Israel, if done with mutual respect and positive agreement . . . can be the correct answer."

And during a debate in the Knesset on Arab terrorism in the territories, Likud Knesset member Amnon Linn said (May 18, 1976): "We should begin mass expulsion of entire communities that participated in demonstrations and riots—and transfer them across the border. This is said for women, men, and children."

They are still a minority of public voices and have not yet understood the totality of what must be done or lack the courage to say so. But they have come a long way. Above all, many Israelis, particularly in the Sephardic communities, do understand and will support a policy of Arab transfer under voluntary or compulsory conditions.

In the meantime, life for the Arabs of Israel must cease to be one of avoiding obligations while enjoying material well-being and waiting for demography to put an end to Israel. Life must be made difficult for them as part of a definite campaign to induce them to leave the country.

There must be an end, first of all, to the wholesale evasion of taxes and land laws. There should be set up an efficient governmental office, working with the Border Patrol, to track down every piece of state land that has been the target of squatters. All illegal buildings must be demolished and stiff fines and prison terms levied, but with the possibility of their being waived in return for a promise to emigrate. All state lands that were leased to Arabs under the government's change of policy in the late seventies should have their leases terminated. The "Judaizing" of the Galilee and Triangle should be openly admitted—with all its good and sufficient reasons—and expropriation of land with compensation vigorously executed. The large number of Bedouins and Arabs from Judea-Samaria-Gaza who have illegally entered Israel must be heavily fined and then deported.

In addition, a special tax department working with the police must see that every Arab pays his fair share of taxes—income, value-added, and others. Stiff fines and levies on property should be the punishments, and justice should be swift and sure.

The Arab youth must prepare to serve for three years in a work corps at the age of eighteen, and for a period of a month each year after that, just as his Jewish counterpart serves in the armed forces and national service. The freedom of the Arab from such service enables him to work and save money during the long periods that the Israeli Jew must sacrifice while in national service. This consideration of no national service, little or no taxes, and land seizure is intolerable, and, of course, it goes far to defeat any incentive for the Arab to leave. This must change, as must the present system of university education for the Arab, regardless of his views. The process whereby Jews allow their universities to be production lines and training grounds for the intellectual leaders of the PLO cannot continue. Any Arab who wishes to study at a university will have to pledge his acceptance and support of the Land of Israel as the exclusive and permanent home—of the *Jewish* people. If he is not willing, he has no place in a Jewish university. The government funds that now go to scholarships for Arab students should be shifted to the Jewish Agency, which will give the money to deserving, needy Jews.

Stiff punishments should be exacted on all employers who hire Arab workers for less than the official or going wage. Similar heavy fines and jail sentences should be meted out for hiring young children and for keeping workers in unhealthy and dangerous working conditions. Morally such things are indefensible, and from an economic standpoint they encourage the hiring of Arabs because of the lower expense to the employer. These employers should be encouraged in every way to hire Jews.

And finally, national insurance, which among other things subsidizes the high Arab birthrate, must be transferred to the Jewish Agency, which as a nongovernmental organ will give benefits only to Jews. The process of encouraging the huge Arab birthrate that is designed to put an end to the Jewish state smacks of irrationality.

The goal of a fair and humane transfer of Arabs from Eretz Yisrael, with full compensation and as part of an exchange of populations, will be immeasurably advanced through the ending of conditions that only encourage Israeli Arabs to remain and comfortably wait for their "Palestine" state to replace "Israel." Life must be made difficult and uncomfortable so that emigration will ultimately by the better of the Arab's choices.

The program of Arab transfer will be the target of unprecedented hate and vilification from both inside and outside Israel. Even so, the great obstacle to its success does not lie in the reaction of the Gentiles, but in the anticipated fanatical extremism of its Jewish opponents.

There is a loud and influential contingent of Israeli Jews who would sooner see Israel come to an end as a Jewish state than transfer the Arabs out of the country. They will be joined by large numbers of American Jewish liberals and the Jewish Establishment. These will be driven both by their gentilized, liberal concepts and by fear of the repercussions of such a move for *them* as a minority in the Exile.

Their presence is already noted in their shrill attack on the Jewish settlements and demands for retreat from large sections of the liberated lands. They are essentially non-Zionists, despite their vigorous denials. Their basic tendencies are toward universalism, not nationalism, and their very ties to Jewishness are tempered with guilt as the contradictions between the particularism and separatism of Judaism conflict with nonbarrier universalism and nonsectarian brotherhood. These contradictions have been sorely tested in the past decade over the Arab issue, in any event. The question of transferring Arabs out of the land will drive them to a frenzied condemnation of Israeli policy. Their danger is their influence on large numbers of simple, good American and Western Jews.

The simplistic and demagogic use of labels such as "immoral," "inhumane," "un-Jewish," and "Nazi-like" is likely to find a troubled, sympathetic ear with the ordinary, decent Jew. Thus, we will pay for all the years of deceit and delusions. For all those decades Jewish and Israeli leaders refused to tell the truth about the remedy of the Arab problem in the Land of Israel. They preferred to avoid it and to lie to world Jewry. It is not surprising that any sudden policy that calls for transfer of the Arabs will meet with astonishment and guilt. It is imperative that there begins, *today*, a campaign among world Jewry to explain the full extent of the Arab hatred and danger. The complete truth must be told to the masses of good Jews both to justify the need to remove the Arabs and to expose the dangers of the liberal Establishment bloc.

The Jewish opposition from within—that is the obstacle to successful transfer of Arabs and the saving of the Jewish state. There is no gentile problem, only the Jewish one of self-destruction.

The problem in the Jew who stupidly equates the transfer of Arabs with Hitler's genocide of the Jews, as if we were advocating gas chambers or the killing of the Arabs in any form! As if the separation of Jews and Arabs will not *save* Arab and Jewish lives both! As if it is not precisely the policy of the perverted moralists that will lead eventually to the horrible bloodbath the Jewish realists see all too well!

How outrageously dishonest is the equation. How they cheapen and demean the terrible historical uniqueness and horror of the Holocaust, those intellectual dwarfs who equate it with any event they cannot abide! Did the Jews of Germany say that the land was really theirs, stolen from them by the Germans, and that they would work until the day they became the majority and take the land and make it "Judea"? If they did, the Jews of Hitler's time can be equated with the Arabs. Did the Jews of Europe massacre Germans, rape their women, burn their settlements, and vow to drive them into the sea? If they did, Europe's Jews and Israel's Arabs are the same.

And if they did—if Germany's Jews killed Germans and sought to take their state from them—Germans would have been justified in removing them from Germany and saving their country. But if, as really happened, the Jews sought, not to destroy Germany, not to separate from Germany, not to be independent of Germany, but to be good, loyal, fervent, assimilated Germans, then what the Germans did was horrible, and what the Jews who equate the murderous Arabs with the murdered Jews do *is obscene*. With no apologies, no defensiveness, no hesitation, the Jew rejects with contempt the gentilized Hebrews and the neo-Hellenists. He knows the Jewish response to threats to destroy people and state: "If one comes to slay you, slay him first" (Sandhedrin, 72d). "Do not be overly righteous" (Ecclesiastes 7). "Said Rabbi Shimon ben Lakish: He who becomes merciful unto the cruel is destined to be cruel unto the merciful."

How cruel are the overly righteous, the carriers of perverted morality, the unthinking, *the gentilized*. How many Jewish women and children will die because of the mercy of the overly righteous to the cruel? The foolish children, the twisted adults, all calling in the name of "humanity" for the destruction of the Jewish state—*they* will be the problem, nothing else.

But there are questions: How can we persuade the Arabs to leave? The answer is: We do not come to the Arabs to request, argue, or persuade. The government that comes to power will remember the past and the hopes of the Arabs to repeat it. It will not request. The Arab will be given the choice of accepting noncitizenship and the difficult new conditions that status will entail, of leaving willingly with compensation, or of leaving unwillingly without compensation. He has no other options, and the election of a strong, iron-handed government whose reputation and determination to implement this program at all cost are known to the Arab will keep resistance to a minimum.

There will be a small percentage who will agree to the conditions of the noncitizen resident stranger. They will be mostly elderly people. They will remain. The majority, however, will accept reality. Knowing that eventually they will have to leave in any event, the largest group will accept the compensation, bonus, and hoped-for visa to the West. They will leave willingly. Ideally, the Western nations will be convinced that it is both the most humane thing *and in their own interests* to accept Arabs in their countries.

A decade ago the United States took in more than a quarter of a million refugees from Cuba. It was more than a display of generosity. Having moved to the brink of nuclear war during the Kennedy-Khrushchev confrontation, Washington saw in the growing tension and antigovernment agitation within Cuba a danger that the United States would become involved yet again in a showdown with the Soviets. This time there was not a chance that the Russians would back away, and America was no longer prepared to go to war for principles. The decision was made to take in large numbers of anti-Castro Cubans who might rise up against the government. *It was a political decision intended to defuse a potential time bomb.*

The same lesson should be taught the Western powers in regard to the Middle East. The Israeli government must make strenuous efforts to convince them that if they truly seek peace and tranquillity in the region so as to ensure stability and the orderly flow of oil, the problem of the Arabs within Israel must be solved.

There will be no peace in the region, no matter what agreements are reached with outside Arab governments, if the Arabs remain within the Land of Israel. They must inevitably rise up, forcing the Arab states to come to their aid. Any and all agreements reached between Israel and her neighborrs will be worthless as the region explodes in war. Oil boycotts will be declared as the anger of the Arab world is directed against the West, and the shaky thrones of the pro-Western, feudal Arab monarchs will come crashing down, with all that that implies for the West.

There will be no peace as long as the Arab-Jewish problem festers in Eretz Yisrael, and it is to the vital interests of the Western nations to agree to accept Arab emigrants from Eretz Yisrael. The United States, though theoretically bound by quotas, makes much immigrant policy on an ad hoc basis. In the past quarter-century more than a million refugees from Cuba, Hungary, the Soviet Union, and other countries have been allowed into the United States under the attorney general's "parole" power. Congress has also made exceptions to the law in response to particularly critical events as they have occurred.

The Arabs of Eretz Yisrael are intelligent and good workers, and there is need in the West for those willing to do the important but unsavory jobs that go begging for lack of local hands. In addition, the shortage of skilled workers in particular sections of the economy is acute, and a careful survey by Israel of the peculiar needs of each Western country could lead to a training program for Arabs tailored to specific skills in demand in the West.

There will be those who will refuse to leave willingly. They will be the worst of haters and the most dangerous of the Arabs, those whose transfer is most urgent. Their removal from the country must be accomplished quickly and without hesitation. These Arabs will be transported to the Lebanese or the Hashemite Kingdom of Jordan, which joins all the rest in working toward the elimination of Israel.

"But what will the world say!"

That is the question that makes Jews tremble. What will the world say? They will condemn Israel universally. And today, of course, they love her. . . .

Dear Jew, look about you; listen. The voices you hear and the hate-filled faces you see are those that prove the wisdom of the rabbis who, millennia ago, pronounced: "It is law; know—Essau hates Jacob." The coat of Jew hatred is of many colors, woven in jealousy, produced in deeply ingrained primeval emotions, now stretching from Mexico to Korea. It is a magical coat. It expands to hold people of all colors and creeds; First, Second, Third and Twelfth Worlds; Communists and Nazis; Soviets and Chinese; Vietnamese and Cambodians; Ayotollah Muslims and Vatican Christians. It is an ecumenical miracle, bringing the worst of enemies together under the unifying banner of Jew hatred.

Let those who fear the gentile world's anger and condemnation know that even without this program Israel faces, in the years to come, international hatred, viciousness, and threat such as no nation, not even South Africa, has encountered. *There is nothing Israel can do about this; for the demands of the world are essentially nothing less than the disappearance of Israel. Nothing that Israel does or does not do affects this hatred.* It is a pathological hate that has its roots in the existence of the Jew. If the nations feel that they can, they will move against Israel, no matter how "kind" the Jewish state is to her Arabs. If they understand Israel's fierce determination to use *all* its deadly weapons against whatever enemy dares to come against her, they will limit themselves to raving.

Israel took in the Jews from the Arab lands; it will give them Arabs from the one Jewish land: an exchange of populations; separation for peace.

In the end, let the Jew forever bear in mind two things. *The first is that Israel has no choice.* To sit and allow the Arabs to grow and destroy Israel from within is unthinkable. Let the Jew never forget the utter and complete hatred of the Arabs for Israel and their determination to destroy her. It may take years, decades, centuries—the Arab will wait. He will use every possible means, but he is obsessed. It was always so, from the beginning of Zionism. It is so today. It will be so tomorrow. Remember the voices: *"Today I am in the minority. The state is democratic. Who says that in the year 2,000 we Arabs will still be the minority? . . . Today, I accept the fact that this is a Jewish state with an Arab minority. But when we are the majority I will not accept the fact of a Jewish state with an Arab majority"* (the teacher Na'ama Saud at the Israeli village of Araba).

Is the Jew prepared to sacrifice his only state on the altar of the democracy the Arabs will use to destroy Israel?

And another voice, that of one of the most famous Arab scholars in his classic 1938 work *The Arab Awakening.* Thus wrote "Palestinian" George Antonius: "The logic of facts is unexorable. It shows that no room can be made in Palestine for a second nation except by dislodging or exterminating the nation in possession."

That is what the Arabs believe and have in mind for us. Never. There is no room for a second nation in Eretz Yisrael. The Arabs must leave. We have no choice, for it is either they or the Jews. *It will not be the Jews.*

On the day following the Land Day Rebellion in 1976, *Maariv* reporter Menachem Talmi (April 2, 1976) reported a conversation between two Jews whose cars had been halted near the Arab village of Kfar Kassem by an Arab roadblock. One of the men said that the only way to deal with the Arabs was with force. The other replied that with such an attitude "we will never reach understanding and settlement with the Arabs."

It is instructive to listen to the reply of the first Jew: "Don't worry, my friend, they have no desire at all to reach understanding and settlement with you. What they want is to see you swimming in the sea. They say it openly, but we don't want to hear.

"There were two villages here in the Triangle, Miski and Tira. All the gangs used to come from there to attack the Sharon plain. We wiped Miski off the map but spared Tira. I have no idea why. The members of Kibbutz Ramat Hakovesh, who ate dung because of them as far back as 1936 and later in the War of Independence, pleaded that they should be expelled after they were captured. But no one listened to them. Now the Arabs there 'thank us.' They throw stones at and burn police cars."

This is a simple Jew who understands that there will be no "understanding and settlement," that only the transfer of the Arabs out of the country will save us heartbreak. That it is either they or we. That it cannot and will not be the Jews.

And the second reply to frightened Jews. What has happened to you? Have you forgotten who the Jewish people are? Have you not the slightest idea of the historical destiny and immutability of the State of Israel? Have you become so gentilized that you so utterly forget the G-d of Israel?

THE RISE OF
RELIGIOUS-CHAUVINIST FANATICISM[5]

The predictable cycle of repression, terror, and violence continues to arouse much concern in Israel, particularly among older, more Europe-oriented segments of the population, who recognize all too clearly what is happening. The first warnings came from Professor Yeshayahu Leibovitz, one of Israel's best-known scholars, who has continued to speak out forcefully against the occupation (also against the war in Lebanon), a fact that has won him little praise. Amnon Rubinstein, former Dean of the Tel Aviv University Law School and a Knesset member, describes a series of actions by "extremist and racist elements," including military rabbis, adding that "all ill wind is blowing against the direction of the Zionist vision, against the character of humanistic Judaism, against all that we had wanted Israel to become." "Perhaps the worst sign of this," he adds, "is that it is becoming hard to distinguish between the lunatic fringe and the mainstream of our political life." He describes anti-Arab terror-

[5]By Noam Chomsky, professor of linguistics at the Massachusetts Institute of Technology and writer on political affairs, from his book *The Fateful Triangle: The United States, Israel and the Palestinians*, Boston: South End Press, 1983, pp. 150–156. Copyright © 1983 by Noam Chomsky. Reprinted with permission from the publisher, South End Press.

ism by student leaders at the Hebrew University who threatened the university authorities with violence if they were disciplined, attacks by "unknown cowardly inhabitants of Kiryat Arba [the religious settlement at Hebron] on the house of an Arab widow," the failure of the authorities to react, the refusal of a construction company to rent an apartment in Jerusalem to a Christian couple, the sentiment among youth that the Arabs must be expelled, etc., concluding that "what we are witnessing is not the action of minor and marginal fringe movements." As internal conflict intensified in Israel in the wake of the Lebanon war, Rubinstein—among many others—warned in still clearer terms of the consequences of the "Nazi storm trooper style" of the agents of "criminal violence," now fortified by "a political ideology of violence" with tacit government support and overt support from Gush Emunim Rabbis who publicly "incite to kill Arab civilians."Again he described how right-wing students "use their fists to control the campuses of the Jerusalem and Tel Aviv universities," using "not only fists but clubs and iron chains," and threatening violence if the university were to attempt disciplinary action. "Large areas of Israel are simply closed to anyone who is not from the Likud" because of the violence of the supporters of Begin and Sharon, which they make no attempt to control. Those who oppose the Likud are threatened with murder, or silenced "by shouting, screaming and threats," and are attacked if they attempt to distribute their materials. Perpetrators of overt violence "are rarely caught." He warns of a sorry fate if these tendencies continue.

What Rubinstein and others fear is a virtual civil war, in which elements of a facist character are increasingly visible—a fact that they do not disguise. But quite apart from the scale of the verbal and physical violence and its socioeconomic, ethnic and religious-cultural roots, there are other indications to support Rubinstein's judgment that the "ill wind" is a serious phenomenon, not confined to the lunatic fringe. The Director General of the Israel Broadcasting Authority (radio and television), who "is a long-time admirer of South Africa and a frequent visitor there," wrote an "emotional article" in 1974 expressing his preference for South Africa over Black Africa, complete "with citations of research proving the genetic inferiority of blacks"—a view which"seems to reflect the feelings of many in the Israeli elite." The journal of Mapam (the left-wing of the Labor Alignment) is capable of publishing an explanation of the superiority of Israeli pilots, based on

American research which has "proven" that Blacks (including, apparently, Arabs) are inferior in "complex, cognitive intelligence" (which is why "American Blacks succeed only in short-distance running"). The same journal also devoted 2 full pages to racist idiocies tracing genetic differences between Jews and Gentiles to Abraham, and explaining the alleged cultural ascendance of the U.S. over Europe in terms of the change in the proportion of the Jewish populations. The article begins by noting that "in the atmosphere prevailing today in the Holy Land, everything is possible, even racist doctrine . . . ," but then proceeds to give a rather sympathetic portrayal of the author of the example they provide, letting the interested reader know how to obtain more information. In the Labor Party journal, we read about "genetic experiments" that have shown that "the genetic differences among Jewish communities [Poland and Yemen are cited] are smaller than those between Gentiles and Jews" (the medical correspondent, reporting research conducted at Tel Aviv University), while the Ministry of Education sponsors a creationist congress organized by Orthodox scientist from Ben-Gurion University in which the theory of evolution is dismissed as "speculation," "secular dogma" and "myth" while most of the participating scientists "reaffirmed their belief in divine creation." It is not too surpirsing, then, to discover that Israel's Christian Maronite allies in Lebanon are really Syrian Jews in origin—though it is likely that they lost this status after the Beirut massacres, a few days after this information appeared.

It is, however, primarily in religious circles that such "Khomeinism" (as it is now sometimes characterized in Israel) is to be found. These circles are increasingly influential as a result of the social and demographic processes noted earlier. There also appear to be efforts to support Islamic fundamentalism in the occupied territories in opposition to secular (and hence more dangerous) forms of Palestinian nationalism. Commenting on this phenomenon in both the West Bank and Gaza, Danny Rubinstein observes that the military authorities—who generally clamp down on demonstrations with an iron hand—allowed busloads of "Islamic fanatics" to pass through IDF roadblocks to join demonstrations at Bir Zeit and al-Najah Universities, one sign of their support for Islamic fundamentalism against left and "nationalist" (read: pro-PLO) trends.

"The uniting of religious fanaticism with extremist national-ism is not an unknown phenomenon in Israel in the past few years." Eliahu Salpeter writes, citing as one example the pro-nouncements of a young Rabbi on the "filth" of mixed marriages and the "hybrid children" they produce, "a thorn in the flesh of the Jewish society in Israel" that may become a real catastrophe unless proper measures are taken—he recommends total school segregation and exclusion of Arabs from the universities. The Rabbi denies that he is prejudiced against Arabs, insisting that he has "close Arab friends"—a remark familiar to Jews, Salpeter comments. Salpeter cites other examples of the dangerous reli-gious-nationalist brew: e.g., the failure to find those responsible for the terrorist attack on Arab mayors, the difference in treat-ment of Arabs who throw rocks and religious Jews who stone peo-ple who drive on the Sabbath.

In earlier years, the Rabbinate had cited biblical authority to justify expulsion of the Arabs (a "foreign element") from the land, or simply their destruction, and religious law was invoked to justi-fy killing of civilians in a war or raid. After the 1973 war, the highly-respected Lubavitcher Rabbi (New York) deplored the failure to conquer Damascus. He also warned against abandoning any of the conquered territories, condemning those "who for the sake of miserable money and honors, and especially in order to be well-regarded by the big Goy [Gentile] in Washington, are ready to threaten the security of the Holy Land by giving up terri-tories against the opinions of military experts," which is "against the Jewish Religion. . . . Another American Rabbi (Rabbi Isaac J. Bernstein, who is identified as "spiritual leader of Manhattan's Jewish Center, . . . an executive member of the Rabbinical Council of America and a lecturer in Talmud at Stern College.") explained that the religious law empowers Israel to "dispossess" the Arabs of the conquered territories: "As long as the war which initiated the conquest was conducted under instructions from the Israeli government, who halachicly [by religious law] possesses the same powers as the biblical king, all territories captured as a result of this war belong to Israel." As for "the argument that by not surrendering the territories, we might be heightening the possibility of a future war," this is "not valid" under religious law which "indicates that, on the contrary, we must start a war to pre-vent even the possibility of permanent settlement nearer our bor-ders than heretofore." After Sadat's visit to Jerusalem, a group of leading Rabbis and religious authorities in Israel and the U.S. warned the government that it is "forbidden" to return any territories of the Land of Israel, and the Supreme Rabbinical Council of Israel later reiterated this judgment, citing biblical obligations and religious law.

The chief Rabbis also gave their endorsement to the 1982 invasion of Lebanon, declaring that it conformed to the Halachic (religious) law and that participation in the war "in all its aspects" is a religious duty. The military Rabbinate meanwhile distributed a document to soldiers containing a map of Lebanon with the names of cities replaced by alleged Hebrew names taken from the Bible, along with the explanation that much of Lebanon belonged to the Hebrew tribe of Asher. They also provided a strategic analysis of the Lebanon war under the heading "Joshua son of Nun to the clearing of the nests of the enemies in Lebanon," referring to the biblical account of the conquest of the Land of Canaan—the phrase "clearing the nests of terrorists" is now a standard way of referring to operations against Palestinian vermin. Speaking to soldiers under the auspices of the *hasbara* ("propaganda"; literally, "explanation") officer, a military Rabbi in Lebanon explained the biblical sources that justify "our being here and our opening the war; we do our Jewish religious duty by being here."

Such pronouncements are by no means novel, and since 1973 at least, they have been taken seriously in significant circles. In the mass-circulation journal *Yediot Ahronot* in 1974, Menahem Barash wrote with much admiration about the teachings of Rabbi Moshe Ben-Zion Ushpizai of Ramat-Gan, who used biblical texts and traditional commentary to explain how Israel should deal with the Palestinians, "a plague already written in the Bible." "With a sharp scalpel and convincing logic" the Rabbi uses the writings of the "greatest sages" to elucidate the commandments, still binding today, as to how to "inherit the land" that was promised by God to Abraham. We must follow the doctrines of Joshua, he explains, referring to the genocidal texts that appear in the book of Joshua and elsewhere. "The biblical commandment is to conquer the land of Israel in its detailed borders, to take possession of it and to settle it." It is "forbidden" to "abandon it to strangers" (Gentiles). "There is no place in this land for the people of Israel and for other nations alongside it. The practical meaning of [the commandment to] possess the land is the expulsion of

the peoples who live in it" and who try to prevent the Jews of the
world from "settling in our land."It is "a holy war, commanded
in the Bible," and it must be fought against Palestinians, Syrians,
Egyptians "or any other people in the world" who seek to block
the divine commandment. There can be no compromises, no
peace treaties, no negotiations with "the peoples who inhabit the
land." "You shall destroy them, you shall enter into no covenant
with them, you shall not pity them, you shall not intermarry with
them," the divine law dictates. Whoever stands in our way must
be annihilated, the Rabbi continues with his "convincing logic,"
citing numerous traditional authorities. All of this is reported
quite seriously, and with much respect.

After the Beirut massacres of September 1982 there was a renewed outpouring of militant support for the war in religious circles. The influential Gush Emunim group, which spearheads
West Bank settlement, published a statement praising Begin,
Sharon, and Chief of Staff Rafael Eitan, describing the war as a
"great act of sanctification of God's name." The statement also
spoke of "the return of the territory of the tribes of Naftali and
Asher to the boundaries of Israel," and of Israel's "responsibility
to act to the limits of its ability to destroy the foundations of evil
in the entire world." Two months before, Rabbi Elazar Valdman
of Gush Emunim wrote in the journal *Nekudah* of the religious
West Bank settlers:

We will certainly establish order in the Middle East and in the world. And
if we do not take this responsibility upon ourselves, we are sinners, not
just towards ourselves but towards the entire world. For who can establish
order in the world? All of those western leaders of weak character?

In Israel, one does not take pronouncements of Gush
Emunim lightly. Their influence has been considerable, and they
have regularly created policy (with state support) by their actions
in the occupied territories. This statement therefore caused some
consternation. One of the founders of the movement, Yehuda
Ben-Meir, sharply denounced it, stating that "according to Gush
Emunim, we must conquer not only Syria and Turkey but with
the blood of our children we must become the guardian of the
entire world." It may seem odd that such ludicrous pronouncements are taken seriously, but in the current atmosphere of
spreading "Khomeinism" among significant circles of the fourth
greatest military power in the world, they cannot be disregarded,
and are not, by serious Israeli commentators. We return to further indications of this grandiose self-image, and its implications.

Those who really deserve the name "supporters of Israel" will not be unconcerned over such developments. Within Israel itself, they have often led to near despair. Boaz Evron writes that "the true symbol of the state is no longer the Menorah with seven candlesticks; the true symbol is the fist." In conformity with his judgment, when West Beirut was invaded, IDF Chief of Staff Rafael Eitan announced:

What must be destroyed—we will destroy. Whoever must be imprisoned—we will imprison.

Aharon Meged writes of his sadness with regard to "the new 'Zionist mentality'," which is coming to reign and "cannot be stopped": "the age of military Zionism." "The old fear of a 'Sparta'—is changing to fear of a 'Prussia'." Like Danny Rubinstein (see note 172), he is much concerned over the ravings of Rabbi Valdman, and offers the hope that return of the territories can still overcome this fate, citing Chief Sephardic Rabbi Ovadiah Yoseph, who agreed that return of territories is legitimate if it would lead to peace. It may incidentally be noted that his Ashkenazi counterpart, Chief Rabbi Shlomo Goren, drew the opposite conclusion from religious law, holding that retaining "Judea and Samaria" takes precedence over the religious duty to save life ("pikuach nefesh"). He "rejects categorically" the idea that achievement of peace would justify territorial compromise. The example once again illustrates the fact that one should be rather cautious in contrasting Ashkenazi doves with Sephardi hawks.

IV. NO WAY OUT? THE PALESTINIAN INTIFADA AND THE TRIUMPH OF THE ISRAELI RIGHT

EDITOR'S INTRODUCTION

The Palestinian intifada, or national uprising, which began in late 1987 and, as of early 1989, showed few signs of abating, was, in the opinion of many observers, whether or not sympathetic to its aims, a long overdue event. Day after day, then month after month, young Palestinian men and women, unarmed except for stones, risked their lives in confronting the heavily armed brutality of the Israeli Defense Forces. Though they did not prevail, they forced both sides to reappraise their positions. The Palestinians realized with a shock that thenceforth their own liberation was up to no one but them: Arab armies were of no further use to them, nor were the PLO commandos in Beirut or Tunis; they had at last to fight their own battles against their oppressors, and in doing so they energized their people. For the Israelis, celebrating their state's fortieth anniversary in the spring of 1988, the shock of the intifada was even greater: After decades of occupation and the resigned expectation in many quarters that the unfortunate occupation would somehow just have to go on forever, supporters of the Jewish state realized that the hundreds of thousands of subject people within and about their borders had aspirations the urgency of which could no longer be ignored or denied. Official Israeli response to the uprising was disorganized, even bewildered, but never less than savage: the IDF, trained for fighting wars, not for controlling unruly civilians, were ordered at various times to beat the demonstrators, not to shoot them, then to break their limbs so they could not throw rocks, then after all to shoot them with plastic bullets; plans were announced or deployed to deport the Palestinians or to bribe them to leave, to close their schools, to knock down even more of their houses, and to lock up their parents. Hundreds of Palestinians were killed outright, thousands were injured or permanently maimed, thousands more were interned in concentration camps without trial. None of these measures had the slightest effect on the intifada, whose time, evidently, had come with a vengeance.

At the same time, the Likud-Labor coalition government was coming to its natural end: Israel faced a momentous general election at the end of 1988. Early indications pointed to a Likud victory, which would entail more official truculence with regard to Palestinian rights, even less chance of a negotiated peace with the surrounding Arab states, and a renewal of unrestricted settlement by Zionists throughout the occupied territories. The election result, however, was a virtual reprise of 1984—a dead heat between the main contenders. Continuation of the Likud-Labor coalition, which was agreed upon in December, will probably involve four more years of stalemate over the question of the occupied territories. The U.S. decision in mid-December to open negotiations with the P.L.O.—recognizing Yasir Arafat as the chief spokesman for the Palestinians—angered the Israeli government. The tortuous road to reconciliation, to the realization, finally, of the Palestinians' hopes as a nation and a people, seemed just as impassable as ever.

In the first article of this section, Henry Cattan, a Palestinian international lawyer and one of his people's most articulate defenders, looks at the future of the conflict. He argues that the very survival of Israel itself depends on the recognition and redressment of the wrongs committed against the Palestinians. Simha Flapan, an internationally respected member of the "Israeli peace camp," as he calls it, attempts in the second article to clarify "the distorted vision on our side" of the conflict. In the third article Joseph M. Hochstein, an American journalist resident in Israel, presents a comprehensive overview of the first few months of the Palestinian intifada, with glances back to the sources of the intensified conflict and forward to the absolute necessity for some form of solution. Note is taken here, in particular, of the impossible demands made upon the normally well-disciplined IDF, ordered to behave as riot police in its own land. Anton Shammas, an Israeli-Palestinian writer, anticipates in the last article his reaction to the creation of a Palestinian state, describing also the toll on the Israeli psyche of a year of intifada.

THE FUTURE[1]

What does the future hold in store for Palestine and the Middle East? In this connection, the future needs to be viewed in terms of decades rather than years. Much of the future can be foreseen in the light of past and present events. What lessons can be learnt from them?

> *The Creation of Israel Was a Historical*
> *Anachronism as well as an International*
> *Wrong Which Has Caused*
> *a Dangerous Upheaval in the Middle East*

No vision of the future can ignore certain tragic facts: the grave error of the Balfour Declaration, the forcing of a massive Jewish immigration on Palestine against the will of its inhabitants, the illegality and injustice of the UN partition resolution, the illegitimate creation of Israel, its usurpation of Palestine and its uprooting of its inhabitants. Nahum Goldmann, late President of the World Jewish Congress and of the World Zionist Organization (and hence by definition not an anti-Semite) wrote:

The Zionist demand for a Jewish state was in full contradiction with all principles of modern history and international law.

Can there be any doubt that to establish a Jewish State in a country which was exclusively Arab for at least 1800 years, to drive out its inhabitants and to usurp their homeland constitutes anything but an international wrong and a great injustice which can only lead to conflict and catastrophe as has happened since 1948?

In addition to the havoc wreaked on Palestine and its inhabitants, Israel also wreaked havoc on the Middle East generally. It was the cause of the five wars of 1948, 1956, 1967, 1973 and 1982 in the region. Each of Israel's neighbours has also suffered from its aggressions: Lebanon's territorial and political unity were shattered by Israeli intrigues, bombings of Palestine refugee camps and invasions; Jordan had to bear the burden of a million

---

[1]By Henry Cattan, Paris-based Palestinian international lawyer, from his book *The Palestine Question*, London: Croom Helm, pp. 353–365. Copyright © 1988 Henry Cattan. Reprinted by permission from Croom Helm.

Palestinian refugees; a part of Syria's territory was occupied and annexed; as to Egypt, Sinai was occupied for a number of years and was evacuated only after Egypt agreed to a peace treaty which Israel imposed upon it during the military occupation of its territory.

Thus, to the Palestine Question, Israel has added two other major problems: the Arab-Israeli conflict with its neighbours and a still wider conflict with the Islamic world that resulted from its occupation and annexation of Jerusalem and its Holy Places.

All those developments weigh heavily on the future and portend more tragedy.

Israeli Illusions

Having seized the whole of Palestine in a way that exceeded the most optimistic expectations of Zionism and having succeeded in evicting the majority of its inhabitants, the Israelis are determined to retain it as their own perpetual possession at whatever cost and by whatever means. This is the policy of the two main political parties in Israel, both Labour and Likud, subject to a minor difference, namely that Labour would return a morsel of the West Bank to Jordan against a peace treaty. They both equally and firmly reject the repatriation of the Palestine refugees, the restitution of their homes, the establishment of the Arab State envisaged by the UN and the implementation of the UN resolutions generally.

Israel's attitude rests upon a number of illusions. It expects that the Palestine Question will evaporate with time, or that it can be treated as a simple refugee problem, or can be settled by a *Pax Hebraica*, such as Security Council resolution 242 or the Camp David formula for 'autonomy'. Israel believes it can, with Jewish and Zionist control over the media, continue to fashion and to warp public opinion in its favour as it has succeeded in doing until now. It is confident that with American support and a strong army and air force, equipped with the most advanced weapons, it can resist redress of the wrongs done in Palestine and maintain peace by force of arms and that by means of the Israeli lobby it can continue to exert its influence upon US policy in the Middle East.

Amnon Kapeliouk, an Israeli journalist, devoted a book to the discussion of Israeli illusions about the Arab-Israeli conflict.

Among those illusions, he cites the following which have become maxims of Israeli policy: "We shall maintain the status quo in the region as long as we desire"; "The Arabs understand only the language of force"; "War is not a game which is known to the Arabs"; "The Arab world is divided and without military perspectives"; "The Palestinians in the occupied territories will resign themselves to their fate"; "Time is in our favour"; "It does not much matter what the Gentiles say, what counts is what the Jews do." The pursuit of such illusions has prevented a serious approach to a settlement. It is likely that Israel will abandon such illusions in the future?

Palestinian Illusions

It is not only the Israelis who harbour illusions about the future; the Palestinians also have illusions. The Palestinians have relied and still rely on the UN to resolve the Palestine Question, on the Arab states, on world opinion and on the principles of justice and international law. Will they continue to harbour these illusions in the future?

It is noteworthy that the illusions of the parties are quite the antithesis of each other: the illusions of the Palestinians seek to obtain redress on the basis of the principles of right and justice while the illusions of the Israelis aim at maintaining their territorial gains and preventing redress through recourse to force and even to nuclear deterrence.

NUCLEAR MENACE

Israeli illusions are not just fanciful for Israel has built up, with American help and money, one of the most formidably equipped armies in the Middle East. In addition, not content with the possession of coventional and most sophisticated weapons, it has also manufactured atomic bombs. Although for a number of years Israel was suspected of manufacturing atomic bombs at Dimona in the Negeb Desert, its activities in this regard were concealed and protected by deceit and a strict censorship. On 5 and 12 October 1986, the *Sunday Times* revealed the secret operation and its magnitude. According to this newspaper's account, the underground plant was established in 1957 with the assistance of the French Atomic Commission and Israel is in possession today of 100 to 200 nuclear weapons, ranking as the world's sixth nuclear power. Moreover, it is presently producing 40 kilogrammes of plutonium a year, enough to make 10 bombs annually. The Israeli technician who made these disclosures, Mordechai Vanunu, was kidnapped by the Israeli secret services and brought to Israel where he was put on trial.

Whether the disclosure of Israeli nuclear activities despite strict censorship was a deliberate leak on the part of Israel to inspire fear and terror among the Arabs cannot be guessed. Israel always maintained that it would not be the first state to introduce nuclear weapons in the Middle East. This is clear deception. The manufacturing of nuclear weapons is dangerous to Israel itself for it will incite other states in the region to do the same, thereby putting its own heavily concentrated population at great risk in case of armed conflict.

An unrestrained Israel in possession of a nuclear potential also constitutes a danger to world peace. Unlike those cases where the Arab-Israeli conflict almost caused a nuclear confrontation between the superpowers, as in 1956 and 1973, now Israel is capable of triggering an independent nuclear attack against its neighbours which may lead to the Third World War. Israel has steadfastly rejected any control by the IAEA (International Atomic Energy Agency) despite the Security Council's directive in its resolution 487 of 7 June 1981 condemning Israel for its raid on the Iraqi nuclear rector at Baghdad. In that resolution the Security Council called upon Israel urgently to place its nuclear facilities under IAEA safeguards, but Israel has not complied. On 12 December 1985 the General Assembly similarly noted in its resolution 40/93 Israel's persistent refusal to commit itself not to manufacture or acquire nuclear weapons and to place its nuclear facilities under International Atomic energy safeguards. It pointed out the grave consequences that endanger international peace and security as a result of Israel's development and acquisition of nuclear weapons and Israel's collaboration with South Africa to develop nuclear weapons and their delivery systems. The General Assembly reiterated its condemnation of Israel's refusal to renounce possession of nuclear weapons, requested the Security Council to take effective measures to ensure Israel's compliance with its resolution 487 of 1981 and reaffirmed its condemnation of continuing collaboration between Israel and South Africa regarding nuclear weapons. It may be observed that the only two states that voted against this General Assembly resolution were Israel and the US which means that the nuclear menace hangs ominously over the Middle East.

In addition to its massive and advanced weaponry and its nuclear capability, Israel pursues the policy of not allowing any Arab state to acquire arms that might threaten or compete with its military power. Thus it has often succeeded, through its influence in the US Congress, to block the sale of arms by the US to Arab countries. Moreover, it has succeeded, by means of the Camp David Accords as well as by American pressure and financial persuasion, in neutralizing Egypt, the strongest Arab power and in removing it from the Arab-Israeli equation. It is now looking for a pretext to knock out Syria from the Middle Eastern chessboard. As for Jordan, it is incessantly manoeuvering to tempt it out from the Arab-Israeli conflict by giving it a morsel of the West Bank. This state of things contains the roots of one or more future wars. Israeli military power coupled with American support portend more tragedy for the Middle East and are not conducive to a settlement of the Palestine Question.

Ironically, despite Israeli military power, one writer observes "that the most dangerous spot in the world for a sizable Jewish community is Israel."

Israel's Disintegration

Although Israel is at the peak of military power and despite the success of its expansionist Zionist programme one cannot help but observe signs of the disintegration of Israel's artificial structure.

Economically, Israel lives on American loans, grants and other financial help. It has the highest foreign debt per capita in the world and requires several billion dollars each year as assistance from the US Government. Without US economic assistance, Israel would collapse.

Politically, its artificial organic structure is cracking as a result of its latent internal struggle between secular and religious Jews and also in consequence of the emigration of its citizens in large numbers. Several hundred thousand Israelis (estimated to be in excess of half a million) have departed and still depart as visitors to the USA and remain there. General Matti Peled wrote in *Hadashot* (3 December 1985) about emigration from Israel:

Last year alone over 96,000 people left without returning. At the same time, only slightly over 17,000 people immigrated formally to this country. . . . The government is feeling powerless in the face of the scale of immigration and rightly so, for emigration figures show a lack of confidence in Israel's future.

Israel has resorted to desperate expedients to secure Jewish immigrants. We have seen how it used its agents to blow up synagogues in Iraq in the 1950s to frighten the ancient and prosperous Jewish community established there for centuries and induce it to move to Israel. It then induced several hundred thousand Jews to emigrate from Egypt, Yemen, Syria, Morocco and Lebanon in which countries they had been living for centuries in security, ease and comfort. When the emigration of Jews from Arab countries came to an end, Israel concentrated on securing the emigration of Jews from the Soviet Union. This move yielded a few hundred thousand immigrants in the 1970s reaching a peak of 51,330 in 1979. Since then the emigration of Soviet Jews to Israel has declined sharply and was reduced to a trickle. Thereupon, Israel mounted a virulent campaign against the Soviet Union charging it with violation of human rights for not permitting a free and unimpeded emigration of its Jewish citizens to Israel. It should be noted, however, that Russian Jews willing or permitted to leave the Soviet Union prefer to go to America rather than to Israel. Yet despite such preference, the Zionists persist in organizing "demonstrations to improve the situation of the Jews in the Soviet Union whereas the real aim is to find immigrants for the Zionist state." In this connection, it is fitting to observe that, in contrast to its campaign for the emigration of Russian Jews, Israel does not consider that its denial of the repatriation of the Palestinians to their *own* homes constitutes a more serious violation of their human rights that the alleged violation of the human rights of Soviet Jews to emigrate out of their own country.

It is relevant to observe that in view of the preference shown by Soviet Jews to go to the US rather than to Israel, the Israeli government urged the US to stop giving special refugee status to Jews emigrating from the Soviet Union so as to force them to proceed to Israel. But the Jewish organizations in the US objected and the American government turned down such a proposal.

In its quest for immigrants Israel turned to the "importation" of Ethiopian Falashas. The American *Naturei Karta* (a Jewish orthodox group) stated recently:

In the 1920s and 1930s when Jewish Americans called for Jews to help the Falashas in Ethiopia, the Zionists emphasized that this was not of interest to them. Now that for the past few years they have run out of Russian Jewish emigrants, the colored Falashas were suddenly one of the main objectives of their support.

In 1984 over 10,000 Falashas were transported to Israel by an airlift at considerable cost to the American taxpayer, but to their distress the Falashas—who consider themselves to be Jews of the earliest times—found on arrival that the Israel Chief Rabbis insisted that they were not authentic Jews but should be "converted" to Judaism.

Israel Rejects Coexistence with the Palestinians

A peaceful future in Palestine by necessity requires coexistence between Arabs and Jews. The Zionist Jews, however, emigrated to Palestine, not to coexist with the original inhabitants, but in order to displace them. This is what they have done and are still bent on doing in the future. Israel's rejection of coexistence with the Palestinians applies both to the creation of a Palestinian state and to living with them as individuals.

Israel is not only hostile to the creation of a Palestinian State by its side in accordance with the UN partition resolution, but it has repeatedly declared that it will prevent its establishment by force of arms.In consequence, it is unwilling to evacuate the territory of the Arab State which it occupied in 1948 and in 1967. Moreover, Israel is unwilling to coexist with the Palestinians as individuals, whether in the territory of Palestine which it calls Israel or in the West Bank and Gaza. Official Israeli policy excludes and resists the repatriation of the Palestine refugees. As to the Palestinians who live under Israeli control they are subject to racist and apartheid practices. These practices, coupled with the anti-Arab education and even the hatred against the Palestinians which is disseminated in religious schools and in the army are incompatible with coexistence with the Palestinian Arabs.

The problem of coexistence is a grave one for the future. Regardless of what constitutional and structural changes would be effected in the State of Israel following the reappraisal of the Palestine Question and the partition resolution, the fact remains that—excluding those Jews who are openly racists or are known to have been responsible for Arab massacres and who should be returned to their country of origin—Jews and Arabs will have to coexist together, whether in one state or in two states. The Palestinians have shown generosity in accepting that the Jews who came as immigrants against their wishes during the British mandate would continue to live with them and enjoy equal rights. On their part, the Israelis have not displayed an equal readiness to coexist with the Palestinians and to recognize their enjoyment of equal rights but, on the contrary, they have manifested, at least in certain quarters, a desire to expel the remaining Palestinians from their own country.

Expulsion is considered by some Israelis as the solution for the increase in the Arab population that would result from Israel's annexation of the West Bank and Gaza. This is the consequence of the organic contradiction between Zionism and Palestinian national rights.

Is the Situation Irreversible?

Influenced by the creation of Israeli settlements in the West Bank and Gaza, Meron Benvenisti, an Israeli land expert, suggests that the situation is irreversible and will inevitably evolve into annexation by Israel of the territories occupied in 1967. Meron Benvenisti further states that if these territories were annexed, the number of Arabs under Israeli rule in the occupied territories and in Israel would reach 38 per cent of the total population and hence "a new equilibrium" is needed. Benvenisti gives no indication as to what "the new equilibrium" would involve. Is it the expulsion of the Palestinians? Some estimate that in the year 2000 the Palestinians would, by reason of their higher birthrate, become the majority of the population. As to Benvenisti's argument that the situation is irreversible, this was rejected by Uri Avnery, Israeli author and politician, in regard to the whole Palestine Question, and not simply in regard to the problem of settlements in the West Bank. Avnery referred to the disappearance from Palestine of the first two Jewish kingdoms as well as of the Crusaders' Latin Kingdom of Jerusalem which had lasted some 200 years and said: "Nothing is irreversible, not even our national existence in this country."

A Peaceful Future Depends on Change
of Zionist Ideology

Jews and Arabs lived in peace for centuries and the Jews found in the Arab and Islamic world a place of refuge from persection by Christians in Europe. This historic harmony was destroyed in the twentieth century by the emergence of political Zionism, its territorial ambitions in Palestine and its creation of a militant State of Israel which has usurped an Arab country and uprooted its traditional population. If peace between Arabs and Jews in Palestine is to be restored, it is essential that certain facts and trends are reversed.

Peace in the future largely depends less upon military considerations than upon psychological factors which would require a basic and radical modification of Zionist ideology, the abandonment of the Zionist plan to possess Palestine to the exclusion of its original inhabitants and a willingness to coexist with them. True peace is not that which is imposed on the battlefield: true peace must exist in the minds and in the hearts. Are the Israelis prepared to give up Zionism and accept coexistence with the Palestinians?

No Future for the Israelis
without Peace with the Arabs

The Israelis cannot hope to usurp Palestine, to uproot and expel its inhabitants, to pillage their homes and to live thereafter in peace. This is perceived by leading Zionists. "Israel has no long-term future without accord with the Arabs," said Nahum Goldmann, late President of the World Jewish Congress. He also quoted Ben Gurion's statement to him in 1956 that "in ten years, fifteen years, I believe there will still be a Jewish state, but (thereafter) the chance of there being a Jewish state would be fifty-fifty." Nahum Goldmann thought that

the Zionist idea is thoroughly irrational: for a people to return to its former lands after two thousand years' absence goes against all reason. If Zionism had been rational it would have had to find another, more or less empty, country, which is what the great English writer Israel Zangwill advocated.

He continued

It is utterly simple-minded to believe that in the end the Arabs will forget our presence in Palestine. . . . They have proved that they will prolong the war until they regain their lands. So this whole policy of the *fait accompli* represents an enormous waste. . . . There is no hope for a Jewish state which has to face another fifty years of struggle against Arab enemies. How many will there be, fifty years from now.

A keen political observer, Lord Mayhew writing in *Middle East International* (17 May 1985) states:

If Israel continues in its present path, relying solely on military firepower and the Washington lobby, its survival as a sovereign Jewish state into the next century seems problematical.

Is Peace between the Palestinians and Israel Conceivable?

The argument is made that the French and German peoples fought three wars in the space of 70 years and yet they have now made peace and are good friends. Why cannot the Palestinians and the Israelis do the same? The answer is that three exists no possible similarity between the two cases. In the Franco-German conflict, each of the two peoples remained in its homeland at the end of each war, with the exception of Alsace-Lorraine which Germany seized in 1870. And the conflict was settled only after the return of Alsace-Lorraine to France. In the Palestinian-Israeli conflict an alien people came to Palestine from the four corners of the world under the protection of British bayonets, forced the Palestinians out of their homeland and took over their homes, their lands and their country. In such circumstances, is peace conceivable unless the Palestinians regain their homes, their lands and their country?

Peace Must Rest on Justice

Peace between the Palestinians and the Israelis is conceivable only on one condition: it must rest on justice. Such a necessary and indispensable condition is absent from the so-called "peace process" that has been pursued during the last few years by the US and Israel which, by the false illusions it creates, has done more harm than good by preventing the deployment of efforts for a just peace.

There exist a small well-meaning groups of Israelis who advocate peace with the Palestinians on terms of Israel's evacuation of the West Bank and Gaza and the creation of a Palestinian State in the evacuated territory. They argue that "half a loaf is better than nothing." But is the giving back of one-fifth of the loaf to one-fifth of the Palestinians a just solution for the theft of Palestine?

Israel Shahak, Professor at the Hebrew University of Jerusalem, stated in one of his periodical publications that:

there is a great dividing line between those who merely want peace, and those who are devoted to justice first. Those who put the emphasis on peace forget that peace which is not based on justice will not be easy to achieve, and even if achieved will not endure.

Other Jewish intellectuals have underscored the concept of justice as an indispensable condition for peace.

Judah L. Magnes, the late Rector of the Hebrew University in Jerusalem, said:

But, as far as I am concerned, I am not ready to achieve justice to the Jew through injustice to the Arab. . . . I would regard it as an injustice to the Arabs to put them under Jewish rule without their consent.

Albert Einstein also declared:

I should much rather see reasonable agreement with the Arabs on the basis of living together in peace than the creation of a Jewish state.

The attempt to establish peace without justice is like building a house on foundations of sand: it will not endure.

Realpolitik *v. Justice*

The peace plan suggested, namely the reappraisal of the Palestine Question, the reconsideration of the partition resolution of 1947 and the implementation of relevant UN resolutions concerning certain basic rights of the Palestinians constitutes a political and peaceful solution based on right and justice. Some critics may consider that it deviates from *realpolitik* which, in their view, has replaced the principles of justice and international law contained in the UN Charter and, according to their argument, should be taken as the criterion for resolving the Arab-Israeli conflict. According to such critics, to expect that Israel, which possesses a most powerful army and enjoys the massive support of one of the superpowers, would accept a reversal of the existing situation on the basis of right and justice is unrealistic and utopian. The answer to such criticism is that the suggested plan offers a viable and logical solution and constitutes the only road to peace because maintenance of the present situation can only lead to catastrophe. Moreover, the suggested plan is less unrealistic and less utopian than the attempt to settle the problem by chimeric means, such as Security Council resolution 242 or the Camp David Accords.

Facing Realities and Wasting a Chance of Survival

The Israelis should face realities: they have wrongfully taken the country of another people, their homes and their lands; they have displaced them by force and terror; such a situation is unnatural and calls for redress. It cannot in the long term be maintained by force of arms because a wrong done to a people by force of arms can be undone also by force of arms.

Until the middle of this century Israel was a Zionist dream. Today it is a nightmare. Its leaders and most Israelis are intoxicated. They are intoxicated with their military victories, with their superiority in armaments, with the massive aid which they receive from one superpower, and above all with their seizure of Palestine and their resurrection of a Jewish state after 25 centuries.

Actually the Israelis do not realize that they live in a fool's paradise if they imagine that five million Palestinians will ever accept the usurpation of their homeland and the theft of all that they own, that over one hundred and fifty million Arabs will forget Palestine and the Palestinians, and that eight hundred million Moslems will abandon to Israel Jerusalem and their Holy Places.

The Israelis have today a choice between peace with justice or perpetual war. By opting for the latter, they may be wasting their chance of survival.

CONCLUSION[2]

My efforts to undermine the propaganda structures surrounding the War of Independence and its aftermath have been motivated not only by a penchant for accuracy and a desire to correct the record but by the relevance of the myths to the present-day situation in Israel. The Labor party and Likud, despite the historical rivalry of their political conceptions within the Zionist movement, have joined together in a "national unity" government that controls up to 90 seats in the 120-seat Knesset. Their union is based not on any consensus about the fundamental problems facing Israel—the continuation of the peace process and the future of the occupied territories—but, rather, on the removal of these problems from the national agenda. Yet clear-cut decisions on these issues cannot be postponed for long.

A choice will have to be made between pursuing the goal of a Greater Israel—which means the annexation of the territories occupied since 1967, continued rule over an unwilling subject population, and increased military activism—and meeting the basic economic, social, and educational needs of the society and preserving its democratic character. Maintaining the status quo can only increase the already devastating polarization of Israel society along with the resulting tensions and conflicts, and erode the moral and ethical values from which Israel traditionally drew its strength. It is clear that the liberal, humanist, and socialist elements that aspire to peace and coexistence with the Palestinians and the rest of the Arab world face a difficult struggle with the ever-growing ethnocentric, militaristic, fundamentalist camp, for whom power and territory are primary objectives, to be achieved, if necessary, by the continued oppression and subjugation of the Palestinian people.

In this struggle, ideology plays a primary role. Menahem Begin justified his invasion of Lebanon in 1982 with the argument

[2]By Simha Flapan (1911–1987), National Secretary (1954–1981) of Israel's Mapam Party and director of its Arab Affairs department, founder-editor of the monthly *New Outlook*, and founder-director of the Jewish-Arab Institute and the Israeli Peace Institute. From his book *The Birth of Israel: Myths and Realities*, New York: Pantheon Books, pp. 233–243. Copyright © 1987 by Simha Flapan. Reprinted by permission of Pantheon Books, a Division of Random House, Inc.

of "historical continuity," referring to Ben-Gurion's policies in 1948. Labor, on the other hand, presents Ben-Gurion's ideas and strategies as the other alternative to Likud's concept of a Greater Israel, pointing out that he totally rejected rule over another people and was unconditionally committed to the perservation of the Jewish and democratic character of the state. As I acknowledged at the outset of this study, an analysis of Ben-Gurion's concepts and strategies during the most crucial and traumatic period in Jewish-Arab relations is not, therefore, a mere academic exercise, and Begin's claim cannot be ignored. Indeed, in spite of the fundamental differences between the two wars and their objectives, the War of Independence (to be exact, its first stage, from November 1947 to May 1948) and the Lebanon War have many features in common that differentiate them from the other Israeli-Arab wars.

The first is the identity of the enemy: the Palestinian people, who claimed the right to independence and statehood in Palestine. In both cases Israel's aim was to thwart such possibilities and eliminate any Palestinian leadership struggling to attain those rights. In 1948 this was achieved by a tactical agreement with King Abdallah, who furthered Israel's aims insofar as he wanted to liquidate the mufti-dominated Arab Higher Committee and annex the West Bank to Transjordan. In 1982 Begin attempted to do the same by liquidating the PLO in Lebanon—seen as the major obstacle to Israeli annexation of the West Bank and to the creation of a collaborationist Arab leadership there that would accept a miserly autonomy, deprived of legislative powers and the right to self-determination.

The second feature the two wars share is that in both instances the Israeli army confronted not only soldiers but a civilian population. True, in the wars of 1956, 1967, and 1973, the civilian populations, especially the Arabs along the Suez Canal and in the Golan Heights, suffered from bombing and shelling, and hundreds of thousands became refugees, but the Israel Defense Forces confronted only regular Arab armies. In 1948 and 1982, on the other hand, Israeli soldiers had to shell villages, blow up houses, schools, and mosques (killing innocent men, women, and children), and detain "able-bodied" men or drive them from their homes into forced exile.

These parallels reveal yet others. In 1948, the Palestinians did not have an army. Their struggle was carried out by scattered

groups of volunteers, mobilized by local leaders or by commanders appointed by the Arab League. In 1982, the PLO did not
have an army either, only arsenals of weapons and fighting units
trained by different political organizations for infiltration, sabotage, and guerrilla warfare. In 1948, the eradication of the Palestinian fighting groups was planned and executed by the
destruction of villages and towns; in 1982, by the destruction of
the refugee camps that served as their bases. In 1948 about 360
Arab villages and 14 towns within the borders of Israel were destroyed and their inhabitants forced to flee. In 1982, the order
given to the Israeli army to liquidate the "terrorist organizations"
in Lebanon meant the destruction of refugee camps and urban
suburbs with a Palestinian population, though the members of
the organizations were also the leaders of the Palestinian communities, their hospitals, schools, workshops, and social and cultural
societies.

In such circumstances, the dehumanization of the Israeli soldiers was inevitable, leading to brutal behavior and violation of
elementary human rights. In a society like Israel's, which claims
the deep sense of justice and respect for life inherent in Judaism,
the erosion of these moral values could not be admitted without
a significant rationalization. In both cases, therefore, the enemy
had to be dehumanized as well. Thus Ben-Gurion described the
Arabs as "the pupils and even the teachers of Hitler, who claim
that there is only one way to solve the Jewish question—one way
only: total annihilation." For his part, Begin described the PLO
fighters as "two-legged animals" and justified the terrible suffering caused by the siege of Beirut by comparing the attacks on
Yasser Arafat's last stronghold in the city to the Allied bombing
of Berlin, aimed at destroying Hitler's bunker.

There was in 1948, as in Israel today, a basic "philosophy of
expulsion." Today it is expressed in the racist ideology of the rab-
ble-rousing rabbi Meir Kahane, with his anti-Arab provocations.
In 1947 and 1948 it was couched in the seemingly more benign
conception of a homogeneous Jewish state struggling for survival.
The man who, with Ben-Gurion's approval, launched a campaign
to persuade the Palestinians to lock their homes, sell their land,
and immigrate, with compensation, to other countries, was the director of the colonization department of the Jewish National
Fund, Joseph Weitz. Weitz did not employ theocratic, racist slo-
gans or propose the abolition of democracy, as does Kahane to-

day. But he and Ben-Gurion did not refrain from harassment by a Military Administration claiming security considerations, and ultimately their aim was the same: a homogeneous Jewish state in all or most of Palestine.

Indeed, it was under Ben-Gurion's leadership in the crucial years 1947 to 1949 that the planks in Zionism's traditional Arab policy became cudgels. Nonrecognition of the Palestinians' right to self-determination turned into an active strategy to prevent, aat all costs, the creation of the Palestinian state as called for in the UN Partition Resolution. The comprehensive social, political, cultural, and economic separation of Jews and Arabs that had always characterized the Yishuv was accelerated, first, by the proposed political partition; second, by the stimulation of a mass exodus of Palestinians from the areas controlled by the Israeli forces; third, by the wholesale destruction of Arab villages and townships to prevent their return; and finally, by the forceful segregation of the remaining Arab minority through the imposition of a Military Administration in Arab areas. The "civilizing mission" of Zionism in the Arab world, as formulated in the Weizmann-Faisal agreement of 1919, was transformed into support for King Abdallah of Transjordan, and the effective political splintering of the Arab movement for independence and unity.

This transformation in Zionist strategy became the model for Israel's policies toward the Arabs in general and the Palestinians in particular. Ben-Gurion's conceptions were molded into the official doctrines of the Israeli establishment, the armed forces, and the political and economic elite—regardless of class or political affiliation.

In retrospect, Ben-Gurion's contribution to the creation of the state cannot be disputed—in the victorious War of Independence, in the absorption of mass immigration, and in the country's successful industrial, technological, and scientific development. But today, in the centenary year of Ben-Gurion's birth, the Labor party is proposing the philosophy of the "state-builder," the "armed prophet," the "prophet of fire" —Ben-Gurionism—as the only ideological, political, and social alternative to right-wing, reactionary nationalism now so entrenched in Israeli society. Indeed, the concept of a democratic Jewish society might conceivably provide such an alternative were it free from the impulse toward territorial expansionism— for whatever reason: historical, religious, political, or strategic.

But the fact is that Ben-Gurion built his political philosophy precisely on these two contradictory elements: a democratic *Jewish* society in the *whole*, or in most, of Palestine.

Israel's success in 1948 and in the armistice talks in 1949 seems to have vindicated Ben-Gurion's policy of not recognizing the Palestinians as a national entity. For a number of years after the war, most Israelis shared the perception that the Palestinian people had ceased to exist; in their view, only the humanitarian problem of the refugees remained (as did, of course, the determination of final borders and the signing of peace treaties with the Arab states). The Palestinian problem was obliterated from Israel's political thinking despite the refugees' struggle for repatriation and the restoration of their rights and property. Between 1948 and 1967, no Israeli studies on the Arab world appear to have predicted the reemergence of the Palestinian national movement in the refugee camps. The fedayeen were seen only as agents of Arab military rulers preparing for wars of revenge. Ben-Gurion viewed them as instruments of the Arab states' deliberate policy of guerrilla warfare, harassment, and violation of the tenuous armistice treaties. In response, he initiated massive retaliations and severe and humiliating punishments intended to force them to stop this policy. As Moshe Sharett wrote in 1955, "In the thirties we restrained the emotions of revenge and we educated the public to consider revenge as an absolutely negative impulse. Now, on the contrary, we justify the system of reprisals out of pragmatic considerations . . . we have eliminated the mental and moral brakes on this instinct and made it possible . . . to uphold revenge as a moral value"

Nearly twenty years had to pass before it became clear that the eviction of the Palestinians from their lands and the creation of the refugee problem only intensified the national aspirations of the Palestinians, whose dispersion and homelessness created a problem greatly resembling that of the Jewish people in past times. Ben-Gurion's policies led to a vicious circle of escalating violence: large-scale battles created dangerous political tensions and rendered the whole area prey to a feverish arms race and great-power rivalry, culminating finally in full-scale wars. The Palestinians themselves became a factor in this sequence of events, seeking to channel political and social unrest into a pan-Arab movement for the restoration of their rights. They became the most committed militants, spearheading the move toward Arab unity and confrontation with Israel.

Thus, Ben-Gurion's nonrecognition of Palestinian nationalism created the very danger he was most afraid of. He knew that the victory of 1948 was achieved not because the Israeli army was more heroic but because the Arab armies were corrupt and the Arab world divided. He became obsessed with the fear that a charismatic leader would modernize Arab education, develop their economies, and unite all the Arab states:

The Arab people have been beaten by us. Will they forget it quickly? Seven hundred thousand people beat 30 million. Will they forget this offense? It can be assumed that they have a sense of hunor. We will make peace efforts, but two sides are necessary for peace. Is there any security that they will not want to take revenge? Let us recognize the truth: we won not because we performed wonders, but because the Arab army is rotten. Must this rottenness persist forever? Is it not possible that an Arab Mustafa Kemal will arise? The situation in the world beckons toward revenge: there are two blocs; there is a fear of world war. This tempts anyone with a grievance. We will always require a superior defensive capability.

This fear led Ben-Gurion to concentrate on building a military force (including a nuclear option) to match the combined force of all the Arab countries and to prevent any unfavorable changes in the political structure of the region. It also led Israel to subordinate its foreign, economic, and social policies to the end of acquiring or producing better and more sophisticated weapons than the Arabs. This in turn involved Israel in the great-power rivalry in the Middle East and required the country to "take sides" in the struggles between Arab nationalism and its adversaries on the principle that "the enemy of my enemy is my friend." This policy has continued unabated till today. Its efficacy, as shown in the Suez War of 1956 and the Six-Day War of 1967, has made its underlying concepts axiomatic for both the public and the political elite. The 1967 victory was so overwhelming that Israelis increasingly came to believe that they could live forever without peace. It induced a demand for new territorial dimensions and new strategic frontiers, enthusiastically acclaimed by the disciples of Jabotinsky, who never stopped dreaming of a Jewish state on both sides of the Jordan, and by the religious nationalists, who insisted on Israel's God-given right to the historical borders of the biblical covenant.

Until 1967, the labor movement in Israel had maintained its hegemony, although its traditional, pre-state social values were being gradually undermined—both in education and in its egalitarian economic conceptions—as a result of the free rein given to capitalist rather than cooperative enterprise and the growth of a large sector of underprivileged people. With the blitz victory in 1967 and the occupation of the West Bank and Gaza, the sudden expansion of Israel's borders gave rise to a more rapid erosion of the socialist and humanist values that had once been the hallmark of labor Zionism: prominent political leaders, poets, writers, and intellectuals, whose roots had been in the labor movement, joined the new, dynamic Greater Israel movement, which sought to turn Israel's most recent conquests into an integral part of the country.

The 1.25 million Palestinians who came under Israeli rule provided cheap labor the the Israeli economy, supplying nearly 100,000 workers for agriculture, public works, construction, light industries, and private services. The Palestinians became Israel's "water carriers and hewers of wood." Jewish workers moved up the social ladder to positions of management, the professions, trade, and public service. The influx of enormous quantities of capital stimulated the growth of a war economy, huge investments in the occupied territories in an Israeli-controlled infrastructure, and a boom in private enterprise. The formerly labor-oriented economy was turned into an unbridled capitalist one, with a typical consumer mentality, out for quick profits, speculation, and tax evasion. Diaspora Jewry, basking in Israel's military glory, provided unconditional moral and financial support, and massive economic and military aid from the United States hastened the further militarization of Israel's political thinking and self-image as a mini-superpower and an indispensable ally of the United States in its global policy of confrontation with the USSR. Chatting with American friends, the late prime minister Golda Meir once said: "I don't know why you fancy a French word like détente when there is a good English phrase for it—Cold War."

The first settlements in the West Bank were built at the inspiration of Yigal Allon, a kibbutz member, a minister in the Labor government, and the former left-wing MAPAM commander of the Palmach; it was also Allon who gave his approval to attempts of the fundamentalist rabbi Moshe Levinger to establish a Jewish community in the heart of Arab Hebron.

In the new circumstances, any attempts made to preach a return to the old values of the labor movement were bound to fail.

Labor leaders did not understand that only by ending the occupation of the Arab territories and reaching a peace settlement with
the Arabs could they reverse this erosion of "pioneering socialist
values."

The religious-nationalistic Gush Emunim, the Bloc of the
Faithful, was not long in emerging as the spiritual leader of new
Israeli expansionism, and with the traumatic experience of the
Yom Kippur War of 1973, when Israel's military superiority was
called into question, the soil was fertile for the appearance of a
gun-toting, messianic, ethnocentric, expansionist movement, of
which Meir Kahane was only the most extreme example.

The Labor government tried to curb the movement for religious and messianic expansion by insisting on "strategic" expansion only, that is, permanent Israeli control over those areas
delineated in the Allon plan and ostensibly necessary for Israel's
security: the Jordan Valley, the Golan Heights, Sharm Al-Sheikh.
But the Labor party both failed to curb the right and continued
to rationalize its own policy of unilateral settlement in the occupied territories by arguing that it would prompt the Arabs to negotiate peace out of a fear that loss of time would mean loss of
territory. This argument was the primary article of faith for
Meir, who, while insisting that there were no Palestinians, be-
moaned the moral decline of Israeli society and the labor movement. Meanwhile, Israeli society as a whole was moving more and
more to the right, and its widespread disregard, both official and
otherwise, of the human and national rights of others was masked
as a return to the religious, traditional, and historical rights and
values of Judaism.

There is no intrinsic connection between Judaism and democracy. There always was an orthodox, fundamentalist current in
Judaism, characterized by racial prejudice toward non-Jews in
general and Arabs in particular. A substantial portion—perhaps
even the overwhelming majority—of the religious movements,
and a growing part of the population in general, came to conceive
of the West Bank not as the homeland of the Palestinian people
but as Judea and Samaria, the birthplace of the Jewish faith and
homeland of the Jewish people. Many people not only became indifferent to the national rights of the Palestinians living there,
they did not even see the necessity for granting them civil rights. Israel's
experience prior to the war in 1967 proved that it was quite possible to exclude the Arab minority from the democratic system by

means of a Military Administration, justified by Arab belligerence and the necessity for a very high level of classified "security" and concomitant measures. Ben-Gurion had maintained such a regime within Israel for eighteen years, and all of his labor successors, before 1967 and after, followed suit: Levi Eshkol, Golda Meir, and Yitzhak Rabin. Little wonder that when Likud came to power in 1977, Menahem Begin had his work cut out for him, especially after Moshe Dayan, the first son of the trail-blazing labor-Zionist Kibbutz Degania, crossed party lines to help him out as foreign minister. Begin hoped to wipe out the "trauma" of the Yom Kippur War and assure the success of Greater Israel by eliminating Egypt from the military confrontation through the return of the Sinai Peninsula and then by giving the *coup de grace* to the Palestinians with the war in Lebanon. Had he succeeded he would have indeed come full circle: Jobotinsky's star pupil and successor would have completed the job the Ben-Gurion, in his own view, had left unfinished.

The Labor party and the labor movement as a whole are now trying to regain the influence they lost in 1977. While Shimon Peres, Ben-Gurion's stalwart lieutenant, shares the offices of prime minister and foreign minister with Yitzhak Shamir, Begin's lieutenant, and the occupation continues unabated, Labor is trying to present Ben-Gurion's idea of a democratic Jewish state as the alternative to a Greater Israel.

But the glorification of the War of Independence and of Ben-Gurion's stategy cannot serve as an alternative. For the line from Ben-Gurion to Begin is direct. Both leaders based their policies on the negation of the binational reality of Palestine: two peoples claiming the same land as a basis for national independence. And in both cases, this negation had doomed their policies. Lebanon became a watershed. It proved that force and oppression cannot eradicate from the hearts and minds of a homeless people its aspiration for freedom and independence. The moral and political failure of that war improved Labor's chances for a return to power. But this would depend heavily on the movement's readiness and ability to submit its own past policies to a serious critical review. Such a step implies an analysis of Ben-Gurion's whole political philosophy and his strategy in the crucial 1947–48 period. He may have assured us of the creation of a Jewish state, but as long as he left the Israeli-Palestinian conflict unresolved, he left us a heritage of war and destruction as well, for which three generations of Israelis and Palestinians are still paying.

The question that remains is this: Can one reasonably hope for a change? The answer is not easy. If there is to be a way out of the present impasse, both Israelis and Palestinians will have to take giant steps in changing their attitudes, priorities, and practices.

There is a consensus among Israeli peace groups that an end must come to the occupation and to Israeli rule over Palestinians. There is also a growing awareness of the fact that the best way to negotiate a real peace is with the PLO. But this will be possible only if both negotiating partners adopt a clear-cut policy in favor of a peace settlement.

There are those who view the Palestine National Covenant—the founding document of the Palestine Liberation Organization—as insignificant and unimportant. I am not of this opinion. In my view, it expresses an ideological credo that became a program for action when al-Fatah assumed leadership of the PLO. The covenant, proclaimed on May 28, 1964, declares that the 1947 partition plan and the establishment of Israel "are illegal and false" and calls for the liberation of Palestine as an Arab homeland. The most controversial points of the covenant are articles 6 and 7, which define Palestinians as "those Arab citizens who were living normally in Palestine up to 1947," and declare that only "Jews of Palestinian origin"—i.e., those living in Palestine before 1948—are eligible to remain. But precisely because the covenant has become a plan of action, one should also take the changes in PLO positions very seriously. They have resulted from failures and setbacks in attempts to implement the covenant.

In the past twenty years most of the PLO's efforts to abide by the covenant—guerrilla tactics in the West Bank and Gaza, the establishment of a territorial sanctuary in Jordan, attempts to maintain their independence from Syria and other host countries, the diplomatic attempt to "de-Zionize" Israel or have it expelled from the UN—failed to produce results. The PLO did succeed in gaining moral and political support all over the world for its claim to be the sole legitimate representative of the Palestinian people in their struggle for self-determination and statehood.

The PLO was deeply affected by the passivity of the Arab regimes during the war in Lebanon, their submission to US pressures, their consent to the dismantling and evacuation of PLO

bases in Lebanon, and the stormy and massive demonstrations in
Israel against the war, the destruction of the refugee camps, and
the massacre of the Palestinians. Against this background one
must view as serious and important the signals and indications
from the PLO of a readiness to negotiate a political solution to
the conflict. The PLO is now compelled to develop a new strategy, and there are already instances of feelers being put out to encourage a dialogue with Israelis—most recently at the conference
of PLO leaders and members of the Israeli peace camp held in
Rumania in November 1986.

Until the Lebanon War, most of the PLO and other Arab
leaders viewed the struggle between Zionists of different out-
looks as a "Jekyll and Hyde" phenomenon. They viewed Jabotinsky, and later Begin, as the true spokesmen of Zionism. Chaim
Weizmann and the labor Zionists were considered merely hypo-
critical cover-ups for Zionism's real expansionist aims. Although
the policies of Israel's successive governments, both Labor and
Likud, have done nothing to alter this view—and the present national unity government only reinforces it—the war in Lebanon
did reveal deep divisions within Israeli society, divisions not always discernible according to party affiliation.

Israel is in the midst of a deep moral, social, economic, and
political crisis, one that will surely become exacerbated if there
in no dramatic change of policy. Many young people, as well as
a substantial number of artists, journalists, and other intellectuals, including a growing number of people from the so-called Oriental communities, find themselves unable to accept the
undemocratic and reactionary religious, military, and moral
codes that are now representative of "official" Israel. The outcome of the struggle between two diametrically opposed visions
of Israel—an enlightened, democratic state or a fundamentalist,
militarist one—will have a significant effect on the future of the
Palestinian people as well as on peace in the region.

The objective asymmetry of the situation places the major responsibility for the solution of the conflict on Israel, but it does
not release the PLO from adopting a strategy that will enable the
progressive forces of peace in Israel to strengthen their positions.

At the same time, it must be recognized that the support of
the Israeli peace camp for Palestinian self-determination, mutual
recognition, and coexistence is not enough. Diaspora Jewry and
friends of Israel abroad must realize that present Israeli policy is

doomed to reproduce over and over again the cycle of violence that shocks our sensibilities every time we read or hear of wanton murder and bloodshed, whether the hand that perpetrates it detonates a bomb or fires a pistol. The collective revenge of an army for the murder of one of its citizens is no more righteous or admirable than the individual revenge of a desperate youth for the murder of one of his people. It is only propaganda and distorted vision that labels one "terrorism" and the other "national defense."

It is, then, in the hope of clarifying the distored vision on our side of the conflict—that is, on the Jewish, Israeli side—that I have written this book.

ISRAEL'S 40-YEAR QUANDARY[3]

It is a pattern that typifies this country, almost continually under siege since its founding in 1948: The crisis atmosphere of the last five months—caused by the Palestinian uprising in the West Bank and Gaza Strip—has failed to interrupt plans for numerous events commemorating Israel's 40th anniversary. (Independence day will be celebrated on April 21. Israel declared its independence on May 14, 1948. As reckoned by the Hebrew lunar calendar, the corresponding date in 1988 is April 21.) But no amount of anniversary hoopla can distract Israelis for long from the violence in the occupied territories. It has already claimed the lives of more than 130 Palestinians, one Israeli soldier and a 15-year-old Jewish girl.

The rioting began December 9 in Gaza and quickly spread to the West Bank, areas that have been occupied by Israel since its lightning victory in the Six-Day War of June 1967. A sense of urgency developed as Israeli troops failed to contain the disturbances. Secretary of State George P. Shultz flew to the Middle East to press for a U.S.-sponsored peace plan that calls for negotiations under the sponsorship of an international conference.

[3]By Joseph M. Hochstein, an American journalist living in Israel, from *Editorial Research Reports*, vol. 1 no. 14, April 15, 1988, pp. 186–198. Copyright © 1988 by Congressional Quarterly Inc. Reprinted by permission.

"The status quo in the region is not a stable option for any of the parties," Shultz said as he arrived Feb. 25 in Israel. Leaving the Middle East a week later after meeting with Israeli and Arab heads of state, he said both sides were being unrealistic and should think in terms of what was possible rather than what was impossible.

Shultz' frustration was understandable given the history of the Arab-Israeli conflict. In the four decades since the Jewish state proclaimed its independence and fought off an invasion by five neighboring Arab nations, war has prevailed over diplomacy. Except for Egypt, which signed a peace treaty with Israel in 1979, no Arab state has recognized Israel's right to exist. In recent years, the focus of the Arab-Israeli conflict has shifted from the Arab states to the Palestinians and their demands for a state of their own.

During more than 20 years of occupation, there have been sporadic incidents of violence and numerous protests by the Arabs living in the Gaza Strip and on the West Bank of the Jordan River, but the current uprising is different. Television news reports showing Israeli soldiers beating Palestinian protesters were broadcast around the world. The government's inability to put down the disturbances without bloodshed has sharpened divisions within Israel about the future of the occupied territories and caused deep anguish among Israel's supporters in the United States, including American Jews. The situation has become so explosive that many Israelis feel that neither they nor the Palestinian Arabs can return to the unresolved tension that existed before rock-throwing Palestinian youths confronted the Israeli army last December.

"I don't know what will happen in the territories," says Israel's foreign minister, Shimon Peres. "No one knows. But we're all aware that there's no going back to the previous situation. The hope for a comfortable and pleasant coexistence, of coming to terms with the situation . . . all this has apparently vanished forever.

Meron Benvenisti, director of the West Bank Data Base Project, which monitors conditions in the occupied territories, says that "the famous dilemma of whether Israel is to be a Jewish state or a democratic state has become an immediate choice."

At issue is how Israel can continue to rule over 1.3 million Arabs in what Israelis call "the territories." These areas, captured from Jordan and Egypt in 1967, are known to outsiders as the West Bank and Gaza Strip, to many Israelis as "Judea, Samaria and the Gaza District," and to Arab activists as "occupied Palestine."

Ebba Eban, the former foreign minister, describes Israel's dilemma this way: "If we insist on maintaining the present territorial structure, which may be possible for a time through physical force, we shall have to give up almost every other attribute of our national vision. If we insist on ruling an entire territory and population . . . we shall soon lose our Jewish majority, our democratic principles, our hope of ultimate peace, the prospect of avoiding war, the maintenance of our international friendships, the durability of the Egyptian treaty relationship and any chance of a national consensus at home. The status quo is the least viable and the most catastrophic of all the available Israeli options."

Benvenisti calls the situation "a new act" of an old tragedy. "Unlike earlier acts," he writes, "it is supported almost exclusively by the two tragic heroes. All supporting actors have withdrawn. The two heroes conduct a dialogue of horrifying deed. The tired audience prays that the tragedy is close to its catharsis, but the actors insist on prolonging the agony. Not all scores been settled. Darkness envelops the strife-torn handscape of the Holy Land. The shadows of rage and fear are deepening."

One issue being debated by Israelis is the latest American peace initiative. They wonder whether intervention by the most friendly U.S. administration Israel has ever known will bring peace closer, or whether the initiative will end in Washington's forcing Israel to make costly concessions, as has happened more than once in the past.

Maj. Gen. Dan Shomron, Israel's military chief of staff, believes that the opening of negotiations will itself increase tension. "Extremists from either side will act . . . so as not to allow negotiations for an agreement which is unacceptable to them," Shomron said. "That is why I believe that once the political process is launched—even though it embodies the solution to the problem—there is no chance that in its early stages the situation will calm down. It would be worthwhile to dispel this illusion, since there are persons who say that the moment a natural dialogue is launched, quiet will prevail."

The feeling that their future may to a large extent be dictated by the decisions of others frustrates many Israelis. "It's a vicious circle," said a Tel Aviv businessman. "The Americans provide weapons to us, but also to the Arabs, who say they will destroy us someday. So we need more weapons, and more American money. The Europeans help the Arabs and close their markets to us. The Russians stir the pot, and everyone tries to pressure us. In the end, it's we who pay the price."

A Double-edged Reaction to Criticism by Others

A pressing issue to Israelis in early 1988 was the impact of the Arab demonstrations on the most highly respected institution within the country, the army. In December the army took on a role that Israeli commentators have called an impossible mission. Soldiers were under standing orders to refrain from using deadly force unless their own lives were immediately threatened. Unprepared to face crowds of jeering civilians whose main weapons were rocks and Molotov cocktails, teenaged combat troops trained for storming enemy strongholds had to learn an unfamiliar crowd-control task virtually overnight.

Israel came under mounting criticism for its failute to handle the situation without loss of life. Prime Minister Yitzhak Shamir retorted Dec. 21: "I doubt that any other state in the entire world dictates to its military forces such restraint and concern for human life."

Commanders said army units were too small at first to control crowds without resorting to firearms. When more troops arrived, the larger units began enforcing curfews on entire Arab communities in an effort to smother the rioting.

Confusion spread after Defense Minister Yitzhak Rabin announced that troops would beat rioters instead of shooting them. Out on the streets, soldiers weren't sure what they were expected to do. An officer remarked that soldiers "need at least a full-time lawyer in the field. . . . They have to remember dozens of prohibitions and restrictions, and they know they will suffer the consequences if they violate orders." A survey by Israeli psychologists found that even soldiers who opposed Israel's continuing occupation of the Arab areas were in favor, nonetheless, of being allowed to use greater force to put down the riots. Palestinian leaflets instructed demonstrators to avoid using firearms, lest the army shoot back in force.

Ze'ev Shiff, an Israeli military expert, commented: "Some soldiers are so infuriated by the situation that they're taking out their frustrations on the Palestinians. It's a process that could morally destroy even the best army in the world, and when the soldiers describe what they saw, their trauma will affect the entire nation."

On Feb. 26, the army announced in had arrested four soldiers after a CBS television crew photographed them beating two captured Arab rock-throwers. Broadcasts of the incident provoked expressions of outrage from many countries. Defense Minister Rabin accused European and American critics of hypocrisy: "Let them look at their own history, in the short term and the long term, before they dare cast aspersions against the state of Israel and our soldiers. . . . Having served in the U.S. for a number of years as ambassador in Washington, I can tell you that what was done in the streets of America during this period to rioters and protesters was far worse than what our boys did." Nevertheless, Palestinians and Israelis continue to be injured and die, and coverage of armed Israeli troops confronting rock-hurling Palestinian youths has focused world attention on the plight of the Palestinians.

Many Israelis charge that the media, and television in particular, are biased in favor of the Palestinians and that camera crews often create the disturbances by their presence. Newsmen counter that criticism of them is only "blaming the messenger." For its part, the Israeli government has considered a total ban on news coverage but has rejected the idea as incompatible with Israeli society. But it has progressively limited coverage of the occupied territories. Local military commanders have increasingly used their power to bar journalists from areas where riots are taking place. On March 28 the Israeli government closed the entire West Bank and Gaza Strip to journalist because of expected Arab demonstrations. Two days later the government closed the Arab-owned Palestine Press Service for six months; the news service had served Western journalists as a major source of information on the uprisings.

Israeli sensitivity to unfavorable press coverage typifies Israel's double-edged reaction to criticism from others. On the one hand, Israelis seek acceptance by outsiders. They have been doing so since at least 1948, when the country's Declaration of Independence appealed to the outside world to "admit Israel into the family of nations." On the other hand, most Israelis believe that experience teaches them to mistrust outsiders. A 1983 opinion survey found that 87 percent of Israeli Jews agreed that "From the [Nazi] Holocaust we learn that Jews cannot rely on non-Jews"; 91 percent of the respondents said Western leaders knew of the mass killings and did little to save the Jews.

In psychological terms, says Dr. Avner Falk, a Jerusalem psychotherapist, Israeli reaction to criticism reflects "group narcissism"—an unconscious attempt by Jews to repair their own self-image, which has been damaged not only by the Nazi Holocaust but by centuries of exile and persecution. "We like to think of ourselves as a "light unto the nations,'" says Falk, who is writing a psychological history of the Jewish people. "The group self becomes part of the personal self, and when [the nation] comes under criticism, members of the group feel personally hurt."

Israeli sensitivity to outside interference also could be seen in the reaction to a March 3 letter sent by 30 U.S. senators, including some of Israel's staunchest supporters on Capitol Hill, to Secretary of State Shultz criticizing Prime Minister Shamir's stated refusal to consider trading occupied territory for peace with the Arabs. Shamir bluntly told the senators not to interfere. "It is the free and democratic people and government of Israel that will have to decide the issues and peace and security," he said. "It is their future and well-being that is at stake."

Current Crisis Born in 1967 Military Triumph

An irony that does not escape Israelis is that the current crisis has its roots in a military triumph. In 1967 Israel astonished the world by defeating Arab armies on three fronts in six days.

On the eve of the war, a vulnerable and isolated Israel appeared in danger of extinction. In May 1967, Egyptian President Gamal Abdel Nasser ordered United Nations Forces out of the Sinai, blockaded Israel's southern sea outlet and supplemented his military union with Syria by military alliance with Jordan and Iraq. "Our basic objective will be to destory Israel," Nasser said on May 26. "This is our opportunity to rectify the ignominy which has been with us since 1948," Iraqi President Rahman Adbel Aref said May 31. "Our goal is clear—to wipe Israel off the map."

The war did dramatically change the map. Destroying Egyptian air power in a first strike June 5, Israel quickly took Gaza and the Sinai Peninsula. When Jordan's King Hussein rejected Israeli appeals to stay out of the fighting, Israel captured the West Bank as well as Jordanian-occupied East Jerusalem. By June 10, the last day of the war, Israel held the Golan Heights, from which Syrian gunners had harassed the Israeli settlements below.

In the heady days that followed, Israeli leaders spoke of returning most of the territory in exchange for a genuine peace to replace the 1949 armistice agreements. All that was needed, they said, was a telephone call from the other side.

One Israeli who saw problems ahead was Hebrew University Professor J. L. Talmon. In an exchange with British historian Arnold Toynbee, a self-styled "Western spokesman for the Arab cause," Talmon wrote July 3, 1967: "I recoil from the idea of Jews lording it over others. It is at variance with the image of Judaism I cherish, and the example of other nations makes me fear the dangers to the moral fiber, the psychological balance, and spiritual values laying in wait for a master race. I pray that we shall not be compelled to assume that role, which may happen if an arrangement with Jordan proves impossible and the other Arab states refuse to establish peace with Israel."

Those fears were realized in August when Arab leaders meeting at Khartoum, the Sudan, announced a formula of "the three no's"—no peace, no negotiations and no recognition of Israel.

This left Israel with the territorial fruits of victory—a deep buffer zone in the Sinai to the west, a natural defense line along the Jordan River to the east, all of Jerusalem (Israel unilaterally proclaimed the unification of Jerusalem under Israeli rule on June 28, 1967. In July 1980, the Israeli Knesset [parliament] declared that "united Jerusalem" was the capital of Israel.) and control of the strategic Golan Heights to the north—but also with a new problem. Israel became an occupying power, ruling over almost a million Arabs in Gaza and the West Bank.

Within a year Jews began to move into formerly Jordanian-occupied areas, only a few minutes' drive from Israeli cities. As early as 1968 a Jewish group established a squatter foothold outside Hebron. Other settlements followed. Some West Bank residents, ignoring Jordan's law that prescribes the death penalty for selling land to a Jew, took part in real estate deals and were sentenced in absentia by Jordanian tribunals across the river.

The possibility of returning to areas where Jews had not lived for centuries—as well as to Jerusalem's Jewish Quarter and ancient Hebron, from which the Jews had been expelled decades earlier—lit a spark not only in religious Israelis but among many secular nationalists. "Occupying these areas, with their old familiar biblical names, resurrected historical memories and gave rise to a feeling of attachment and reluctance to part with them," wrote Yehoshaphat Harkabi, a former chief of military intelligence.

The 1977 Israeli election that brought Menachem Begin to the premiership changed the complexion of Israeli policies toward the occupied territories. The victory by Begin's Likud bloc meant the socialist Labor alignment was out of power for the first time since 1948. The Likud viewed the West Bank as the Jews' inheritance from biblical times. Consequently it advocated policies to promote permanent Jewish settlements in the West Bank. Although Israel's Labor Party agreed in principle that Jews had a right to settle in these areas, it had been more willing to make territorial compromises with Israel's Arab neighbors. Security was the foremost concern of the Labor alignment with regard to the territories. Successive governments led by the Labor Party had established settlements in strategic locations to provide early warning of any possible attack.

The goal of the Likud bloc, on the other hand, was to ensure that Israel retained control over the occupied territories by creating "facts on the ground" that could not be ignored in any future peace negotiations. To accomplish this, the Likud implemented policies that encouraged settlement in the territories. The party tried to expand the pool of potential settlers by offering subsidies and government-sponsored mortgages at good terms. The government hoped to attract Israelis who could not afford to buy a place in the crowded cities along Israel's coastal plain.

Another aim of the Likud, beside creating numbers in the area, was to build settlements near existing population centers. Likud promoted settlements throughout the territories to establish a Jewish presence everywhere, thus giving weight to Israel's over the area.

Although Likud was disappointed in the number of Israelis who took advantage of the economic incentives to move to the territories, between 1982 and 1984 the Jewish settlements' population doubled. By the end of 1984, according to a report published by the West Bank Data Project, there were 114 settlements with 42,600 inhabitants, up from 71 settlements and 20,600 people in 1982. By 1988, more than 150 Jewish settlements with a population estimated at around 60,000 had been established in Judea, Samaria and Gaza.

One result of the 1987–88 Arab rioting has been a growing realization among Israelis of the extent to which their lives have become interlocked with the Palestinians in the past two decades. A whole generation of Israelis and Palestinians grew up with little or no awareness of the so-called "Green Line," the 1949 armistice line on the map distinguishing Israel from the now-occupied territories.

Until last December, the Green Line, if not erased, had at least been blurred by day-to-day economic and social developments. Integration went beyond the growing number of Jewish settlements in formerly Arab-held lands. New roads interlinked Israel and the territories. Israelis became accustomed to traveling and shopping in the West Bank and Gaza.

Soon after Israel captured the economically depressed West Bank and Gaza, Arabs from these territories began finding work in Israel. When the riots began in December, approximately 100,000 Arabs from the territories were commuting to jobs in Israel. About 30 percent of all employed West Bank Arabs worked in Israel, along with more than 40 percent of all employed Gazans. They represented more than 6 percent of the labor force in Israel and were concentrated in lower-paid jobs such as construction laborers and restaurant helpers.

Another feature of the occupation has been increased interaction between Israeli Arabs and the Palestinians in the West Bank and Gaza. During the recent rioting, Israeli Arabs openly expressed support for the rioters across the Green Line. Some threw rocks at Israeli civilian vehicles. This, too, was a change. In the past, Israel's Arab citizens had remained passive, expressing political disaffection by voting Communist or engaging in cautious protest, but habitually avoiding violence or disruption.

Public Deeply Divided over the Territories

Since 1967, Israel's unwillingness to withdraw from territories it acquired in the Six-Day War has sometimes given an illusory appearance of unity to Israeli policy. An overwhelming majority of the Knesset, Israel's one-chamber parliament, rejects Arab demands for a complete Israeli withdrawal. But there the appearance of Israeli unity stops.

Long before the Shultz initiative, Israel's internal debate had focused on the territories. As the key issue dividing the country, it cannot be resolved without a basic shift of voters, to the left or to the right.

Deeply divided in their views of what to do about the territories, Israelis even disagree on what to call them. To the ideological and political bloc led by Prime Minister Shamir, the widely used term West Bank is unacceptable. To these Israelis, the land captured from Jordan in 1967 is known as Judea and Samaria—terms that were used in the British mandate that immediately preceded Israeli independence, and also in biblical times. The term West Bank is a political rather than geographic designation, adopted by Jordan in 1950 to signify the Hashemite Kingdom's annexation of most of the Samaria and Jerusalem districts of the former British mandate. And many Israelis use the term West Bank not to dispute history or support Jordan's claim, but to express their disagreement with the substance of Shamir's policy.

There is less disagreement over military security. Israelis of almost every political view share the concern expressed by Prime Minister Menachem Begin in a Sept. 5, 1982, letter to President Reagan: "Geography and history have ordained that Judea and Samaria be mountainous country and that two-thirds of our population dwell in the coastal plain dominated by those mountains. From them, you can hit every city, every town, each township and village and, last but not least, our principal airport in the plain below."

But security is not the sole concern that impels Israel to remain in the territories. Israelis of varying political persuasions feel that Jews have a legitimate and long-established right to live there. Some, like Rabbi Moshe Levinger, who led the return of Jews to Hebron in 1968, base the Jewish claim on biblical tradition. They say that no Jew, and no Israeli government, has a right to abandon the land to other sovereignty.

David Landau, assistant managing editor of the *Jerusalem Post*, has criticized the Jewish community in Hebron and neighboring Kiryat Arba as containing "some of the toughest nuts of the rabid right, violent racists." Even so, Landau has proposed creating a sovereign Jewish enclave in Hebron, although he would have it be in return for a similar Moslem enclave in Jerusalem. "Jews poured out their hearts at the Tomb of Machpela in Hebron a thousand years before Mohammed was born, and King David made it his capital city before Jerusalem," Landau wrote, concluding that "the moderates' determination to be rid of the occupied territories . . . is historically and politically insensitive."

The central issue on which Israelis have been divided for two decades is not whether Jews have rights in the territories, but, simply, whether these rights are negotiable. In political terms, the issue is whether Judea and Samaria are an inseparable part of the Land of Israel, or whether they can be used as bargaining chips.

The concept of territorial compromise on the part of Israel for a guarantee of peace from the Arabs was embodied in United Nations Security Council Resolution 242, adopted Nov. 22, 1967. Both sides have continued to disagree over the meaning of the resolution, which contains an intentional ambiguity. The resolution called for Israeli withdrawal "from territories occupied in the recent conflict." It did not spell out whether this meant all territories, or only some. The formula resulted from negotiations in which the United States backed Israel's refusal to accept the word "the" in front of "territories."

Prime Minister Shamir has said in the past that Israel has already fulfilled Resolution 242, by withdrawing from the Sinai in 1982. According to this contention, neither Gaza nor the West Bank is subject to the withdrawal requirement, because Jordan and Egypt acquired these territories in violation of Resolution 242's preamble, which emphasizes "the inadmissibility of the acquisition of territory by war."

The Likud bloc led by Shamir continues to support Israeli sovereignty over all of the occupied territories. Marking Israeli Arbor Day at a Jewish settlement in Samaria on Feb. 3, Shamir said the planting of trees "means that the settlements in this location will grow, flourish and develop. I refer to Judea, Samaria and the Gaza Strip, and also the Golan Heights."

To the surprise of many, it was a Likud-led government that agreed to return the Sinai Peninsula to Egypt and to dismantle all the Jewish settlements there, as part of the September 1978 Camp David Peace Accords. In an article published in a recent issue of *Foreign Affairs* magazine, Shamir described why Israel took a more conciliatory position toward the Sinai: "While we were willing to dismantle the towns and villages we built in the Sinai desert and to relinquish every inch of the Sinai, it is quite unthinkable that we should allow Judea and Samaria, the cradle of our nation and culture to revert to being *Judenrein*, forbidden to Jews, which was the case during the Jordanian occupation of 1948–67. . . . The security problem, too, is quite different on our eastern border. In the case of Egypt, the 300 miles of desert separating the population centers of the two countries make agreements on demilitarization, separation of forces, multinational peace-keeping forces, listening posts and warning systems viable substitutes for strategic depth. But the borders of Judea and Samaria are within rifle range of pedestrians in the streets of Jerusalem and Tel Aviv. The Judea-Samaria mountain range dominates Israel's population centers, main industrial zones, its rail and road arteries and international airport. Relinquishing Israel control over these ridges can only turn the clock back to the pre–June 1967 days when the Arab regimes felt that destroying Israel was a feasible option."

The Labor alignment led by Foreign Minister Peres would give up Arab-populated parts of the territory acquired in 1967, while keeping strategic terrain for defense. Peres told a student group Feb. 8 that the principles for negotiations with Jordan should be "that the Jordan River will be Israel's security border—in other words, no Arab or foreign army will cross the Jordan—that the Israel army will be deployed along the Jordan River, that Jerusalem will remain a united city, the capital of Israel; and, again, that the borders [with Jordan] will remain open."

Neither of these two main Israeli viewpoints would meet the Arab demand for full Israeli withdrawal.

Israel's Right to Exist Is Still the Main Issue

Writing in 1967, American journalist I. F. Stone described the Arab-Israeli dispute as "a tragedy . . . a struggle of right against right." "Stripped of propaganda and sentiment," he wrote, "the Palestine problem is, simply, the struggle of two different peoples for the same strip of land. . . . [T]o find a solution that will satisfy both peoples is like trying to square a circle. . . . If God, as some now say, is dead, He no doubt died trying to find an equitable solution to the Arab-Jewish problem." One thing unites the Arabs and Israelis, Stone said: a belief "that only force can assure justice. . . . [T]his sets them on a collision course. For the Jews believe justice requires the recognition of Israel as a fact; for the Arabs, to recognize the fact is to acquiesce in the wrong done them by the conquest of Palestine."

More than 20 years later, the central issue in the conflict is still the recognition of Israel by its Arab neighbors. After 1967, many Arab leaders abandoned calls for Israel's destruction and spoke instead of regaining "occupied territories." Israelis contended, often in vain to disbelieving Westerners, that the "occupied territories" sought by the Arabs included all of Israel. Israelis pointed out that the Arab governments could have set up an independent Palestinian state any time from 1949 to 1967, while the West Bank was part of Jordan and Egyptian troops held Gaza. (The United Nations, on Nov. 29, 1947, voted to partition Palestine into separate, independent Jewish and Arab states, effective Oct. 1, 1948. As a result of the 1948–49 Arab-Israeli war, the Arab Palestinian state envisaged by the U.N. never came into being. The land allotted to it was taken over by Israel, Transjordan and Egypt. Transjordan annexed the West Bank and half of Jerusalem and transformed itself into the state of Jordan. Egypt took control of the Gaza Strip, but did not formally annex it. Israel incorporated the remaining territory into its boundaries.)

At a meeting in Rabat, Morocco, in October 1974, the heads of state of the 20 Arab League nations voted to recognize the Palestine Liberation Organization (PLO) as the "sole legitimate representative of the Palestinian people." Although some Middle East experts have said that PLO leader Yasir Arafat has moderated his long-stated position calling for the elimination of Israel through armed struggle, there is little hard evidence to support this. "The greatest obstacle to peace in the Middle East still is the insistence of Arab governments that the organization whose charter stipulates the destruction of Israel is the sole representative of the Palestinian people," says Prime Minister Shamir.

Although both wings of Israel's National Unity Government refuse to negotiate with the PLO, other Israelis contend that no other potential negotiating partner exists. A 1987 survey with Palestinian cosponsorship showed that 93.5 percent of respondents in the territories endorsed the PLO as a sole representative of the Palestinian people. "The choice before Israel is not between good and bad, but between bad and worse," says former intelligence chief Yehoshaphat Harkabi, who urges Israel to press for negotiations that could provide a safe exist from the territories.

Yaron Ezhari, a professor of political science at the Hebrew University of Jerusalem, says Israel should agree to talk to "any authentic Palestinian leader." This means, he says, "that Israeli leaders must be prepared to talk with members or supporters of the PLO who have perpetrated unconscionable acts of terror. Even this, however, is a lesser evil than prolonging the present impasse, thereby forcing both peoples further along the road toward mutual destruction."

Ezrahi, founder of a new movement of academicians opposed to the occupation, also has some advice for the Palestinians: Give up violence and terrorism. "If the Palestinians choose the political option, they will discover, as did Egypt's late President Sadat, that nothing changes Israeli attitudes and convinces us to make concessions more effectively than credible Arab moves toward renouncing violence," he writes. "When Palestinians resort to violence they revive our collective memories of atrocities and unite us behind our military leaders. But Palestinian restraint could crate a new dynamic—a reciprocal deescalation of violence that would reinforce the political momentum necessary for a true peace process."

And there is also the question of the ultimate authority of anyone negotiating on behalf of the Palestinians. Journalist Yosef Goell of the *Jerusalem Post* put it this way: "The tragedy of the Palestinians in the territories is that just as they were not the ones to actively foment the war that led to their being occupied, neither do they have it within their power today—even if they wanted to, which is questionable—to provide the essential security guarantees to Israel, which alone can be expected to persuade a majority of Israelis to agree to get off their backs.

Many Israelis, including the major political blocs, contend that a Palestinian homeland already exists east of the Jordan River, in the Hashemite Kingdom of Jordan. More than half of Jordan's population is Palestinian and a majority of all Palestinians hold Jordanian citizenship. The area that makes up the kingdom was originally designed as part of the Palestine Mandate that the League of Nations awarded to Britain after World War I for establishing a "Jewish national home."

But Israelis are aware that Palestinian Arabs show little desire to return to Jordanian rule. A survey released by two Israeli sociologists Dec. 25, 1987, showed that only 19 percent of Palestinian men under age 35 viewed a confederation with Jordan as acceptable.

The concept of "the return" to Palestine is deep and widespread among the Palestinians. Palestinian children are taught that their homeland is this or that village in Palestine—a homeland that most have never seen. David Grossman, the Israeli author of a book on life in the West Bank. *The Yellow Wind* (1988), writes, "[T]he Palestinians . . . are making use of the ancient Jewish strategy of exile, and have removed themselves from history. They close their eyes against reality and stubbornly fabricate their Promised Land. . . . Everything happens elsewhere, in some splendid past or longed-for future. The one thing most present here [on the West Bank] is absence. One senses that people here have voluntarily turned themselves into doubles of the real people who once existed in some other place. Into people who hold in their hands only one real asset: the ability to wait."

Internal Conflicts Dominate the Pre-election Scene

Israelis recognize that they face extremely difficult decisions with regard to the occupied territories. If Israel absorbs them, the nation's population balance could shift eventually to the Arabs. Relatively high Arab birth rates, (The annual birth rate among Israeli Jews is about 21 per 1,000 population. Among Israeli Arabs, it's about 33 per 1,000 population; among West Bank Palestinians, 40 per 1,000, and among Gaza Palestinians, 47 per 1,000.) a decline in Arab infant mortality since 1967, a decline in Arab out-migration and a decline in Jewish immigration are fueling this population shift.

By 1988, the population of Israel and the occupied territories west of the Jordan River included more than 3.6 million Jewish and 700,000 Arab citizens of Israel, and 1.3 million non-Israeli Arabs in the West Bank and Gaza. For the past 20 years, the Jewish-Arab population balance has remained almost unchanged. Jews constituted 62.3 percent of the total population west of the Jordan in 1986, compared with 63.7 percent in 1967. Israel's Central Bureau of Statistics has projected that by the year 2000 the Jewish majority west of the Jordan will drop to 55 percent. By the year 2010, says Meron Benvenisti of the West Bank Data Project, Jews and Arabs will be equal in number.

At stake are Israel's Jewish character and its democratic principles. If Israel annexes the occupied territories and their Arab populations, it would dilute the state's Jewish majority, unless it denies the Palestinians full political rights. "If present trends continue," Lance Morrow writes in the April 4 issue of *Time* magazine, "Israel will have to choose between its democratic principles—which would eventually require political power with Arabs—and its other profound ambition, to offer to Jews around the world a land they can always call their own."

Faced with this dilemma, Israelis often display more emotion toward one another in verbal conflict than toward their Arab foes. Each of the two major Israli political camps accuses the other of ignoring reality. Those who want to maintain the status quo or annex the territories are charged with pretending the demographic problem does not exist. Those who favor a territory-for-peace approach are accused of deluding themselves into imagining that Arab hostility would abate if Israel withdrew to less favorable lines. Each group denounces the other as pursuing policies that would jeopardize the nation's survival.

The Palestinian uprising has heightened an already high level of frustration in Israeli society. "To be an Israeli these days is, for many of us, to live with the sense that our world has begun to crumble, that our deepest beliefs and most cherished dreams are being shattered . . . ," says Hebrew University Professor Yaron Ezrahi. "The military, political, psychological and moral costs of the occupation are now impossible to ignore, even for those who have succeeded in doing so for 20 years."

The current unrest in the occupied territories has tended to divert public attention from other unsolved problems in Israel. These include an unwiedly coalition government, continuing religious-secular tensions and an annual inflation rate now running at about 16 percent. Israelis bear the highest per capita military burden in the world, depend heavily on American aid, (Israel receives $3 billion a year from the United States in military and economic aid.) are diplomatically isolated and have repeatedly failed to derive political gains from military victories.

Israel is accustomed to achieving national unity in moments of crisis and lapsing into divisiveness in quieter times, but the crisis of 1988 finds the country with a deadlocked National Unity Government and a sharply divided public.

The country's two major political blocs, Likud and Labor, currently govern together in an unusual power-sharing arrangement. They agreed in 1984, after elections left neither side able to organize a working coalition, to form a government together and rotate the top jobs between them. This National Unity Government quickly achieved the two main goals on which its partners agreed—withdrawing from Lebanon (Israel invaded Lebanon in June 1982 and attacked the armed forces of the PLO that had used Lebanon as a base for attacking Israel. The Israeli army advanced all the way to West Beirut. The military capacity of the PLO was destroyed and PLO forces were evacuated from Beirut under the supervision of a multinational peace-keeping force. For all its success in routing the PLO, the war was a costly one for Israel. It lasted three years, until June 1985, with financial burdens that contributed to Israel's sizeable foreign debt and runaway inflation rate. It also was the first Israeli war for which there was significant domestic oppostion.) and stopping runaway inflation, which had reached an annual rate of more than 400 percent in 1984. It could not agree on other major issues.

Paralysis in the government was not the only result. With neither major party playing an opposition role in the Knesset, parliamentary debate suffered, and new national policies did not take shape.

Before the Arab uprising dominated the scene, unresolved tension between religious and secular Jews was often described as the country's outstanding problem. This religious-secular conflict has its roots in the Israeli institution of coalition politics. In 1948, in return for supporting his secular, socialist-dominated government coalition, Prime Minister David Ben-Gurion gave the religious minority certain concessions. These included embodying religious principles, such as Sabbath observance, in public law. Since then, religious-secular conflict has erupted from time to time as one side or the other tried to press beyond the bounds of the 1948 arrangement. Violent confrontations flared in Jerusalem in 1987, as religious elements tried to prevent secular Jews from increasing the showing of movies on the Sabbath.

Israel's religious parties hold only 10 percent of the seats in the current Knesset; they are expected to decline slightly in the next elections. But their power is sometimes much greater than their numbers. The two major political blocs hold only 81 of the Knesset's 120 seats. Recent polls point to their losing five or more of those seats this year. Thus, in a new Knesset the extreme elements on both the right and the left are likely to have increased bargaining power. And when it comes to the West Bank, the ultranationalists on the right will not be alone; a high proportion of Israelis—44.4 percent, according to a poll taken in December 1987—are unwilling to yield any land in Judea and Samaria in exchange for peace with Jordan. An even higher percentage was unwilling to evacuate Jewish settlements in these areas.

Both Likud and Labor agree that peace must be reached through direct negotiations with Israel's Arab neighbors. Months before the Shultz initiative, Peres' Labor alignment endorsed a proposed international conference as a route to direct negotiations between Israel and Jordan. Shamir continues to oppose such a conference. "The complex and sensitive nature of the issues between Israel and Jordan are such that only direct, independent, openended, face-to-face negotiations can provide the unpressured atmosphere that is absolutely vital for reaching an agreement," he wrote in *Foreign Affairs*.

Shamir expressed little sympathy for Jordan's King Hussein. "We are told that King Hussein needs an international umbrella to protect himself from the radical forces in the Arab world. But a country that cannot defy the radicals on matters of procedure cannot be expected to defy them on matters of substance," he wrote. "Indeed, there cannot be any doubt that an international conference would be reduced to the lowest radical denominator, and present a united front against Israel."

Transcending all election-year issues—beyond the Palestinian question, religious-secular disputes and all other matters that can be reduced to rhetoric—is a continuing internal struggle for power. No party has ever won a majority of seats in the Knesset. A constitution has not yet been adopted.

Power means more in Israel than is ordinarily the case in tiny nations with few natural resources. On a day-to-day basis, the men and women who govern Israel preside over a rapidly developing nation that has become a leader in various fields of research and technology, a center of vigorous activity in culture and the arts, and outstanding practitioner of democracy and a nuclear-armed military power whose pilots and ground troops are regarded as among the finest in the world.

For many politicians in the world, these might be only the trappings of power. For Israelis, they can be much more. They can be a chance to make history. But after 40 years, Israelis have yet to render a political verdict on themselves. They have yet to decide whether the Jewish state will reflect the socialist views of its founders, the moral heritage that shaped the founders' socialism or the religious rituals that preserved the moral tradition through centuries of exile—or some future fusings of all of these streams.

THE MORNING AFTER[4]

It has been a scorching summer in Israel: both sides have been playing with fire. Fire was set to forests all around the country, allegedly by Palestinian arsonists; then it was set to three Gazan workers sleeping in Or Yehudah near Tel Aviv, by Jewish youngsters. "Facing the Woods," a story written by Abraham B. Yehoshua twenty-five years ago, suddenly took on a fresh meaning. It is about a Jewish student who is staying in a watchtower overlooking the woods, writing a paper about the Crusaders, and watching out for fire. A tongueless old Arab, who lives downstairs with a little girl, is assisting him in his job, yet secretly accumulating kerosene cans in order to set the forest ablaze. Eventually the Jewish student helps the old Arab set fire to the woods, and they find the ruins of the Arab village, which has been long covered up by the trees.

One interpretation of that story observes that the only language tongueless Arabs can speak is the language of fire. Why, then, should the tongueless, oppressed, battered, and dispossessed Palestinian speak in a language other than that of fire? Then the name Emmwas this summer began more and more to be heard. The inhabitants of Emmwas (supposedly the biblical Emmaus) and of two other adjacent villages were expelled from their homes in the wake of the battles of the Six Day War, four years after Yehoshua's story was published. The villages were located in what the Israelis regarded at the time as a very sensitive

[4]By Anton Shammas, Israeli-Palestinian novelist and writer on political affairs, from *The New York Review of Books*, vol. 35, no. 14, September 29, 1988, pp. 47–52. Reprinted by permission from *The New York Review of Books.* Copyright © 1988, Nyrev, Inc.

spot, a cigarette away, as the Arabs say, from the Green Line, and the scene of heavy fighting in 1948. The villages were bulldozed, and, later, trees were planted on top of the ruins. The once populated hills of Emmwas became "Canada Park," and Yehoshua's student, who exists somewhere in every Israeli Jewish mind, wondered if one day this park, and similar forests, would be set on fire.

However, the Palestinian issue, in recent months, has not been on the front burner, so to speak, of the lame-duck policy makers in Israel or in the United States. The uncertain time preceding the November elections in both countries has somehow obscured the issue, which must wait for clearer days. But the Palestinians have always been notorious for bad timing. The *intifada*, long overdue as it is, erupted at a bad time. The PLO procrastinated far too long in taking a definite position on Israel. Finally, at June's Arab summit in Algiers, Bassam Abu Sharif, Arafat's adviser and spokesman, came out with an explicit political extension to the *intifada*, a statement that called upon the PLO to hold direct talks with Israel, and implicitly recognized Israel's right to exist. "All nations," Abu Sharif wrote, "Jews and Palestinians among them, have the right to expect not only nonaggression from their neighbors, but also a political and economical cooperation of sorts." Some Palestinian leaders criticized this statement, but Abu Sharif repeated the gist of it on August 13, and told the Reuters news agency that the PLO is ready to trade peace with Israel for an independent state in the occupied West Bank and the Gaza Strip. Furthermore, *The Wall Street Journal* of August 24 reported that

while the document drew condemnation from extreme PLO factions outside the occupied territories, Palestinians in the West Bank and Gaza did not repudiate it. Indeed, interviews with scores of Palestinians, from refugee youths to university professors, reveal an overwhelming majority in favor of recognition.

Then the second-highest PLO official, Abu Iyad, in an interview on August 14 in the Paris *Journal du Dimanche* issued the most unequivocal PLO announcement in years. He called for a provisional state in the occupied territories, whose political program would be "completely different" from that of the current Palestinian Charter. "My solution for peace," he said, "is a Palestinian state, a discussion to establish the frontiers of that state and the mutual recognition of Israel and Palestine." He also said the Palestinian state would be set up with reference to UN Resolution 181 of 1947 calling for the partition of Palestine. "I did not say it was necessary to accept the frontiers mentioned in article 181," he told the interviewer. "I said it was necessary to refer to it since it is the only one that asserts the agreement of the United Nations on the creation of two states." A day before, on August 13 in Amman, a member of the Palestinian National Council told *The Washington Post* that the PLO's acceptance of the 1947 UN resolution

could be the basis for negotiations and would give the PLO international legitimacy, which also means you accept the state of Israel without the need to say it. The [council] may come out and say it. This is the bottom line.

Three days later, on August 17, in an interview with Radio Luxembourg, Ibraheem Sous, the PLO representative in Paris, conceded that the PLO is ready to accept the UN Partition Resolution of 1947,

as a judicial ground, or as a starting point for negotiations with Israel. . . . What is meant is the principle that lies behind the resolution and not necessarily the boundaries between the Jewish state and the Arab state as drawn some forty years ago.

As for the Palestinian charter calling for an end to Israel, which long stood in the way of negotiations, Sous said that it

lacks validity because of all the decisions taken by the Palestine National Council ever since, decisions that reflect the changes in the PLO standpoints. There is no reason why the Charter should be an obstacle for negotiations.

Abu Iyad's announcement was pushed aside in the Israeli media, and hardly mentioned in the US. Five days had elapsed before John Kifner of *The New York Times* referred to it briefly in a report published on August 19; and an editorial on the Israeli occupation published on the same day made no mention of it. Shamir's office called the announcement a "conjuring trick" and Peres referred to it as a "crossword puzzle." Decoded, this arcane language means that now that the Palestinians have got their tongues back and seem to be giving up on the language of fire (and terror for that matter), the Israelis turn a deaf ear.

Talking about the morning after in the Middle East these days sounds like worrying about a hangover while the Molotov cocktails are still being smashed. Still, since a would-be Palestinian state will probably have to deal with many similar problems and challenges that the Jewish state of Israel has been facing since the day it was established, it might be enlightening to try to outline the ready-made Israeli pitfalls that the Palestinian state should try to evade. Now that a Palestinian state, provisional or otherwise, is within a stone's throw, one might indulge in examining what the morning after the establishment of the state would be like.

One is drawn to these analogies if only by sheer rhetoric. There is a stunning similarity between the language used by Jewish organizations during the Forties and the language that could be used these days by, say, the leaders of the uprising, in their clandestine pamphlets:

Terrorism is for us a part of the political battle being conducted under the present circumstances, and it has a great part to play; speaking in a clear voice to the whole world, as well as to our wretched brethren outside this land, it proclaims our war against the occupier.

This is taken from a article published in the summer of 1943, in the Stern Gang's publication *Hahazeet* ("The Front"), written by the current prime minister of Israel, Yitzhak Shamir. "Neither Jewish ethics nor Jewish tradition," Shamir wrote, "can disqualify terrorism as a means of combat."

And between the counter-rhetoric of violence used by the authorities of the British Mandate for suppressing the Jewish "terrorists" and that used by the Israeli authorities today against the Palestinian "terrorists" in the occupied territories, there is more than a similarity—the violence is carried out according to the same regulations. However, I am afraid the similarity between Palestinian and Jewish experience is more than rhetoric-deep: if the Palestinians do not try to learn from the errors of the Jews, they will end up establishing a duplicate of the Jewish state on the other side of the Green Line, another ethnic state that will self-righteously call itself, as Israel does, "the only democracy in the Middle East."

The UN Partition Resolution of 1947, which after more than forty years is beginning to appeal to the Palestinians, talked about two states in Palestine/Eretz Israel, a Jewish state and an Arab state. World Jewry at the time accepted the resolution. The late Simha Flapan (in his recent *The Birth of Israel*) argues that it was meant to be a tactical step on the part of Ben-Gurion. However, the resolution forms the backdrop of the "Declaration of the Establishment of the State of Israel." "On the 29th of November, 1947, the United Nations General Assembly passed a resolution calling for the establishment of a Jewish State in Eretz Israel," Ben-Gurion writes in the "Declaration," failing to mention that the resolution also called for the establishment of an Arab state. He then proceeds:

Accordingly we, . . . by virtue of our natural and historic right and on the strength of the resolution of the United Nations General Assembly, hereby declare the establishment of a Jewish state in Eretz Israel, to be known as the state of Israel.

Thus the state of Israel was not established in 1948; rather, a Jewish state was. And that is, apparently, what the Palestinians are going to do. Instead of a "secular democratic Palestine," as the PLO has been declaring for years, what will be eventually established is a purely ethnic Palestinian state, not the state of Palestine.

When talking about their conflict, Zionists and Palestinians (there is no Israeli-Arab conflict) tend to begin with the Book of Genesis. There are people on both sides who seem to believe that the Book of Genesis quotes God as saying, "Let there be a Palestinian problem," and that the only solution for this conflict, in the spirit of that book, would be to throw the other side into the sea, or the desert, respectively. People from both sides have made a Gordian knot out of the emotions, arguments, and counterarguments that have accumulated for nearly a century. However, the solution is rather simple. It lies in drawing the line between the Homeland and the State—between the Land of Israel (Eretz Israel) and the State of Israel, between the Land of Falastin and the State of Palestine—which simply means a two-state solution. So the Palestinian prime minister will probably write the following entry one day in his diary:

One does not demand from anybody to give up his vision. We shall accept a state in the boundaries fixed today—but the boundaries of Palestinian aspirations are the concern of the Palestinian people and no external factor will be able to limit them.

This derives from David Ben-Gurion's diary of 1937; but he, of course, was talking about the "boundaries of Zionist aspirations."

Seventy percent of the 700,000 Palestinians who are Israelis by citizenship and Arabs by nationality were born after the establishment of the state of Israel. They are the descendants of the 156,000 Palestinians who tried to cling to their homes and lands during the year 1948. I was born two years afterward, in a small village in the Galilee, far away from the village of Emmwas, in the safer north. I left that village twenty-five years ago, not as a refugee but as a disoriented villager, in pursuit of what my father had considered, surprisingly enough, the most effective Palestinian weapon of all—education. Whenever I go back to the village, I go back to something that exists only in my memory, and I keep reciting to myself an aphorism that is excessively used by the modern, identity-seeking writers in Israel. It is the famous opening lines of a poem written in 1923:

> Man is nothing but a little plot of
> land
> Man is nothing but the image of his
> native landscape.

The above lines were written by one Tchernichovsky, a fine Hebrew poet. Incidentally, the word "image" ("Man is nothing but the image of his native landscape") is translated from the Hebrew "*tavneet*," which could also mean "a baking mold, a baking pan." So whenever I think of these lines I wonder which parts of me have, by any chance, stuck to the baking pan of my "native landscape." Then I recall that I was only half-baked in that distant landscape, or "half made," as V.S. Naipaul loftily describes third world societies.

My generation, if you will pardon the broad usage, was helped out of its past, of its landscape. We were lucky, in a way, because we could have been born, if we were born at all, within the landscapes of the refugee camps, among the people who were flung out of their respective landscapes, out of their respective, scorching baking molds. So to some extent, Israel's Palestinians to this very day are still ashamed of having been privileged, of having been spared the fate of the wanderers. However, also to some extent, they feel that the Palestinian refugees are somehow closer to perfection, so to speak, more at peace with themselves, than they are. Nevertheless, I doubt if there is any Israeli Palestinian who would be willing to trade his affected, imperfect being for that of a Palestinian refugee. I have more than one reason for believing that the latter may not be inclined to exchange places with him either.

Thirty years ago, at the end of my first year of primary school, which happened to be the second anniversary of the foundation of the public school in my village, we children were sent to bring laurel branches from the tree shading the village spring, to decorate an enormous Star of David that one of the teachers had built from six planks. Our Arab principal wished to make a good impression on the Jewish inspector of schools who had, apparently, invited himself to have a close look at the achievements of the young school. The huge Star of David, covered in laurel branches, was hung carelessly and loosely above the stage front, where, as it swayed, it frightened the children taking part in the program, and also frightened their proud parents in the first rows who thought it might topple down on them. (It didn't.)

I sometimes wonder whether we were not seared by that star, whether it wasn't a branding iron after all. A branding iron to all the Arabs who were left, for some reason or another, inside the borders of Israel, in the year of our Lord Balfour 1948, henceforth to be referred to as the Green Liners. For nineteen years, between 1948 and 1967, the Green Liners were living in a cultural quarantine. In a way, they were illicitly experiencing being Arabs, as they tried to adjust to the new Israeli order. After 1967 they were all of a sudden given the lung that had been amputated from their body twenty years before, and were thus exposed to an overdose of oxygen. Now they were no longer cut off from their fellow Palestinians. Since 1948 they had been exposed to the state, which had defined itself, from the very beginning, politically and culturally, as a Jewish state. This sudden exposure after 1948 knocked the ground—in the literal sense of the word too—from under their cultural confidence. Those were the days of the military administration and land expropriations.

My father in those days needed a special permit, like all the Arab fathers of his generation, to move around in his homeland in the Galilee, which had turned, overnight, into the homeland of the Jewish people. But no such permits were available for moving around among the different cultures. For once branded, you cannot move around freely. My father's native landscapes were no longer open to him, and new books printed in Arabic did not make their way any longer to our shelves. The state of Israel put us in isolation.

When you brand someone, you are actually telling him two equally painful things. First, that he belongs to you, that he must abide by your laws, wander only in the regions that you had put under his disposal and keep away from the ones that are out of bounds. Second, you're telling him that this searing of the skin is just a searing of the skin; you are not after his heart. When he, too, realizes that you do not seek his utter loyalty, then you both break even, confining yourselves to a position lacking any mutual anticipation. You both acquiesce in the rules of the game: Don't call us and we won't call you.

I have already discussed the astonishing fact that there are no Israelis in Israel (*The New York Review*, March 31) for the simple reason that the rubric "nationality" (in Hebrew, *Leom*) on Israeli identity cards reads either "Jew" or "Arab." The term "Israeli nationality" does not exist in any Israeli official document, and it is used only by the Israeli Jews because Israel, as defined by its laws, is "the state of the Jewish people" and not the state of its citizens. In other words, the state of Israel, like the state of Palestine, has not been established yet. So "the morning after" has a double effect.

The Israeli Law of Return is still considered by nearly all Jewish Israelis to be the backbone, the raison d'être, of the Jewish state. It means, among other things, that the state of Israel cannot choose its citizens according to a particular immigration law, as is the case in most democratic countries of the Western world, but, rather, the citizen (i.e., the strictly Jewish citizen) is the one who makes the choice. If we exclude its application to those Jews in the Diaspora who are still persecuted because of what they are—an application that should not be excluded—the Israeli Law of Return is in effect a racist law. Twenty-five years, more or less, are enough time for anybody to make up anyone's mind about where she or he wants to spend her or his life. So I would suggest—if anybody would bother to ask—that a Palestinian Law of Return be applied primarily to those Palestinians who do not hold citizenship of any country. Then it should, after twenty-five years or so, become an ordinary immigration law, allowing the state to choose its citizens, and not vice versa. In other words, the Palestinian state that I dream of is a state that after two or three decades of its establishment will cease to be the Palestinian state and become the state of Palestine, i.e., a state where anybody who wishes to have a Palestinian nationality will have the right to apply for it.

On the morning after the establishment of the Palestinian state I, as an Israeli citizen, will no longer accept the fact that Israel does not belong to its citizens. Likewise, I will not accept the fact that my fellow Palestinians will regard me—as does Israel—as a potential citizen of their state, as one who is expected to "make *aliyah*" to Palestine. Since I am against the unlimited, absolute Law of Return in Israel, I decline to accept a possible, unlimited Palestinian law that will, after twenty-five years, grant more rights to, say, an American Palestinian than it will to an American Jewish professor who wishes to teach modern Hebrew literature at Beir Zeit University and make Ramallah his home—not because he wants to strike an old but still raw nerve, but because he simply wants to apply for Palestinian nationality.

Surprisingly, the left-wing intellectuals in Israel, when imagining the morning after, tend to insinuate that my place, as someone who considers himself to belong to the Palestinian people, should be in the Palestinian state and that I, too, "should make *aliyah* to Palestine. Of course if you want to stay, then you're most welcome. But please bear in mind that this is and will always be a Jewish state." Abraham B. Yehoshua for one told me two years ago, bluntly and publicly, that because he strongly supports the establishment of a Palestinian state beside Israel, with the old city of Jerusalem as its capital (and this is, one must admit, a very unusual statement from an Israeli Jew), he expects me, if I want to fulfill my national identity, to move to that state. This view unfortunately overlaps, to a certain extent, with that of the extreme right in Israel, with one substantial difference; when it comes from the right, racist camp, it means that the Palestinian state is already established in the kingdom of his majesty King Hussein of Jordan. Incidentally, when I discussed the question with a Palestinian friend of mine he told me that I would be most welcome in the new state provided I came along with the Galilee. "Otherwise," he said, "who needs more refugees?"

The hidden premise in Yehoshua's argument was that no Israeli Zionist would, on the morning after, accept that even after the establishment of the "Arab State" in Eretz-Israel/Palestine there would be Palestinians who would be brazen enough to ask the Jews for their share in a narrow strip of land called the state of Israel.

What should be done, then, on the morning after, with the 700,000 Palestinian Israelis? Who are they, and where should they go? (Seven hundred thousand is also the number of the Palestinian refugees who are euphemistically said to have left their homes duing 1948. Chaim Weizmann, we should bear in mind, said of the departure of those refugees in 1948 that is was "a miraculous simplification of the problem.")

Imagine, then, that the long conflict has come to an end, and the long-awaited Palestinian dream has come true, and there is a Palestinian state in the West Bank and the Gaza Strip. And imagine that you are a Palestinian of the Green Line, an Israeli by citizenship, according to your passport, but an Arab national according to your identity card. And imagine that the state of Israel, which considers you an Arab by nationality, gives no sign of being able to carry out the promise made in its Declaration of Independence about equal social and political rights, since it continues to be strictly a Jewish state. As a nonconstitutional Jewish state it can only promise to give you social rights, such as the right to equal employment opportunity, only to find out, after applying for a certain job, that preference is given to those who served in the army. You will also have to make do with some limited quasi-political rights such as the right to vote for the Knesset and even to be elected to it, while being unable to run for office: there has never been an Arab minister in the Israeli cabinet, nor will there be. But you will find yourself dependent for protection on the enlightened tolerance of Israeli society, which has been drifting recently more and more to the right. Israeli Arabs do not have any access to key positions in government departments, let alone to the sensitive places where their daily life is dealt with and decided upon. Every single detail of their lives, from cradle to grave, is virtually controlled by the Jewish ruling majority. Even Arab departments in every government office are run by Jewish managers. With all this in mind, what is your next step?

Or imagine that you are an American Palestinian with a US passport. You belong to the Palestinian people, but you are actually an American by nationality, and a well-off one for that matter (say, a professor at the University of Michigan)—will you practice the right given to you according to the Palestinian Law of Return and make *aliyah* to the Palestinian state? And if you don't, how deep is your involvement in that state to be—if you were asked, some day, by your fellow Palestinians who consider you a potential citizen of their state, to be the Palestinian equivalent of Jonathan Pollard, would you accept?

Or imagine that you are a Palestinian refugee at Ein el-Hilweh refugee camp in Lebanon, devastated by Israeli air raids and the ghastly whims of Lebanese politics. Would you be happy to trade places and pick up your shattered life at a "designer refugee camp" in the West Bank? Or would you rather stick to the good old desolate life, to the good old Lebanese civil war, instead of having to adjust to the new, vehement rules of, say, a Palestinian civil war in the West Bank? Because who, in the fickle Middle East, can assure you that the morning after will be a nice one; that the hangover will be mild; that a Palestinian identity card is the best of shelters amid the turmoils of Middle East politics?

Jerome M. Segal, a research scholar at the University of Maryland, who helped found the Jewish Committee for Israeli-Palestinian Peace some six years ago, published an article last April in the Palestinian Arabic daily *Al-Quds* (the original in English was published in *The Washington Post* of May 22), and also in the English version of the Palestinian daily *Al-Fajr*. Surprisingly enough, the article was approved by the otherwise very strict Israeli censorship, despite its proposal of an "alternative strategy" for attaining an independent Palestinian state, a strategy that "will overnight transform the political agenda, and place the two-state solution in center stage as the only peace option." This "Radical Plan for Mideast Peace," as the article was titled, apparently was partly responsible for the draft proposal for an independent Palestinian state, later to be known as "The Husseini Document," which was seized by Israeli authorities at the end of July at the Arab Research Institute in Jerusalem, whose director is Feisal Husseini. The authorities leaked it to the press, hoping that it would be attacked, but they inadvertently made a pivotal event out of it.

The draft Palestinian declaration proclaimed the establishment of an independent Palestinian state, according to the UN Partition Resolution of 1947, a state that will "live in peace side by side with the state of Israel" and whose provisional government would negotiate its final borders with the state of Israel. This declaration was to be announced in a press conference that would have been held in Jerusalem by Palestinian intellectuals and political activists, had not Husseini been arrested.

There are two major discrepancies, though, between Segal's and Husseini's propositions. Whereas Segal suggests that the PLO issue "a declaration of independence and statehood announcing the existence of the State of Palestine," Husseini suggests that this declaration should be made by the unified leadership of the *intifada*, thus slightly pushing the PLO aside. As for the territory of this proposed state, it consists of the West Bank and the Gaza Strip according to Segal, and is indicated by the Partition boundaries according to Husseini; however, the boundaries of the Palestinian state would be the first item on the agenda of peace negotiations between the PLO and Israel.

In a report in *The New York Times* of August 8, some Palestinians who said they were in contact with the PLO headquarters in Tunis claimed that the Husseini document is actually five years old, and that

the document was prepared by the PLO's research arm, . . . when Palestinian academics and economists met at PLO headquarters in Tunis at the invitation of the Palestine Research Center. Among them were a number of university professors of Palestinian origin from the United States.

Be that as it may I tried to read between the lines of the Husseini document, but it seemed that my worries were left unanswered: How does this would-be state relate to me as a Palestinian citizen of Israel? Am I supposed to start tuning up my Jewish guilt feelings about not making *aliyah* to Palestine?

Then the Segal article put me on the alert:

The state of Palestine will allow dual citizenship. Palestinians who are citizens of other states are encouraged to apply for and travel on Palestinian passports.

This means that the relation between Israel and the Diaspora is applied to the Palestinians. Not only does an American Palestinian with a green card have the same rights as a ragged, devastated refugee from Ein el-Hilweh in Lebanon, but I also am "encouraged" to keep my Israeli citizenship and apply for a Palestinian passport. In other words, the state of Palestine, like the state of Israel, will also maintain a situation in which citizenship does not coincide with nationality. In practical effect, this very likely means that the state of Israel will have every right to deprive me of my political rights inside its jurisdiction, arguing that I am able at any time to pursue my national fulfillment next door, since I am automatically wait-listed as a Palestinian citizen. Some

Israeli officials from the Ministry of the Interior might argue, in the years to come, that since I have access to a Palestinian passport and, consequently, to a Palestinian nationality, this would annul my claims for an Israeli nationally, because it was meant solely for Jews in the first place, and now that I have an outlet why should I cling to the old deadlock between Jews and Arabs? Palestinians throughout the world, including the Arab states, will face the same reproach.

King Hussein, sly and shrewd as he is, has already foreseen the problem. In his July 31 announcement that he was severing his ties with the Palestinians on the West Bank, he made the following statement about his Palestinian subjects:

Our steps apply only to the occupied Palestinian territories and their inhabitants, but not to the Jordanian citizens of Palestinian origin inside the Hashemite Kingdom. Needless to say that those citizens enjoy full civil rights, and, like any other citizens, they carry all the obligations, regardless of their ethnic affiliation (origin). These citizens form an integral part of the Jordanian state, to which they belong . . . [since] Jordan is not Palestine and the independent Palestinian state should be established in the occupied Palestinian land after its liberation, in God's will, [that is] where Palestinian identify should be fulfilled.

On August 14 in Amman, the hot potato in the discussions between the PLO representatives and the senior Jordanian officials was the issue of the political loyalties of Palestinians living in Jordan. A PLO official, according to *The Washington Post* (August 14), indicated that sharp disagreements had emerged over the national identity of Palestinians who carry Jordanian citizenship. However, at the end of the discussions on August 15, the PLO seemed to accept the King's view. "The [1.5 million] Palestinians who live in Jordan," the joint statement said, "are Hashemite citizens with full rights and obligations. The Palestinian State established, they will have the right to live in it."

Around the same time in Israel, M. K. Abdel Wahab Darawsheh, the founder of the new Democratic Arab Party, which is exclusively Arab, told a reporter of Israeli Radio (on August 18) that with "the Palestinian state established, there will be no problem of national identity for the Arab population in Israel." Another member added: "My citizenship is Israeli but my nationality is Palestinian; I want to be a loyal Israeli citizen but at the same time I want to celebrate the establishment of the Palestinian state which could be my national home." It was not clear though whether this Arab party had taken account in its platform, or in its plans, of Israel's Basic Law (Knesset, Amendment Number 12) that the state of Israel is the state of the Jewish people.

Still, it is worth observing that as far as personal freedoms are concerned, the Palestinians who live in Israel proper, nonconstitutional as it is, are much better off, relatively speaking, than the Jordanian citizens, Palestinians or otherwise. For no matter how unequivocal a Bill of Rights could be, the boundaries of freedom for a member of a minority will eventually depend on the enlightenment of the society in which he lives. Nevertheless, the Black experience in the US proves, if proof is needed, that a constitution, even when it is not meticulously observed, is the best of shelters for minorities. That is exactly why Israeli Palestinians are consumed with worries; they live in a nonconstitutional Jewish state whose enlightened Jewish communities are on the wane. At the very least they are in danger because they, as a "national minority," are perceived by the majority as a perpetual threat to its political and cultural hegemony.

All the questions I have raised have never been faced, except by such people as Akiba Ernst Simon, who died last month in Jerusalem. He was one of the less prominent members of *Brit Shalom*, a group of wise Zionists that included, among others, Martin Buber and Judah L. Magnes. As early as the Twenties they believed that the only solution west of the Jordan was a binational state, in a federation that would include Jordan, Syria, and Lebanon. "If and when this Federation comes into being," Magnes wrote in September 1942, "the whole question of numbers in Palestine loses its present primary significance for the Arabs." Magnes, who was called a "starry-eyed idealist" by the Jewish press at the time, tried in the early Forties to involve the American consulate in Jerusalem in his crusade, hoping that "America's moral and political authority [would] be thrown into the balance." Starry-eyed as he was, Magnes was one of the first to understand that

Palestine as a Jewish State means Jewish rule over the Arabs; Palestine as an Arab State means Arab rule over the Jews. Palestine as a bi-national state must therefore provide constitutionally for equal political rights and duties for both the Jewish and the Arab nations, regardless of majority and minority.

According to one of Simon's obituaries, after backing the plan for a bi-national state in Palestine he supported the Palestinian demand for separate statehood while "in his pursuit of reconciliation, he worked for friendship between the youth of both nations" (*The Independent*, London, August 26). Whether his approach acquires any serious following in Israel will determine the country's future.

Moshe Arad, the Israeli ambassador to the US, was on *Evans & Novak* (CNN) some seven months ago (Saturday, February 20). He was asked by Mr. Novak to comment on an article by an American Jew, Robert Zelnick, which had been published in *The Washington Post* three days earlier. "The heart of the problem," Mr. Zelnick contended at the end of his rather fierce article, "is the greed, the extremism, the opportunism that have increasingly driven Israel policy in the occupied territories." The ambassador, managing to muffle his diplomatic anger, gave the familiar Israeli response: Who are these people, sitting in Washington in their air-conditioned offices, telling us what to do at the front line?

Both interviewers failed to remind the ambassador that Mr. Zelnick's article was written in response to a previous publicly released letter that the president of Israel, Chaim Herzog, had sent to Rabbi Alexander Schindler, president of the Union of American Hebrew Congregations, inviting American Jews who are critical of Israeli actions in the West Bank and the Gaza Strip "to offer a different approach." The letter, apparently, didn't make it clear that only proposals congenial to the government should be made—otherwise American Jews should confine themselves to their air-conditioned offices.

This might explain, in the future, the conduct of the Palestinian ambassador to the United States, lashing out at a Palestinian Zelnick who has been living in Washington for all his life but has enough chutzpah to criticize the measures taken by the Palestinian government against, say, the remaining Jewish settlers who, according to the peace treaty between Israel and the Palestinian state, preferred to become Palestinians by nationality and Jews by ethnic affiliation but now are demonstrating because they feel they are being treated as second-rate citizens. Or, better still, against a group of Palestinian dissidents who have incurred the authorities' wrath by advocating the now long-forgotten political ideas of Judah L. Magnes, by calling for a federation with the state of Israel, and by denouncing the narrow ethnic system.

Despite what Ambassador Arad believes, the state of Israel is by law "the state of the Jewish people," so Robert Zelnick was certainly entitled to criticize the Israel government. Arthur Hertzberg (in the January–February 1988 issue of *Present Tense* defined, rather brilliantly, this special relationship between the Jewish state and its long-distance sponsors:

> The diaspora has long ago agreed that whether Israel is socialist or capitalist remains its own business. It has not agreed that reversing [the commitment to] partition is a matter for Israel alone to decide, at the very least because it was not Israel alone that accepted partition. That decision was made in 1947 by world Jewry.

If the Palestinian national movement follows the steps of Zionism, and there is more than one indication that it will, then in a generation's time the situation of the Palestinian state will completely conform to that of the Jewish state, even in the minutest details of its magnificient failure. Except that Palestinian Zionism, in the spirit of "history repeating itself," could be more tragic. An ethnic, non-pluralistic Palestinian state would not appeal to most of the Palestinians living in the western Diaspora. having been exposed to many different national cultures and societies, they would not be attracted to yet another Middle Eastern state in which individual freedoms are stifled, political dissidence is suppressed, and cultural minorities are confined to narrow, isolated quarters. They will probably wait for better times. But then again, we Palestinians were always notorious for our bad timing.

After helping the old tongueless Arab set fire to woods, the Jewish student in Yehoshua's story rescues the little Arab girl from the burning watchtower. That is something to reflect on.

BIBLIOGRAPHY

The Israeli-Palestinian conflict is one that is far better understood by referring to books than to periodicals. The conflict's causes are many and complex, and these are seldom noted in accounts found in weekly or monthly magazines. This bibliography concentrates on those books of the last several decades that best describe the conflict's origins and course. The articles listed at the end, with their abstracts, are examples of recent journalistic comment.

BOOKS AND PAMPHLETS

Abu-Ghazaleh, Adnan Mohammed. Arab cultural nationalism in Palestine during the British Mandate. Institute for Palestine Studies. '73.

Abu Iyad. My home, my land: a narrative of the Palestine struggle. Quadrangle/New York Times Book. '81.

Abu-Lughod, Ibrahim, ed. Palestinian rights: affirmation and denial. Medina Press. '82.

Amad, Adnan, ed. Documents and reports on Israeli violations of human and civil rights. Palestine Research Center. '75.

Amad, Adnan, comp. Israeli League for Human and Civil Rights (the Shahak papers). Near East Ecumenical Bureau for Information and Interpretation. '73?

Antonius, George. The Arab awakening. Hamish Hamilton, '45; Putnam. '65.

Arabs under Israeli occupation, 1981. Institute for Palestine Studies. '84.

Arnon, Itzhak. From fellah to farmer: a study on change in Arab villages. Agricultural Research Organization, The Volcani Center. '80.

Aruri, Nasseer, ed. Occupation, Israel over Palestine. Zed Books. 1984.

Ashabranner, Brent K. Gavriel and Jemal: two boys of Jerusalem. Dodd, Mead. c'84.

Avineri, Shlomo. The making of modern Zionism: intellectual origins of the Jewish state. Weidenfeld & Nicolson; Basic Books. '81.

Avneru, Uri. My friend, the enemy. L. Hill. '86.

Bailey, Clinton. Jordan's Palestinian challenge, 1948–1983: a political history. Westview Press.'84.

Bailey, Sydney Dawson. The making of Resolution 242. M. Nijhoff. '85.

Barbour, Nevill. Nisi Dominus. Harrap. '46.

Bark, Dennis L., ed. To promote peace: US foreign policy in the Middle East. Hoover Institution Press. '84.

Bar-Zohar, Michel. Ben-Gurion. Weidenfeld & Nicolson; Delacorte. '78.

Ben-Ami, Yitshaq. Years of wrath, days of glory: memoirs from the Irgun. Robert Speller & Sons. '82.

Ben-Dor, Gabriel, ed. The Palestinians and the Middle East conflict. Turtledove. '78.

Berger, Earl. The covenant and the sword. Routledge & Kegan Paul. '65.

Begin, Menachem. The revolt. Nash. '77.

Bein, Alex. Theodor Herzl. East and West Library, '57; Atheneum. '70.

Bendt, Ingela. We shall return: women of Palestine. L. Hill. '82.

Ben-Gurion, David. Israel: a personal history. Funk & Wagnalls. '71.

Ben-Meir, Alon. Israel: the challenge of the fourth decade. Cyrco Press. '78.

Benvenisti, Meron. The West Bank Data Project: a survey of Israel's policies. American Enterprise Institute. '84.

The bitter years: Arabs under Israeli occupation in 1982. The American-Arab Anti-Discrimination Committee. '83.

Braunthal, Julius. The significance of Israeli socialism, and the Arab-Israeli dispute. Lincolns-Prager. '58.

Breslauer, S. Daniel. Meir Kahane: ideologue, hero, thinker. E. Mellen Press. '86.

Brown, Leon Carl. International politics and the Middle East: old rules, dangerous game. Tauris; Princeton University Press. '84.

Burns, E. L. M. Between Arab and Israeli. Harrap '62; Astor-Honor '63.

Cameron, James. The making of Israel. Secker & Warburg. '76.

Caplan, Gerald. Arab and Jew in Jerusalem: explorations in community mental health. Harvard University Press. '80.

Carter, Jimmy. The blood of Abraham: insights into the Middle East. Houghton Mifflin. '85.

Cattan, Henry. Jerusalem. Croom Helm. '81.

Cattan, Henry. Palestine and international law: the legal aspects of the Arab-Israeli conflict. Longman. '76.

Cattan, Henry. The Palestine question. Croom Helm. '88.

Chacour, Elias. Blood brothers. Chosen Books. '84.

Chomsky, Noam. The fateful triangle: the United States, Israel and the Palestinians. South End Press. '83.

Clifford, Clark M., ed. The Palestine question in American history. Arno Press. '78.

Cohen, Mitchell. Zion and state: nation, class, and the shaping of modern Israel. B. Blackwell. '87.

Cohen, Richard I. The return to the land of Israel. World Zionist Organization. '86.

Controversy in the Middle East: U.N. Resolution 242 and the October War: documents and analysis. IDOC-North America. '74.

Cooley, John K. Green March, Black September: The Story of the Palestinian Arabs. Frank Cass. '73.

Curry, Jerry R. Israel's treatment of its major ethnic groups: an individual research report. U. S. Army War College. '73.

Curtis, Michael et al., eds. The Palestinians: people, history, politics. Transaction Book. '75.

Curtiss, Richard H. A changing image: American perceptions of the Arab-Israeli dispute. American Educational Trust. '82.

Darwish, Mahmud. The Palestinian chalk circle. Lebanese Association for Information on Palestine. (n.d., 1970s?)

Davis, John H. The evasive peace. John Murray. '68.

Davis, Uri. The Golan Heights under Israeli occupation, 1967–1981. Centre for Middle Eastern and Islamic Studies. '83.

Day, Arthur R. East Bank/West Bank: Jordan and the prospects for peace. Council on Foreign Relations. '86.

DeVore, Ronald M. The Arab-Israeli conflict: a historical, political, social and military bibliography. Clio. '76.

Dimbleby, Jonathan. The Palestinians. Quartet Books. '84.

Douglas-Home, Charles. The Arabs and Israel. Rev. ed. Bodley Head. '70.

Draper, Hal, ed. Zionism, Israel, and the Arabs: the historical background of the Middle East tragedy. Independent Socialist Press. '67.

Dupuy, Trevor N. Elusive victory: The Arab-Israeli Wars, 1947–1974. Harper & Row. '78.

Eisenman, Robert H. Islamic law in Palestine and Israel: a history of the survival of Tanzimat and Shari'a in the British Mandate and the Jewish state. Brill. '78.

El-Asmar, Fouzi. To be an Arab in Israel. Frances Pinter. '75.

El-Yacoubi, Hassan Hasan Sheikh Salim. The evolution of Palestinian consciousness. '73.

Epp, Frank and Goddard, John. The Palestinians: portrait of a people in conflict. Herald Press. '76.

Feinberg, Nathan. On an Arab jurist's approach to Zionism and the state of Israel. Magnes Press, Hebrew University. '71.

Feinberg, Nathan. Studies in international law, with special reference to the Arab-Israel conflict. Magnes Press, Hebrew University. '79.

Flapan, Simha. The birth of Israel: myths and realities. Pantheon Books. '87.

Flapan, Simha. Zionism and the Palestinians. Barnes & Noble. '79.

Fraser, T. G. The Middle East, 1914–1979. St. Martin's. '80.

Freedman, Robert O., ed. World politics and the Arab-Israeli conflict. Pergamon. '79.

George, Donald E. Israeli occupation: international law and political realities. Exposition Press. '80.

Ghabra, Shafeeq N. Palestinians in Kuwait: the family and the politics of survival. Westview Press. '87.

Gilmour, David. Dispossessed: the ordeal of the Palestinians. Sphere Books. '82.

Ginat, J. Women in Muslim rural society: status and role in family and community. Transaction Books. '82.

Glubb, John Bagot. The Middle East crisis. Hodder & Stoughton. '67.

Golan, Galia. Soviet-PLO relations and the creation of a Palestinian state. Hebrew University of Jerusalem, Soviet and East European Research Centre. '79.

Goldring, Benjamin. Treatment of Palestinians in Israeli-occupied West Bank and Gaza: report of the National Lawyers Guild. 1977 Middle East Delegation. '79.

Graham-Brown, Sarah. Education, repression, liberation: Palestinians. World University Press. '84.

Grangvist, Hilma Natalia. Portrait of a Palestinian village: the photographs of Hilma Grangvist. Third World Centre for Research and Publication. '81.

Gruen, George E., ed. The Palestinians in perspective: implications for Mideast peace and U.S. policy. Institute of Human Relations Press, the American Jewish Committee. '82.

Gvati, Haim. A hundred years of settlement: the story of Jewish settlement in the Land of Israel. Keter. '85.

Hacohen, David. Time to tell: an Israeli life, 1898–1984. Cornwall Books. '85.

Hadawi, Sami. Bitter harvest: Palestine between 1914 and 1979. Caravan Books. '83.

Halabi, Ratile. The West Bank story. Harcourt Brace Jovanovich. '82.

Haron, Miriam Joyce, Palestine and the Anglo-American connection, 1945–1950. P. Lang. '86.

Hardie, Frank and Herman, Irwin. Britain and Zion: the fateful entanglement. Blackstaff. '80.

Harris, William Wilson. Taking root: Israeli settlement in the West Bank, the Golan, and Gaza-Sinai, 1967–1980. Research Studies Press. '80.

Har-Shefi, Yoella. Beyond the gunsights: one Arab family in the promised land. Houghton Mifflin. '80.

Herzog, Chaim. The Arab-Israeli wars. Random House. '82.

Hirst, David. The gun and the olive branch: the roots of violence in the Middle East. 2d ed. Faber & Faber. '84.

Howe, Irving, ed. Israel, the Arabs, and the Middle East, Quadrangle Books. '72.

Howley, Dennis C. The United Nations and the Palestinians. Exposition Press. '75.

Hudson, Michael, ed. Alternative approaches to the Arab-Israeli conflict: a comparative analysis of the principal actors. Croom Helm. '83.

Hurewitz, Jacob Coleman. The struggle for Palestine. Greenwood. '68.

Hussaini, Hatem I., ed. The Palestine problem: an annotated bibliography, 1967-1980. Palestine Information Office. '80.

Hutchison, E. H. Violent truce. Devin-Adair. '56.

Ingrams, Doreen, ed. Palestine papers, 1917-1922: seeds of conflict. John Murray '72; Braziller '73.

Israeli, Raphael, ed. PLO in Lebanon: selected documents. Weidenfeld and Nicolson. '83.

Jackson, Elmore. Middle East mission. Norton. '84.

Jbara, Taysir. Palestinian leader, Hajj Amin al-Husayni, mufti of Jerusalem. Kingston Press. '85.

Jefferson, H. R. The American solution to Middle East problems: wars and oil. Exposition Press. '75.

Johnson, Nels. Islam and the politics of meaning in Palestinian nationalism. Kegan Paul. '82.

Jurays, Sabri. The Arabs in Israel. Monthly Review Press. '76.

Jurays, Sabri. Democratic freedoms in Israel. Institute for Palestine Studies. '72.

Jureidini, Paul and William E. Hazen. The Palestinian movement in politics. Lexington. '76.

Kahane, Meir. They must go. Grosset & Dunlap. '81.

Kahane, Meir. Uncomfortable questions for comfortable Jews. L. Stuart. '87.

Kaufman, Menahem. America's Jerusalem policy, 1947-1948. Institute of Contemporary Jewry, Hebrew University of Jerusalem. '82.

Kayyali, A. W. Palestine: a modern history. Third World Center for Research & Publishing. '81.

Kayyali, A. W. Zionism, imperialism, and racism. Croom Helm. '79.

Kazziha, Walid. Palestine in the Arab dilemma. Barnes & Noble Books. '79.

Khalidi, Rashid. Under siege : P.L.O. decisionmaking during the 1982 war. Columbia University Press. '86.

Khalidi, Walid. Before their diaspora: a photographic history of the Palestinians, 1876-1948. Institute for Palestine Studies. '84.

Khalidi, Walid and Jill Khadduri, eds. Palestine and the Arab-Israeli conflict. Institute for Palestine Studies. '75.

Khouri, Fred J. The Arab-Israeli dilemma. 2d. ed. Syracuse University Press. '76.

Kimmerling Baruch. Zionism and economy. Schenkman Pub. Co. '83.

Kimmerling, Baruch. Zionism and territory: the socio-territorial dimensions of Zionist politics. Institute of International Studies, University of California. '83.

Klein, Herbert Arthur. The people of Israel: fifty-seven centuries of presence. Pangloss Press. '86.

Knox, D. Edward. The making of a new Eastern Question: British Palestine policy and the origins of Israel, 1917–1925. The Catholic University of America Press. '81.

Kozodou, Neal, Ed. The generations of Israel. CBS Records. '68.

Kuniholm, Bruce. The Palestinian problem and United States policy: a guide to issues and reference. Regina Books. '86.

Kuroda, Alice K. and Yasumasa Kuroda. Palestinians without Palestine: a study of political socialization among Palestinian youths. University Press of America. '78.

Kurzman, Dan. Ben-Gurion, prophet of fire. Simon and Schuster. '83.

Landau, Jacob M. The Arabs and the Histadrut. Ranot Printing Press. '76.

Langer, Felicia. These are my brothers: Israel and the occupied territories. Ithaca Press. '81.

Laqueur, Walter and Rubin, Barry, eds. The Israel-Arab reader: a documentary history of the Middle East conflict. Penguin '84; Facts on File '85.

Lesch, Ann M. Arab politics in Palestine, 1917–1939: the frustration of a national movement. Cornell University Press. '79.

Lesch, Ann Mosely. Political perceptions of the Palestinians on the West Bank and the Gaza Strip. Middle East Institute. '80.

Litvinoff, Barnet, ed. Israel: 2500 B.C.–1972; a chronology and fact book. Oceana Publications. '74.

Living conditions of the Palestinian people in the occupied territories. (prepared for, and under the guidance of, the Committee on the Exercise of the Inalienable Rights of the Palestinian people) United Nations. '85.

Lucas, Noah. The modern history of Israel. Weidenfeld and Nicolson. '75.

Lukacs, Yehuda., ed. Documents on the Israeli-Palestinian conflict, 1967–1983. Cambridge University Press. '84.

Lustick, Ian. Arabs in the Jewish state: Israel's control of a national minority. University of Texas Press. '80.

Mallison, Sally V. and W. Thomas Mallison. The Palestinian problem in international law and world order. Longman. '83.

Mandel, Neville J. The Arabs and Zionism before World War I. University of California Press. '76.

Mansfield, Peter. The Arabs. Harmondsworth; Penguin. '85.

Mansour, Atallah. Waiting for the dawn: an autobiography. Secker and Warburg. '75.

Ma'oz, Moshe. Palestinian nationalism: The West Bank dimension. Wilson Center, International Security Studies Program, Working Paper 18. '80.

Ma'oz, Moshe with Mordechai Nisan. Palestinian leadership on the West Bank: the changing role of the mayors under Jordan and Israel. Frank Cass. '84.

Marks, Shannee. Where is Palestine?: the Arabs in Israel. Pluto Press. '84.

Marlowe, John. The seat of Pilate: an account of the Palestine Mandate. Cresset; Dufour. '59.

Mendes-Flohr, Paul R., ed. A land of two peoples: Martin Buber on Jews and Arabs. Oxford University Press. '83.

Merhav, Peretz. The Israeli left: history, problems, documents. A. S. Barnes. '80.

Migdal, Joel, ed. Palestinian society and politics. Princeton University Press. '80.

Miller, Ylana N. Government and society in rural Palestine. 1920–1948. University of Texas Press. '85.

Mohammed, Franklyn Aphzal. The role of the United Nations in the establishment of Israel. F. Mohammed. '73.

Moore, John Norton, ed. The Arab-Israeli conflict: readings and documents. Princeton University Press. '77.

Morris, Benny. The birth of the Palestinian refugee problem, 1947–1949. Cambridge University Press. '87.

Nakhleh, Emile A., ed. A Palestinian agenda for the West Bank and Gaza. American Enterprise Institute for Public Policy Research. '80.

Nakhleh, Khalil. Palestinian dilemma: nationalist consciousness and university education in Israel. Association of Arab-American University Graduates. '79.

Nakhleh, Khalil and Elia Zureik, eds. The sociology of the Palestinians. Croom Helm. '80.

Nashif, Taysir N. The Palestine Arab and Jewish political leaderships: a comparative study. Asia Pub. House. '79.

Nasir, Jamal. A day of justice: the truth about the Arab case in Palestine. The Modern Press. '56.

Nazzal, Nafez. The Palestinian exodus from Galilee, 1948. Institute for Palestine Studies. '78.

Newman, David. Jewish settlement in the West Bank: the role of Gush Emunim. Centre for Middle Eastern and Islamic Studies. '82.

Nassib, Selim. Beirut, frontline story. Pluto Press. '83.

Niv, David, ed. Know the facts: a historical guide to the Arab-Israeli conflict. Department of Education and Culture, World Zionist Organization. '85.

Nuseibeh, Hazem Zaki. Palestine and the United Nations. Quartet Books. '82.

O'Brien, Conor Cruise. The siege: the saga of Israel and Zionism. Simon and Schuster. '86.

O'Neill, Bard E. Armed struggle in Palestine: an analysis of the Palestinian guerrilla movement. Westview. '79.

Ott, David. Palestine in perspective: politics, human rights, and the West Bank. Quartet Books. '80.

Ovendale, Ritchie. The origins of the Arab-Israeli Wars. Longman. '84.

Owen, Roger, ed. Studies in the economic and social history of Palestine in the nineteenth and twentieth centuries. Macmillan. '82.

Parkes, James William. Israel in the Middle-East complex. Anglo-Israel Association. '72.

Parkes, James William. Whose land? A history of the people of Palestine. Gollancz; Taplinger. '71.

Peretz, Don. Israel and the Palestine Arabs. The Middle East Institute. '58.

Peretz, Don. A Palestine entity? Middle East Institute. '70.

Persecution of the Arabs in Israel: facts that every American should know about the tragedy of the Holy Land. Palestine Arab Refugee Office. '56.

Peters, Joan. From time immemorial: the origins of the Arab-Jewish conflict over Palestine. Harper & Row. '84.

Plascov. Avi. The Palestinian refugees in Jordan, 1948-1957. F. Cass. '81.

Pogany, Istvan S. The Security Council and the Arab-Israeli conflict. St. Martin's. '84.

Porath, Yehoshua. The emergence of the Palestinian-Arab national movement, 1918-1929. Frank Cass. '74.

Porath, Yehoshua. The Palestinian Arab national movement: from riots to rebellion, 1929-1939, vol. 2. Frank Cass. '77.

Pryce-Jones, David. The face of defeat: Palestinian refugees and guerrillas. Holt, Rinehart and Winston. '73.

Quandt, William B., Jabber, Fuad, and Lesch, Ann Mosely. The politics of Palestinian nationalism. University of California Press. '73.

Rabinovich, Itamar and Reinharz, Jehuda, eds. Israel in the Middle East: documents and readings on society, politics and foreign relations, 1948–present. Oxford University Press. '84.

Regan, Geoffrey B. Israel and the Arabs. Cambridge University Press. '84.

Reich, Walter. A stranger in my house: Jews and Arabs in the West Bank. Holt, Rinehart, and Winston. '84.

Rfouh, Faisal Odeh Matlag, Quest for peace: United Nations and Palestine. National Book Organisation. '86.

Report on Israeli human rights practices in the occupied territories. ADC Research Institute. n.d.

Richardson, John P. The West Bank: a portrait. Middle East Institute. '84.

Rodinson, Maxime. The Arabs. Croom Helm; University of Chicago Press. '81.

Rodinson, Maxime. Israel and the Arabs. Pantheon '69; Penguin '82.

Rosen, Harry M. The Arabs and Jews in Israel; the reality, the dilemma, the promise. American Jewish Committee. '70.

Rossel, Seymour. Israel: covenant people, covenant land. Union of American Hebrew Congregations. '85.

Royal Institute of International Affairs. The Middle East: a political survey. Oxford University Press. '58.

Rubenberg, Cheryl. The Palestine Liberation Organization, its institutional infrastructure. Institute of Arab Studies. '83.

Rubinstein, Alvin Z., ed. The Arab-Israeli conflict: perspectives. Praeger. '84.

Rubner, Michael. Conflict in the Middle East from October 1973 to July 1976: a selected bibliography. (Political Issues series, vol. 4, no. 4.) Center for the Study of Armament and Disarmament, California State University. '77.

Sachar, Howard Morley. A history of Israel: from the rise of Zionism to our time. Knopf. '76.

Sahliueh, Emile F. The PLO after the Lebanon war. Westview Press. '86.

Said, Edward. The question of Palestine. Times Books. '79.

Said, Edward. Orientalism: Western concepts of the Orient. Routledge & Kegan Paul; Pantheon. '78.

Said, Edward W. After the last sky: Palestinian lives. Pantheon Books. '86.

Sandler, Shmuel and Hikel Frisch. Israel, the Palestinians and the West Bank: a study in intercommunal conflict. Lexington Books. '84.

Sayeqh, Fayez Abdullah. Do Jews have a "divine right" to Palestine? Research Center, Palestine Liberation Oraganization. '67.

Sayigh, Rosemay. Palestinians: from peasants to revolutionaries. Monthly Review Press. '79.

Schnall, David J. Beyond the Green Line: Israeli settlements west of the Jordan. Praeger. '84.

Scholch, Alexander, ed. Palestinians over the Green Line: studies on the relations between Palestinians on both sides of the armistice line since 1967. Ithaca Press. '83.

Segre, V. D. Israel: a society in transition. Oxford University Press. '71.

Seldin, Ruth R. The Arab minority. American Association for Jewish Education. '73.

Shadid, Mohammed K. The United States and the Palestinians. Croom Helm. '81.

Shehadeh, Raja. Samed: a journal of a West Bank Palestinian. Adama Books. '84.

Shehadeh, Raja. The third way: a journal of life in the West Bank. Quartet Books. '82.

Sherman, John, ed. The Arab-Israeli conflict, 1945–1971: a bibliography. '78.

Shokeid, Moshe. Distant relations: ethnicity and politics among Arabs and North African Jews in Israel. Praeger. '82.

Simson. H. J. British rule in Palestine and the Arab rebellion of 1936–1937. Documentary Publications. '77.

Sinai, Anne, ed. Israel and the Arabs: prelude to the Jewish state. Facts on File. '72.

Slann, Martin Wayne. The political integration of East and West Jerusalem: Arab and Jewish community cooperation. '70.

Smith, David. Prisoners of God: the modern-day conflict of Arab and Jew. Quartet. '87.

Smith, Pamela Ann. Palestine and the Palestinians, 1876–1983. St. Martin's. '84.

Smooha, Sammy. The orientation and politicization of the Arab minority in Israel. University of Haifa, Jewish-Arab Center, Institute of Middle Eastern Studies. '84.

Sobel, Lester, ed. Palestinian impasse: Arab guerrillas and international terror. Facts on File. '77.

Peace-making in the Middle East. Facts on File. '80.

Soshuk, Levi, ed. Momentous century: personal and eyewitness accounts of the rise of the Jewish homeland and state, 1875–1978. Herzl Press. '84.

Spielmann, Miriam. If peace comes—: the future expectations of Jewish and Arab Israeli children and youth. Almaqvist & Wiksell. '84.

Stein, Leonard. The Balfour Declaration. Vallentine Mitchell; Simon & Schuster. '61.

Stendel, Ori. Arab villages in Israel and Judea-Samaria: a comparison in social development. Israel Economist. '68?.

Stewart, Desmond. The Middle East: Temple of Janus. Doubleday. '71.

Stewart, Desmond. Palestinians: victims of expediency. Quartet Book. '82.

Stone, Julius. Israel and Palestine: assault on the law of nations. Johns Hopkins University Press. '81.

Sykes, Christopher. Crossroads to Israel, 1917-1948. Indiana University Press. '73.

Tal al-Zaatar. The fight against fascism. P.L.O. Unified Information, Foreign Information Dept. '77?.

Tanber, George J. Life under Israel occupation. National Association of Arab Americans. '81.

Tawil, Raymonda Hawa. My home, my prison. Zed Press. '83.

Taylor, Alan R. Prelude to Israel: an analysis of Zionist diplomacy. Philosophical Library. '59.

Teveth, Shabtai. Ben-Gurion: the burning ground, 1886-1948. Houghton Mifflin. '87.

Thorpe, Merle. Prescription for conflict: Israel's West Bank settlement policy. Foundation for Middle East Peace. '84.

Tillman, Seth. The United States in the Middle East: interests and obstacles. Indiana University Press. '82.

Touval, Saadia. The peace brokers: Mediators in the Arab-Israeli conflict, 1948-1979. Princeton University Press. '82.

The United Nations and the question of Palestine: a compilation of essays, 1980-1982. United Nations Division for Palestinian Rights. '83.

Turki, Fawaz. The disinherited: journal of a Palestinian exile. Monthly Review Press. '72.

Van Arkadie, Brian. Benefits and burdens: a report on the West Bank and Gaza Strip economies since 1967. Carnegie Endowment for International Peace. '77.

Van Horn, Carl. Soldiering for peace. Cassell. '66.

Venn-Brown, Janet, ed. For a Palestinian: a memorial to Wael Zuaiter. Kegan Paul International. '84.

Vital, Daniel. The origins of Zionism. Clarendon Press; Oxford University Press. '75.

Waines, David. The unholy war: Israel and Palestine, 1897-1971. Chateau Books Ltd. '71.

Wallach, Jehuda Lothar. Israeli military history: a guide to the sources. Garland Publishing. '84.

Ward, Richard Joseph. The Palestine state: a rational approach. Kennikat Press. '77.

Weisfeld, Abie H. Sabra and Shatila: a new Auschwitz. Jerusalem International Pub. House. '84.

Weizmann, Chaim. Trial and error. Hamish Hamilton; Schocken. '66.

Wilson, Harold. The chariot of Israel: Britain, America, and the state of Israel. Weidenfeld and Nicolson. '81.

Yaniv, Avner. P.L.O. (Palestine Liberation Organization): a profile. Israel Universities Study Group for Middle Eastern Affairs. '74.

Zayid, Ismail. Zionism, the myth and the reality. American Trust Publications. '80.

Zeigler, William H. United States reaction to the 1970 Jordanian crisis. U.S. Army War College. '73.

Zionism is racism: documents and articles on the Palestinian people's national liberation struggle. Norman Bethune Institute. '75.

Zucker, David et al. Research on human rights in the occupied territories 1979-1983. International Center for Peace in the Middle East. '83.

Zureik, Elia. The Palestinians in Israel: a study in internal colonialism. Routledge and K. Paul. '79.

SUPPLEMENTARY READING

Readers who require a comprehensive list of materials on this topic are advised to consult the *Reader's Guide to Periodical Literature* and other Wilson Indexes.

Losing the West Bank war. Micah Morrison *The American Spectator* 21:17-20 Je '88

Israel has suffered losses on several fronts in the West Bank war, making the prospects for peace less likely in the short term. The Palestinian uprising in the occupied territories can be contained, but Israel has lost the moral high ground. It is also losing whatever diplomatic agreements have governed its relations with Arabs. Israel's losses might be recovered, however. By the end of 1988, there will be new Israeli and U.S. governments, and the Palestinians in the territories will have had time to absorb their victory. The key questions are whether a strong Palestinian leadership will emerge from the uprising and how it will approach Israel.

An Israeli and an Arab tour for peace. James M. Wall *The Christian Century* 104:427-8 My 6 '87

Mattityahu Paled, a member of the Israel Knesset, recently toured the United States, speaking in favor of the establishment of a Palestinian state. The West Bank and the Gaza Strip, annexed by Israel following the 1967 Six-Day War, are inhabited by more than 850,000 Arabs and only 50,000 Jews, but the idea of turning the occupied territory into an independent Palestinian homeland is unpopular among most Israelis. Peled agrees with the sentiments of the late David Ben-Gurion, who insisted that peace was more important than real estate. Peled would also like to see the end of the $3 billion annual subsidy provided to Israel by the United States because he believes that this aid has forged a partnership that is harmful to both nations.

The expulsion of Mubarak Awad. Charles A. Kimball *The Christian Century* 105:675-7 Jl 20-27 '88

The June 13 deportation from Israel of Mubarak Awad, a nonviolent Palestinian-American activist, has sparked considerable debate in the United States and Israel. Awad, the founder and director of the Palestinian Center for the Study of Nonviolence, has been portrayed by the Israeli government as an underground leader of the Palestinian uprising. He has never been formally charged with any crime, however. He supports the PLO as the only legitimate organization of the dispossessed Palestinian people, not as a force for the destruction of Israel, as the Israelis have charged. His groundless deportation is an alarming indication of the growing power of the extreme right in Israel.

Where Arabism and Zionism differ. Elie Kedourie *Commentary* 81:32-6 Je '86

Zionism differs from Arabism in that Israel has less powerful origins, and its institutions proceed from, respond to, and attempt to minister to the body politic. Both Arabism and Zionism are ideologies that have arisen in the meeting of the Arab and Jewish worlds with modern European political thought. The relationship between Arabism and Islam and between Zionism and Judaism is not a simple one of conflict but of ambivalence. Although the political and military ventures of Zionism have yielded mixed and ambiguous results, politics are nonetheless necessary. The political ideologies of Arabism represent a vain attempt to compensate for oppressive, though no longer compulsive, institutions that are unable to evoke loyalty. Zionism depends on the support and trust of its citizens; such support comes from a solidarity much older than that aroused by modern ideologies.

The occupied territories: deeper realities. Gwyn Rowley *Focus* 37:34-6 Wint '87

Two matters are posing increasing problems on the West Bank and in the Gaza Strip: Jews are taking a disproportionate share of the land, and Israel is overpumping the water tables, distributing 95.5 percent of the water to Israel and only 4.5 percent to the West Bank. The fighting that broke out in December 1987 was partially caused by the Israeli Defense Force's decision to raze Palestinian housing in certain places in Gaza to permit the rapid retreat of military patrol vehicles that might be caught in an ambush. Israel wants a return to law and order, but as long as it builds settle-

248 The Reference Shelf

ments in and controls the water of the occupied territories, problems will
continue.

Intifadeh: the Palestinian uprising. Don Peretz *Foreign Affairs*
66:964–80 Summ '88

While the Palestinian uprising has united the people of the West Bank
and Gaza, it has deepened divisions between Jews and exacerbated Israeli
anxieties about whether an independent Palestine would be a peaceful
neighbor. The culmination of years of economic, social, and political frustration, the uprising began as a sporadic protest, but it soon became an
organized resistance movement with an underground leadership, a clear
political objective, and a well-planned and integrated strategy. The previously fragmented Palestinian community closed ranks quickly and issued
a united demand for self-determination and an end to occupation, creating political turmoil in Israel and focusing world attention on the Palestine problem.

No choice but activism. Abba Eban *Foreign Policy* 57:3–7 Wint
'84/'85

There has been no progress toward resolving the Arab-Israeli conflict
since the signing of the 1979 peace treaty. Israeli leaders have remained
inflexible on the central question of Palestinian autonomy. But new developments suggest the possibility of a breakthrough and active participation
by the United States could encourage a renewal of the peace process. Israel is ready to remove its forces from Lebanon, and if the United States
can reverse its antagonistic relations with Syria it could influence a negotiated settlement in Lebanon. Moreover, the newly elected Israeli government has not endorsed the Begin government's drive to settle the
disputed areas of the West Bank and the Gaza strip, and this policy change
could encourage a resolution of the Palestinian question with Jordan. Jordan and Egypt's resumption of diplomatic relations may also prove a positive factor.

Return to Geneva. Hassan bin Talal: Crown Prince of Jordan
Foreign Policy 57:8–13 Wint '84/'85

Jordan suggests that the United Nations sponsor an international peace
conference in Geneva under the joint supervision of the two superpowers.
Other states and organizations support the plan, which would offset Israeli dominance in the region and the United States' present role as sole ne-
gotiator. Jordan favors an approach based on U.N. Security Council
Resolution 242, which outlines the principle of exchanging peace for territory. The basic issues remain the right to national self-determination for
Palestine; the illegality of Israeli settlements on the West Bank, the Gaza
Strip, and the Golan Heights; Israel's annexation of Arab East Jeruslaem
in 1967; and extremist activities that could undermine social stability. A
resolution of the conflict would encourage economic development,

which, along with financial aid from Jordan and the implementation of some kind of approach similar to the Marshall plan, would further stabilize peace in the region.

Myths about Palestinians. Kathleen Christison *Foreign Policy* 66:109-27 Spr '87

An ingrained mythlogy has led many Israelis and their allies to believe that Palestinian nationalism is not a legitimate political movement. Israelis often argue that Palestinian nationalistic feelings were weak or nonexistent before Israel was created, that the Palestinians were never a distinct people, that Palestinians already have a home in Jordan, that they never attempted to gain their independence while Jordan controlled the West Bank, that they fled Israel voluntarily during the 1948 fighting, that the PLO is a terrorist organization unrepresentative of the Palestinian people, and that Israel needs the West Bank for security reasons. These inaccurate and irrelevant arguments ignore the growing radicalism of Israel's Arab population, which could create an explosive situation for Israel in the future.

Letter from Jerusalem. Milton Viorst *Mother Jones* 13:21-3+ Ap '88

Unlike previous confrontations in the occupied territories, the latest Palestinian uprising against Israel has given the Arabs a distinct advantage over their adversaries. For the first time, the Palestinians are using an approach of nonviolent confrontation that has given them the moral high ground over Israel's brutal attempts to squelch the rebellion. A key player in this new strategy has been Mubarak Awad, a Christian Arab whose arrival in Jerusalem in 1983 seemed to coincide with a cohesion of diverse strains of nonviolence. Through his Palestinian Center for the Study of Nonviolence, he has designed a program of civil disobedience that encourages Palestinians to refuse to carry identity cards, obstruct the movement of equipment, and participate in mass arrests, among other tactics. By portraying themselves as victims and by forcing Israel to defend its actions before a global audience, they have won their greatest victory since Israel's founding in 1948.

Force for change in the West Bank (Palestinian labor movement). Joost R. Hiltermann *The Nation* 245:338-40 O 3 '87

The Palestinian labor movement in the West Bank and Gaza Strip has long been the target of Israeli repression and is one of the chief targets of Israeli defense minister Yitzhak Rabin's Iron Fist policy, which began in August 1985. Israeli authorities fear the unions' potential for organizing Palestinian nationalist resistance. There are currently more than 100 active unions in the West Bank, and leaders estimate that 10-35 percent of West Bank workers now beling to a union. Many of the new recruits are workers who cross into Israel each day in search of jobs and who, while receiving adequate wages, encounter harsh working conditions and discrimination. Palestinians are prohibited from joining the Histadrut, Israel's largest trade union organization, even though reduced membership dues are deducted from their wages.

No land, no peace for Palestinians. Robert I. Friedman *The Nation* 246:562-4+ Ap 23 '88

The Palestinian uprising has increased mainstream support for Israel's radical right wing, a powerful religious-nationalist movement bent on annexing the occupied territories and expelling Israel's Arabs. Polls indicate slowly growing support for the ultraright Kach and Tehiya parties. The fundamentalist movement Gush Emunim is also gaining influence. Calls for wholesale deportation and even extermination of the Arabs have entered into the country's public debate. This political atmosphere has given rise to vigilante violence by Jewish settlers in the occupied territories. The Far Right is strengthened by Israelis' powerful emotional attachments to the West Bank and by the government's reluctance to criticize Gush Emunim, which has spearheaded the West Bank settlement drive. One observer notes, however, that continued violence and increased international pressure could isolate the Far Right from its more moderate allies.

The demons of the Jews (M. Kahane). Leon Wieseltier *The New Republic* 193:15-21+ N 11 '85

The rise of rabbi Meir Kahane, recently elected to the Israeli parliament, reflects the darker side of contemporary Israel. Kahane, an odious extremist who favors the expulsion of all Arabs from the state of Israel, harbors tremendous hatred that impels him to promote ideas reminiscent of Nazism, such as the legal prohibition of sexual relations between Jews and Arabs. He is the product of three powerful forces in Israel today: radical nationalism, militant millenarianism, and social resentment. Kahane could not have gained prominence without the ascendancy of Menachem Begin and Ariel Sharon, who promoted extremism and irrationality. Begin glorified militarism and his own terrorist past and sanctioned paranoiac politics. To gain support, Kahane has played upon the discontent of the Sephardic Jews. The Jews must defeat Kahane just as they have overcome external enemies.

Make money, not war (proposal to bribe Palestinians to leave occupied territories). *The New Republic* 198:4 F 29 '88

However impracticable such a plan might be, bribing the Palestinians in the occupied territories to go elsewhere cannot rightly be considered immoral. Indeed, there is precedent for such a free market approach: the Jews gained possession of most of the land that the Palestinians now want back by buying it, not through military force. If each of the Arabs in the occupied territories were given a million dollars to leave, the tab for the whole package would come to about a trillion dollars, which is probably not much more than the world is already paying for the Arab-Israeli conflict. Although some maintain that money should be kept in its own sphere, the moral logic of capitalism suggests that there is nothing wrong with using economic means to address spiritual complaints.

Profits of peace (economic solution to Arab uprisings). Daniel Doron *The New Republic* 198:22+ My 30 '88

Israel could improve relations with its resident Arabs and with those living in the West Bank and Gaza by removing government obstacles to economic opportunity. Because Israelis have become so accustomed to their politicized economic system, they tend to overlook the economic factors that aggravate Arabs. While Israelis excuse or accept their nation's onerous economic policies and rely on networks and organizations for protection, Arabs are unable to defend themselves from the system. Mostly organized laborers and small entrepreneurs, Arabs lack political clout and feel excluded and discriminated against in an economy in which most resources are allocated according to political access. Although good economic conditions would not resolve all political disputes, Israel could ease tensions with its Arabs if it would remove impediments to the free functioning of the markets.

The new anti-Semitism. Bernard Lewis *The New York Review of Books* 33:28-34 Ap 10 '86

In current Arab writing about Israel and in mainstream Arab intellectual life, a hatred of the Jews as virulent as Nazi anti-Semitism threatens any hope of peaceful accommodation between Israel and the Arab nations. The intractable Palestinian refugee problem and, even more, Israel's repeated victories over the Muslim Arabs have inspired deep humiliation and outrage, which fuel the longheld Arab desire for Israel's utter destruction. In the forty years since Israel's inception, only Egypt and Lebanon have broken free of the Arab lock step to engage in talks, and both have suffered ostracism. Unlike Israel, a liberal democracy with a free press, the Arab countries are authoritarian and command rigid loyalty. Few can speak out in defense of reason and tolerance in the government-controlled press. But if Arab leaders follow Sadat's example and engage Israel in dialogue, and if Israelis can respond appropriately, perhaps the bigotry can be exorcised.

A stone's throw. Anton Shammas *The New York Review of Books* 35:9-10 Mr 31 '88

Although it has been recognized as a state for 40 years, Israel has not yet been technically established. The Israeli Declaration of Independence was created on May 14, 1948, but today there is still no constitution and no sense of Israeli nationality. Israel still thinks of itself as an entity that is not confined to any given territory. Instead, it belongs to Jews wherever they may reside, be it in the Soviet Union or the United States. Thus, most American Jews, part owners of Israel by its laws and their own consent, share in the responsibility for Israel's recent policy of force in the occupied territories. No citizens are accorded nationality in Israel, a fact that creates a problem for its Arab citizens. They are expected to be faithful to Israel, but they are not allowed to participate in the country's political process. If they seek political fulfillment elsewhere, they are branded as subversives.

From the uprising. Amos Elon *The New York Review of Books* 35:10-14 Ap 14 '88

An incredible lack of foresight, imagination, and empathy by successive Israeli political leaders has led to the present Palestinian uprising in the West Bank, the Gaza Strip, and East Jerusalem. If nothing else, the status quo that Likud politicians have long trumpeted as the ideal situation in the area has been shattered forever. The most dramatic evidence of this change is in Jerusalem, which again has become a divided city. Clearly the city was never as united as the politicians had claimed. As the Israelis apply more repressive measures in an attempt to weaken the Palestinian cause, Israel's image abroad becomes tarnished. Israel's position in Washington has also weakened, and it could become even more precarious after the U.S. presidential election. Moreover, a wild gulf has developed between Israeli ministers Peres and Shamir concerning the uprising.

Understanding the uprising. Avishai Margalit *The New York Review of Books* 35:17-20 Je 2 '88

David Grossman's article on daily life in the West Bank—which was published as a special issue of the Israeli magazine Koteret Rashit in May 1987 and later issued as a book, *The Yellow Wind*—portrays the story of occupation as essentially one of honor and humiliation and accurately shows the political conflict as more a clash of virtues and vices than of interests. The Israeli occupation of the last 20 years was basically humiliating, and the Palestinian uprising that began in December was directed against that humiliation and designed to regain lost honor. Now that the Israelis have begun to consider every Palestinian an enemy, however, the occupation has moved beyond humiliation to severe repression. In part because of Grossman's work, some Israelis are now beginning to take an interest in Palestinian views and aspirations.

An open letter to Elie Wiesel (American Jewish response to uprising). Arthur Hertzberg *The New York Review of Books* 35:13-14 Ag 18 '88

The writer challenges Jewish author Elie Wiesel's public comments about Israel's behavior in response to the Palestinian uprising in the West Bank and Gaza. He accuses Wiesel's position, which deplores the extremists in both camps but dismisses the measured criticisms of Jewish moderates, as amounting to an elegant defense of the Likud hard line. He contends that if Wiesel is not prepared to defend Likud policies publicly, he should stop dismissing the political and moral views of the many moderate Jews who reject hard-line politics and morality.

Arabs and Jews in Israel. David K. Shipler *The New York Times Magazine* 22–9+ Ag 10 '86

The minds of the young have become the new battleground for the war between Jews and Arabs in Israel. In their determination to preserve their national identities while living side by side, both Jews and Arabs pass on prejudices and negative stereotypes to their children. Although many view any mingling as a threat to their individuality, scattered efforts are being made to promote communication and coexistence. Neve Shalom, an interfaith Israeli community created in the 1970s, sponsors workshops that bring Arab and Jewish highschoolers together to further mutual understanding. An ambitious program aimed at reforming the curriculum of Israel's schools has also made progress, as has a program that promotes joint Arab-Jewish ventures.

Breaking the deadlock: a Palestinian view. Sari Nusseibeh *The New York Times Magazine* 26+ F 21 '88

Negotiations between the Palestinians and Israelis can yield a fair and lasting settlement only if both nations recognize each other and formally acknowledge that each can exercise its sovereign rights in its homeland of Palestine/Israel. Once such basic principles are accepted, any number of political arrangements might prove workable. A catalyst, such as the U.S. government or the American Jewish community, will be needed to bring the parties together and keep the negotiations running smoothly. Before negotiations commence, however, the leaders of each nation should make a direct appeal to their opponent's constituency, which might help improve the psychological climate.

Breaking the deadlock: an Israeli view Yaron Ezrahi *The New York Times Magazine* 27+ F 21 '88

The Israelis and the Palestinians must renounce violence if the current deadlock is to be broken. As the weaker party in the conflict with Israel, the Palestinians can communicate most effectively through political acts and symbols. It would be tragic if they failed to take the initiative in addressing both their national aspirations and Israel's security problems. By acting with restraint, the Palestinians could precipitate a reciprocal deescalation of violence that would add impetus to the political momentum that a true peace process requires. The Israelis can do their part to break the deadlock by acknowledging the Palestinians as the other party to the conflict and by agreeing to talk to any authentic Palestinian leader. The advocates of force currently command greater public support than the advocates of compromise. Ultimately, however, compromise is the only

solution, since continued occupation of the territories can only weaken
Israel.

Encounter in Gaza. Michael Rosenblum *The Progressive* 50:32–4
Je '86

The Gaza Strip has been the home of Palestinian refugees since 1948,
when they were displaced by the war that erupted over Israel's independence. Isolated from the rest of the world by the Sinai and Negev deserts
and the sea, Gaza is the closest thing there is to a Palestinian state even
though it is technically part of Israel. The residents of the Strip have little
contact with the Israeli nation except through the occupation forces. In
the camps, the temporary housing built by the United Nations Relief
Works Agency in 1948 has become permanent. The water supply and
sewage system are woefully inadequate, and there has been no discernible
improvement in recent years. Terrorism is born out of the squalor and
hopelessness of Gaza, but the camps remain hidden from the eyes of Israelis and American tourists. It they were to see how people live in Gaza, they
might change their view of the Palestinians.

**Deporting their troubles (Israel attempts deportation of Pales-
tinians from occupied territories).** Michael S. Serrill *Time*
131:30+ Ja 18 '88

Hours after Israel announced the deportation of nine Palestinians from
Israeli-occupied territories, rioting broke out in Gaza and the West Bank.
Three of the deportees were accused of direct responsibility for the
month-long rebellion in the Gaza Strip and the West Bank. The others
are accused of being hard-core agitators. Israel says that 876 Palestinians
have been deported since 1967. The Arabs claim that the number is
2,500. The United States joined the other 14 members of the United Nations Security Council in declaring that the expulsions violated the Geneva Convention and demanding that Israel retract the orders. All nine
Palestinians have filed appeals.

Behind barbed wire (Palestinians detained in prison camps).
Johanna McGeary *Time* 131:34–5 Je 13 '88

About 5,000 Palestinians and their sympathizers are being held in Israeli
detention camps as punishment for alleged participation in insurrections
against Israeli rule in the West Bank and Gaza. Most of the detainees have
not been tried or even officially charged with a crime. Few of those who
have appealed their detention have won release. Among the inmates are
doctors, lawyers, labor leaders, students, and members of the outlawed
Palestine Liberation Organization. Some Israelis, including staff members of the now-defunct left-wing newspaper Derech Hanitzotz, have also
been detained.

Arabs vs. settlers in the Gaza Strip. Almut Hielscher *World Press Review* 34:56–7 Ja '87

Excerpted from the October 27 *Stern* of Hamburg. Since the occupation following the Six Day War, Israeli authorities have seized almost a third of the Gaza Strip, according to an Israeli-American study. Israeli settlers in the occupied territory are pleased that Likud leader Yitzhak Shamir has taken over as prime minister, since Shamir considers the West Bank and Gaza Strip indisputably part of Israel and has announced his desire to increase the number of Israeli villages in Arab territory. The local Arab population is subjected to frequent roundups, arrests, and interrogations by Israeli soldiers. Israelis have not, however, eradicated Palestinian sympathy for the Palestine Liberation Organization.

Rage against Israel. *World Press Review* 35:11–14+ Mr '88

A special section examines the Palestinian uprising in the West Bank and Gaza. Excerpted from the *Economist*, a London newsmagazine. If Israel rejects peace with willing Arabs, the state will gradually decline until time and demography bring its demise. Although a consensual division of Israel-Palestine only recently seemed within reach, it is possible that the champions of compromise have become irrelevant. While the Palestinian rioters appear detetmined to expunge Israel in the name of Islam, Israel's frightened majority has become larger and more intransigent. An immediate Israeli withdrawal from the occupied territories is a poor alternative to an intelligent restoration of order there, since withdrawal would encourage further polarization. To bolster the forces of compromise, European leaders should advise Israel on intelligent policing techniques and join the United States in urging it to deal with any Palestinians prepared to deal with it.